Sex and Pregnancy in Adolescence

**MELVIN ZELNIK
JOHN F. KANTNER
KATHLEEN FORD**

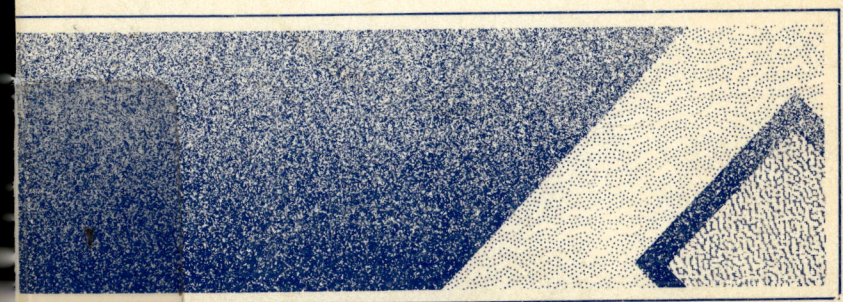

Sage Library of Social Research   133

SEX AND PREGNANCY IN ADOLESCENCE

Volume 133, Sage Library of Social Research

RECENT VOLUMES IN
SAGE LIBRARY OF SOCIAL RESEARCH

95 Roberts **Afro-Arab Fraternity**
96 Rutman **Planning Useful Evaluations**
97 Shimanoff **Communication Rules**
98 Laguerre **Voodoo Heritage**
99 Macarov **Work and Welfare**
100 Bolton **The Pregnant Adolescent**
101 Rothman **Using Research in Organizations**
102 Sellin **The Penalty of Death**
103 Studer/Chubin **The Cancer Mission**
104 Beardsley **Redefining Rigor**
105 Small **Was War Necessary?**
106 Sanders **Rape & Woman's Identity**
107 Watkins **The Practice of Urban Economics**
108 Clubb/Flanigan/Zingale **Partisan Realignment**
109 Gittell **Limits to Citizen Participation**
110 Finsterbusch **Understanding Social Impacts**
111 Scanzoni/Szinovacz **Family Decision-Making**
112 Lidz/Walker **Heroin, Deviance and Morality**
113 Shupe/Bromley **The New Vigilantes**
114 Monahan **Predicting Violent Behavior**
115 Britan **Bureaucracy and Innovation**
116 Massarik/Kaback **Genetic Disease Control**
117 Levi **The Coming End of War**
118 Beardsley **Conflicting Ideologies in Political Economy**
119 LaRossa/LaRossa **Transition to Parenthood**
120 Alexandroff **The Logic of Diplomacy**
121 Tittle **Careers and Family**
122 Reardon **Persuasion**
123 Hindelang/Hirschi/Weis **Measuring Delinquency**
124 Skogan/Maxfield **Coping With Crime**
125 Weiner **Cultural Marxism and Political Sociology**
126 McPhail **Electronic Colonialism**
127 Holmes **The Policy Process in Communist States**
128 Froland **Helping Networks and Human Services**
129 Pagelow **Woman-Battering**
130 Levine/Rubin/Wolohojian **The Politics of Retrenchment**
131 Saxe/Fine **Social Experiments**
132 Phillips/Votey **The Economics of Crime Control**
133 Zelnik/Kantner/Ford **Sex and Pregnancy in Adolescence**
134 Rist **Earning and Learning**

Sex and Pregnancy in Adolescence

**MELVIN ZELNIK
JOHN F. KANTNER
KATHLEEN FORD**

Volume 133
SAGE LIBRARY OF
SOCIAL RESEARCH

 **SAGE PUBLICATIONS**   Beverly Hills   London

Copyright © 1981 by Sage Publications, Inc.

All rights reserved. No part of this book may be reproduced or utilized in any form or by any means, electronic or mechanical, including photocopying, recording, or by any information storage and retrieval system, without permission in writing from the publisher.

For information address:

    SAGE Publications, Inc.　　SAGE Publications Ltd
    275 South Beverly Drive　　28 Banner Street
  Beverly Hills, California 90212　London EC1Y 8QE, England

Printed in the United States of America

Library of Congress Cataloging in Publication Data

Zelnik, Melvin.
  Sex and pregnancy in adolescence.

(Sage library of social research ; v. 133)
Bibliography: p.
  1. Premarital sex--United States.　2. Pregnant
schoolgirls--United States.　3. Young women--
United States--Attitudes.　4. Youth--United States
--Sexual behavior.　I. Kantner, John Frederick,
1920-　　. II. Ford, Kathleen, 1950-
III. Title.　IV. Series.
HQ27.5.Z44　　306.8'088055　　81-13541
ISBN 0-8039-1733-3　　　AACR2
ISBN 0-8039-1734-1 (pbk.)

FIRST PRINTING

CONTENTS

Foreword by John Scanzoni	9
Preface	11
1. Introduction	15
The Problem	15
The Approach	21
The Data: Procedures, Cost, Quality	24
Perspective	29
How This Book Is Organized	29
2. The World of the Teenager	35
Family Background: Structure and Stability	35
Familism	38
Family and Friends	39
Religion	42
Social Life	44
Perceptions of Society	45
The Future	54
3. Premarital Intercourse	63
The Prevalence of Premarital Sexual Activity	64
Variables and Analysis	67
The Initiation of Premarital Intercourse	75
Total Number of Premarital Sexual Partners	79
Frequency of Intercourse	85
Summary	89

4. Contraceptive Use — 95

- Use at First Intercourse — 96
- Use at Last Intercourse — 101
- Patterns of Contraceptive Use — 113
- Ever Use of Medical Contraception — 118
- Source of Pill and IUD — 123
- Reasons for Nonuse — 125
- Summary — 126

5. Premarital Pregnancy — 133

- Prevalence of Premarital Pregnancy — 140
- Mean Age at First Premarital Pregnancy — 147
- Outcome of First Pregnancy — 149
- Marriage During First Premarital Pregnancy — 154
- Illegitimacy — 157
- Summary — 161

6. Summary and Conclusions — 167

- Pathways to Pregnancy and Beyond — 167
- The Nub of the Matter—Illegitimacy — 169
- Methodological Caveats — 170
- Results — 172
- Conclusions — 178

Appendix A: History and Design of the Study — 183

- Preliminary Efforts — 183
- The 1971 and 1976 Samples — 187

Appendix B: Methodology and Validity Issues — 203

- Consent Procedures — 203
- Differences Between the Two Studies — 204
- Response Consistency — 210

Validity of Responses on Premarital Intercourse	215
Comparisons of Estimates Based on Sample Data with External Data	217
Appendix C: Data from the Study	233
Bibliography	265
About the Authors	271

FOREWORD

For many years, research and applied professionals have been reading with great interest the many articles published by Jack Kantner and Mel Zelnik reporting results of their national studies of adolescent female sexuality and fertility control. Anyone who had the slightest interest at all in the topic is familiar with their work. And all of us have been eagerly awaiting the time when they would compare their two studies and provide us with the kinds of interpretations and explanations their rich and unique data deserve.

This book fulfills our expectations by providing detailed analyses of the sexual activity, contraception, and pregnancy outcomes of adolescent women during 1971 and again in 1976. The authors supply numerous insights in helping us to try to grasp these complex phenomena; but they also point out that, as yet, we possess no "easy answers" as far as guiding social policy addressing the matter of unwed motherhood is concerned. I am very pleased to welcome this long-awaited contribution into the NCFR-Sage Series. I am sure that the reader will become as convinced as I that it is an important step on the road toward developing meaningful social policy regarding adolescent sexuality and unwed motherhood.

John Scanzoni
Series Editor
National Council on Family Relations
Book Series

PREFACE

The facts and figures presented in this book are based for the most part on two national surveys of young women aged 15 through 19, the first survey conducted in 1971, the second in 1976. Previously published articles based on these two surveys were concerned largely with levels, trends, and group differences in premarital sex, contraceptive use, and pregnancy-related behavior, and with the probability of the occurrence of certain of these events. In this book we attempt to see behind these findings, and in the concluding chapter look briefly at changes since 1976 as revealed by a third, yet-to-be-analyzed, survey carried out in 1979.

Prior to the publication of this book, we published very little that attempted to explain these different aspects of adolescent behavior. Our decision to proceed as we did, that is, by suspending efforts to account for the behavior until we had rather fully described it, was not one we reached easily or without some subsequent misgivings. We did feel, however, an obligation to respond to the demands of those concerned with helping young women who are faced with the risk or the reality of a premarital pregnancy that we make available as quickly as possible information about levels and differentials in adolescent reproductive behavior—information that prior to these surveys was not available. Thus, for example, we gave first priority to the question of the magnitude of the problem of how many young women have had intercourse and second priority to the factors that "cause" premarital intercourse. Even though many readers may not be familiar with our earlier publications, we have kept to a minimum the presentation of material contained there. However, each of the analytical chapters in this book begins with a set of purely descriptive tables that characterize the behavior in question as to levels, trends (1971 to 1976), and selected group differences. These tables will be of interest to those whose policy or programmatic interests require that they know about the dimensions of the problem in terms of the estimated prevalence of sex, contraception, pregnancy, and the weighted distribution of cases by age, race, socioeconomic status, religion, and family background. This leads to an unavoidable redundancy, since the second part of each chapter takes up these variables again, but this time the aim is to be analytical rather than descriptive. The analytical part involves the unweighted sample rather than the data which has been weighted to conform to the distribution of these events in the population. The aim of the analysis, for which we employ a technique known as Multiple Classification Analysis, is to establish the relative influence of the variables as they operate in the presence of each other. Readers interested in this question—that is, in how these variables relate to the behavior in question when they are considered all together—may want to skip lightly over those parts that describe and comment on the weighted distributions and go directly to the discussion of the "adjusted" data.

The selection for study of young women aged 15 through 19 is arbitrary and, if one likes, arguable. From a technical, demographic viewpoint, there is reason to select this group, since data on young women from public sources are more often published for this age category than for any other. This is an important consideration, for it permits us to check some of our results against other, independently collected, figures. A study of sexuality for its own sake, rather than as a necessary condition leading to pregnancy and childbirth, might well lower the age of eligibility for its subjects.

Increasingly, professionals who concern themselves in a practical way with adolescent reproduction focus on young women under 18 years of age, frequently dropping the lower age boundary to 12 or 13. We have no quarrel with that under certain conditions and safeguards. However, given the relatively insignificant amount of reproduction among young women under the age of 15—granted it can be overwhelmingly significant for the individuals so involved—it does not appeal to us as efficient, necessary, or ethically warranted to raise this issue among very young women in the relatively insensitive setting of a large-scale household survey. Most will not yet have become sexually active and thus would have little to contribute to the study. It would take a very large and expensive study to obtain a sufficient number of pregnancies and births to be able to say much that would be dependable about reproductivity under age 15. This is not to say that sex and reproduction among the very young cannot or should not be studied, but rather that great care should be exercised in how it is done—and very strong reasons advanced for doing so. A national sample

Preface

survey, however sober its purpose and well trained its interviewers, is not the way to do it.

The English language, even its slovenly cousin, American-English, does not have the precise collective term that both sounds right and has the correct connotations for this group. Adolescence, while a loose term, nevertheless generally begins earlier than age 15 and ends before age 20. Despite this poor fit, we sometimes use the term in its adjectival form (adolescent) as inclusive of our subjects. Demographic formalism would suggest "females aged 15 through 19"; we tend to avoid that usage as too aseptic for the subject and subjects at hand. Some who react against the embalmment of strict demographic delineation prefer to speak of "girls." In our view this sacrifices the sobriety our academic peers expect of us at no gain, and indeed a significant loss, of accuracy. The term covers females of all ages and conditions and recently has acquired a faint odor among emancipationists. And so we have settled for "young women"—less elastic and more neutral than "girls," less precise but also less pretentious than "females aged 15 through 19," and a better fit than "adolescents" or "teenagers."

The major source of funds supporting this study has been the National Institute of Child Health and Human Development, DHEW; both the 1971 and 1976 field activities were carried out under Grant HDO5255, although, in the case of the latter survey, additional funding without which the study might have foundered was received from the Ford Foundation. The fieldwork for the 1971 survey was carried out under a subcontract with the Institute for Survey Research, Temple University; the 1976 survey was subcontracted to the Research Triangle Institute. Preliminary work undertaken prior to the 1971 survey, designed to determine whether such a survey was feasible, was supported by the Social and Rehabilitation Service, DHEW (Grant 10-P-56012/3); the various field activities involved in that preliminary work were carried out, under subcontract, by the Institute for Survey Research, Temple University.

Over the years, additional assistance of various kinds has been received from the Population Council, the General Service Foundation, the Andrew Mellon Foundation, and the William and Flora Hewlett Foundation. The final analysis and writing of this book were funded in part under a contract from NICHD (HD82848). The conclusions and comments in this book do not necessarily reflect the views or policies of DHEW or of our other sponsors, none of whom, it is worth commenting, ever sought to inflict on us anything more annoying than a benign and beneficial impatience to see the final results. We have complained when, in our estimation, our sponsors were more stinting in their support than we thought they should be. We would like it in print that at the same time we have appreciated their forebearance. We hope they find satisfaction with what they have helped to create.

We are greatly indebted to a number of people, including Farida Shah and Judy Gehret who, if not progenitors, were indispensable midwives to the project. The integrity of the work owes much to them. We are indebted also to those graduate students who used the surveys as sources of data for their doctoral dissertations. Although none of them worked on this book, their questions, criticisms, and suggestions made us more aware than we might otherwise have been of some of the defects of the surveys. Nelva Hitt, Marta Pramschufer, and Ruth Skarda banged out typescripts draft after draft without audible protest and with a skill which at times verged on the cryptographic. We alone are responsible for the shortcomings of the book.

Melvin Zelnik
John F. Kantner
Kathleen Ford

CHAPTER 1

INTRODUCTION

The Problem

This is a book about the fertility of young American women and about certain choices that precede childbearing, particularly for the unmarried woman—whether or not to have sex, whether or not to use contraception, whether to have a birth or an abortion, whether or not to marry before the birth. In discussing these alternatives, we avoid speaking of the "decision" to have sexual intercourse, to use contraception, and so on, for, while the phrase is common in current discussion, it confers a greater degree of ratiocination than these acts generally receive. We prefer to think of this sequence of alternatives as a series of forks in the road, as possible pathways; while some individuals will consciously consider which forks to take, others will drift one way or the other without considering alternatives or the consequences of the choice.

The book is a study of a fascinating facet of recent history: the early stages of sex and childbearing among young women who were 15 to 19 years of age in 1971 and their replacements 5 years later in 1976. Their entry on the American scene was itself demographically dramatic. Born on the plateau of the post-World War II surge in American fertility, the "baby boom," which crested in 1961,[1] they numbered, counting both sexes, more than 40 million. In those 10 years (1952-1961), 8.5 million more children were born than in the previous 10 years (1942-1951) and 3.6 million more were born than in the following 10 years (1962-1971) to a considerably larger population.[2] Inescapably, such a demographic magnitude became a force for change in American society.

The influence of these swollen cohorts on the character of American life began before they could be aware of it. As children they helped underwrite the market for four-bedroom suburban homes and station wagons, which in turn changed the morphology of American cities; their entry into school crowded classrooms, strained the budgets of local governments, and built the PTA into something approaching a social movement.

They came of age during the turbulent and tumultuous sixties, when, according to some observers, American society became more permissive toward youthful dalliance.[3] As they passed into early and then late adolescence, they elevated the crime statistics, flooded colleges and universities, swarmed in hedonistic pursuits, and became the collective patrons of a raucous musical revolution heavily laced with sexual innuendo. Their collective purchasing power created new industries and dramatically altered others. The tastes and preferences of older members of American society were crowded aside or revamped in an effort to be part of the younging of America.

In retrospect, the period of their advent, the fifties and the opening years of the sixties, appears to have been molded partly in reaction to the deprivation and denial of the war years. Family building resumed, indeed it flourished, into a celebration of familism. Sociologists rediscovered the family, which they had previously characterized as functionless and vestigal in contemporary society, as an abiding and necessary institution even in "postindustrial society."[4]

It was with some surprise and dismay then that society watched this loaf of contentment begin to fall in the sixties. The birthrate declined, ultimately reaching levels even lower than those experienced during the Depression years; and it fell at all ages, signifying a pervasive reconsideration of values, at least those relating to the quantitative and temporal aspects of family life.

The theories that have been advanced to explain the nature of U.S. fertility since World War II and to predict its future path are, whatever their merits or shortcomings in regard to the fertility of the married, essentially mute as regards the childbearing of young, unmarried women.[5]

The most widely discussed theory, the so-called Easterlin Hypothesis, asserts:

> that the post-World War II baby boom in the United States was the result of the decline in the birth rate that occurred 20-25 years earlier. Correspondingly, the current baby bust is due to the rise in the birth rate 20-25 years earlier, that is, to the post World War II baby boom. And if the current baby bust is the product of the previous baby boom, then looking to the future, the baby bust may itself produce a new baby boom [Easterlin et al., 1978a: 18].

By way of explanation for this cyclical pattern of boom and bust, the authors state that:

> stripped of various qualifications and elaborations, the argument is a simple one. When young adults are in increasingly short supply, their

labor market situation improves and their relative well-being increases; when they are in growing surfeit, their labor market situation deteriorates, and their relative well-being diminishes. A growth in relative well-being encourages earlier marriages and childbearing; conversely, when relative well-being deteriorates, marriage and childbearing are postponed [p. 16].

Thus marriage and childbearing, with the former presumably preceding the latter, are a function of relative well-being, which is itself a function of the labor market situation. Almost completely outside the scope of this hypothesis are the activities of the unmarried.

A variant of the labor market theory of fertility trends since World War II has been developed by Butz and Ward (1979). Their model stresses the demand and supply of both male *and* female labor and to that extent is more satisfactory than the Easterlin version. As a noncyclical model, the Butz-Ward system cannot penetrate the future, since the economic conditions that drive it are exogenously given. It has been able to predict short-run blips in fertility. Since it deals implicitly with intended fertility within regular marital unions, it also is not well suited to the explanation of teenage fertility.

Other analyses of fertility trends pay less heed to short-run alterations of relative advantage or disadvantage in the labor market, stressing instead the long-term strain toward equilibrium in vital rates. Modern societies, having undergone a transition from high levels of fertility and mortality, will eventually stabilize with birth rates that match their death rates. In this view, the baby boom that reached its apogee two decades ago was a demographic aberration attributable in large part to coinciding but independent trends not likely to be in the same conjunction in the foreseeable future: an upsurge in marriages, a shifting of fertility toward the younger ages while at the same time older women resumed or extended disrupted childbearing careers. Since then, according to this account, there has been a trend toward delaying marriage and fertility, which, already quantitatively diminished, has been concentrated roughly into the first half of the childbearing years. This concentration, by age and parity, is ensured by better and more readily accessible methods of birth control (including abortion and sterilization). The number of children wanted by women of childbearing age comes closer to the number they have, and this number, as if guided by a hidden hand, converges to a replacement level of fertility.

The noncyclical, secular trend of fertility change, with its appeal to historic inevitability, projects a future for young Americans in which the requirements for extended education, the availability of reliable means for avoiding unwanted births, and the increased pressure for alternative careers for women, especially those careers that can outlast childbearing, will conspire to limit marriages and fertility and to keep them that way.[6] A recent presentation of this argument also sees the likelihood of increasing levels of illegitimacy (but within the context of low fertility) as a consequence of unmarried couples living together (Westoff, 1977). The author notes the increase in this phenomenon in Sweden and sees it as significant that:

> in the United States in 1975 there was a record high proportion (14.2 percent of all births) of illegitimate births, in which the greatest increases occurred among white women 20-29 years old [Westoff, 1977: 83].

Unstated and unacknowledged but implicit in this discussion is the belief that the increase in illegitimacy in Sweden and among U.S. women over age 20 represents largely wanted (and planned) births—and to that extent is amenable to the same explanatory frameworks as those devised for fertility within marriage. Childbearing among the young is ignored except to note that:

> we are fast approaching the perfect contraceptive society in which unwanted births will become nonexistent, although teenage childbearing continues to constitute a major problem [Westoff, 1977: 58].

In this context it is worth raising the question whether this or any society can significantly reduce illegitimacy among women under age 20 while the taboo on having children out of wedlock is progressively weakened among older women.

The lack of attention to the fertility of young, unmarried women is not surprising. Most childbearing occurs among older and married women and, in the United States, knowledge about the causes of fertility relates almost exclusively to their rather well regulated fertility. The fertility of young, unmarried women, by contrast, is unplanned, largely unwanted, and, until recently, was not seen as amenable to scientific scrutiny. Therefore, explanations that rely on deliberative models of behavior are at best relevant to the resolution of marital pregnancy. Clues to premarital fertility must account for factors which lead to premarital sex and which determine the character of contraceptive use. For married couples regular sex is a reasonable assumption and thus in large measure falls outside the scheme of explanation; the regularity of sex in turn provides a stable context for decisions regarding the use of contraception. In short, two of the most problematic aspects of teenage fertility, the prevalence and regularity of

Introduction

sex and the nature of contraception, are qualitatively different matters among married couples.

Birth rates among young women have fallen in recent years, although less than the rates for older women. Nevertheless, there are still about 1 million pregnancies annually to young women under the age of 20. In a society such as ours, where these events generally are disapproved if they occur outside of marriage, the result is much human damage—to the plans and prospects of the young, to parents' hopes, to family relations, and many times to the innocent, unintended products of adolescent passion. There are, in addition, the economic costs involved, borne by both individuals and society.

Illegitimacy, which has continued to rise among young women, even as their birth rates declined somewhat, casts a long economic shadow. A number of studies have detailed the persistent problems that stem from such disruptions of the "normative schedule" (Furstenberg, 1976). Among the young in the United States, illegitimacy is of substantial proportions and rising as the increase in sexual activity more than keeps pace with advances in contraceptive usage or pregnancy interruptions. In 1977, for example, 2 out of 5 births to women under the age of 20 were illegitimate and, of course, a much larger proportion were conceived outside of marriage. Unseen in these numbers are the 350,000-375,000 legal abortions to women under age 20, without which both the illegitimacy rate and the number of premature marriages undoubtedly would have increased.

The major problem in American fertility today, then, is the problem of teenage pregnancy and childbearing. Unwanted fertility among adult women is becoming a marginal phenomenon even if we include births that are unwanted only in the sense that they occur at the wrong time. Short of programming fertility by Orwellian measures (Djerassi, 1970), it seems unlikely that there can be much greater perfection in the planning of births than adult women in the United States have achieved. But such is far from true for females under the age of 20, especially those who have never married. It is our aim here to investigate the factors associated with the fertility of young women who reached age 15 between 1967 and 1976, that is, who were born between 1952 and 1961, in the center of the postwar baby boom.

As we have said, studies of the fertility of married women can assume some regularity of sexual activity. Intercourse within marriage is not only condoned, it is expected. And, until recently at least, social pressure encouraged having "at least 2 children." Not so with the young and unmarried. Premarital sex among teenagers may be "expected"—despairingly by parents—even tolerated, but seldom condoned. The many who are sexually active have sexual lives that are irregular, episodic, and unplanned—factors which presumably play some part in whether contraception is used, what kinds are used, and with what degree of effectiveness.

Many young women, regardless of whether their sexual lives are regular or irregular, appear to be woefully uninformed about relatively simple facts relating to sex and pregnancy. A number of impediments, some obvious and explicit, others more subtle, prevent sexually active young women who want contraceptives from obtaining them. Some, relying perhaps on observation or on their own limited experience, believe themselves immune to pregnancy; some regard contraceptive preparedness as "too calculating" and tending to dispel the sudden overpowering passion which the script calls for; for some, being prepared for sex conflicts with their self-image, which has not yet incorporated the expectation of sexual activity.

There are, in fact, myriad reasons why sexually active young women, even those who do not want to become pregnant, do not use contraception. Some of these reasons are applicable to married women; many are not. It is as naive as it is common to believe that the solution to the problem of teenage pregnancy is simply the availability of a new and better contraceptive, even one more suited to the particular needs of teenagers. If such a contraceptive were to appear, reasons for not using it would still exist. Davis (1972), in an insightful sociological analysis of premarital sex and pregnancy, relates changes in premarital sex and illegitimacy to changes in social control and social discipline. The development of new contraceptive techniques neither promotes nor prevents such behavior or the events that stem from it.

Our investigation of the factors associated with the fertility of young women starts with an investigation of those factors associated with the antecedents of fertility—sex and contraception. We cannot answer all questions, but we can and do answer some. Equally important, we clear away some of the intellectual debris that surrounds discussions of this aspect of teenage life. Adolescent fertility is a substantial social fact. Young women under 20 currently contribute about 600,000 births annually, or about 17 percent of the nation's total; teenage women also account for one-third of the more than 1 million legal abortions that have been performed annually in recent years in the United States. Our aim is to learn what lies at the root of these events and the reasons for the inability of most young women to deal effectively with this part of their lives. Perhaps if we and others succeed in this endeavor, the cohorts that are coming on line will be able to navigate this stretch of the life course more nimbly.

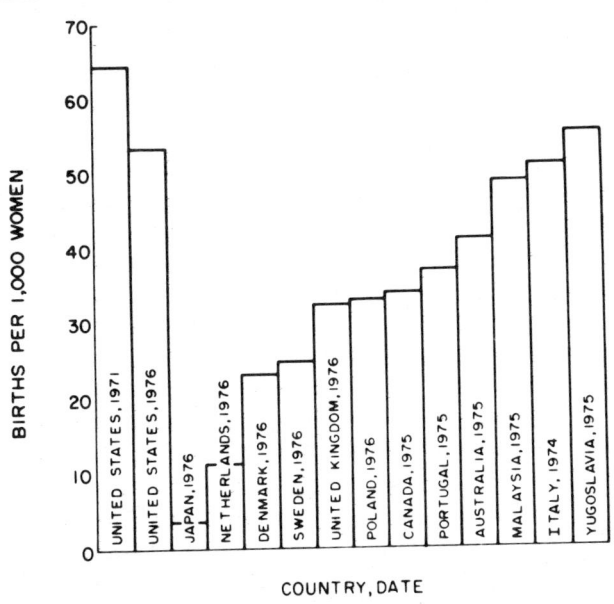

Figure 1.1 Fertility Rates for Women 15-19 Years of Age, United States, 1971 and 1976, and Selected Countries, Mid-1970s

SOURCES: United States: National Center for Health Statistics (1975, 1978a). Other countries: United Nations (1978: Table 11).

The Approach

The approach we take is limited in several respects. To explain why requires a brief digression. The United States stands out among industrialized nations in relation to the fertility of its young women. Compared to Japan, our rates are 15 times higher; they are more than twice the rates for the sexually emancipated Scandinavians; and they are higher than the rates in Canada and Australia (Figure 1.1). By confining our observations to the United States, we cannot expect to understand completely the reasons for the high level of fertility among our teenagers. In this respect our problem is no different from that encountered in studies of married women. We can, however, learn a good deal from the variations among teenagers in the behavior associated with early pregnancy and early childbearing.

Since we shall not return to a comparison of U.S. adolescents with those of other countries, we caution here against facile interpretations of variation in adolescent fertility rates among countries. Such differences as one finds do not appear to be simple expressions of differences in the surface manifestations of modernization, such as degree of industrialization, level of education, urbanization, or the like. Nor is it wholly a matter of how liberal a country is in matters associated with sex and reproduction. It is not difficult to think of societies more liberal than ours in regard to sex where the rates of teenage fertility are substantially lower. So complex are the processes, so varied the pathways leading to pregnancy and affecting its resolution that liberality insofar as it leads to more open, instructive discussion of sex and fertility control may actually help to avert unintended births. For example, a study of Baltimore teenagers concludes that the condemnation of premarital sexual relations leads to the concealment of such behavior by the teenager and provides parents, seldom eager to bring up the subject, with an excuse for failing to impart any useful information about the prevention of pregnancy beyond the most oblique warnings. According to Furstenberg (1976: 52), "premarital pregnancies do not stem from permissive attitudes ... but may instead be a consequence of restrictive standards about premarital sexual activity."

In order to advance beyond the fragmentary, highly speculative state which has characterized knowledge of teenage fertility, we have had to cast a wide empirical net. We sought as subjects for study not merely young women who have delivered babies, nor even those who have ever been pregnant, but a sample of all young women, including those who have never been involved in sexual intercourse. As in epidemiological inquiries, one must study the "cases," that is, those who have a given condition, as well as those who are free of it. Unless these two groups are found to differ with respect to suspected causal factors, one hasn't learned much. This is not to say that useful information about certain aspects of fertility-related behavior cannot be learned by the study of cases only, but such information cannot stand in a causal or explanatory relationship to the "index" behavior.

The behavioral sequence running from sexual intercourse through the use, nonuse, and misuse of contraception to pregnancy and its resolution needs to be examined at each juncture. Working along this behavioral chain, one soon runs out of readily served up populations that include cases as well as noncases or "controls." On occasion, investigators finding cases readily available, for example, pregnant clients of a prenatal service, may select "controls" from some convenient population, such as nonpregnant school classmates, and proceed to contrast the cases and controls with respect to factors suspected to be associated with pregnancy. A well recognized limitation of such an approach is that it fails to be informative about the distribution of the phenomenon being studied in the general population.[7] It can be revealing about, in this example, the relative risk of pregnancy among a selection of cases, but these cases may or may not

Introduction

resemble those in the population at large. Thus, when little is known about the prevalence of a condition, case control studies, as these are called, can be misleading. To study premarital intercourse, the use of contraception, the extent of pregnancy, abortion, and childbirth, we needed a random selection of teenagers. The time-honored way of achieving this is through a household sample survey—an enormously exacting and expensive operation when one is looking for something not found in most households. Such a survey, conducted in the spring of 1971 among 4392 young women, provides the baseline information for the present investigation.[8]

Though, as we have emphasized, the population of U.S. teenagers is large as an absolute quantity, most households do not contain a young woman aged 15 to 19. Parenthetically, we are often asked why we did not choose our respondents from high school populations. While this can be a useful source of cases for certain kinds of study, the association between pregnancy and dropping out of school is sufficiently important to seek an approach that includes those not in school. In addition, there are other problems: securing the cooperation of school authorities for a study dealing with the intimate matters touched on in this study, the vulnerability to community opposition in having the schools so used, obtaining signed parental consent in a location other than the home, the subtle abridgement of the strictly voluntary nature of the study that might be fostered if conducted at school, and a host of other problems.

To isolate the social, familial, and individual factors associated with the pathways leading to pregnancy or childbirth requires knowing something about the temporal ordering of events—what precedes what. Obtaining such information retrospectively may involve distortion due to inaccuracy of recall, complete forgetting, or the recasting of events and the circumstances under which they occurred in the light of subsequent developments. For example, a pregnancy unwanted at the time it occurred may in time, especially if "it" is now a member of the family, come to be remembered as wanted. The only certain way around this is to be there at the time—that is, to follow events prospectively rather than retrospectively.

The present investigation actually began as a prospective study, but the longitudinal aspect was aborted for lack of funds.[9] Were it not that conditions affecting reproduction among young women changed significantly after 1971, the survey of that year might have ended our investigation. However, because of the liberalization of abortion subsequent to the original survey and the increase in expenditures for family planning services, which rose from $80 million in 1971 to an estimated $197 million in 1975 (Alan Guttmacher Institute, 1976: 46), while the illegitimacy rate for young women increased from 22.4 to 24.2, a further look was warranted. In the spring of 1976, five years after the original survey, a second survey was launched. Because of tight funding, the 1976 sample was less than half the size of the 1971 survey.[10]

Two national samples of young women taken five years apart, even though not ideal for testing causal hypotheses, do nevertheless provide data of considerable utility to those who deal with the problem of adolescent fertility. They enable us to gauge the magnitude of the problem, to describe the various behavioral sequences from the initiation of sexual activity to pregnancy, abortion, or childbirth, and to identify correlates of sexual and reproductive behavior[11]—all of this during a period of rapid change.

The questions put to respondents in the two surveys were similar, but there are some important differences which will be noted as we go along.[12] Experience from the first survey led to certain modifications in the second survey—in particular to be more situationally specific in asking about the use of contraception. This means that in some instances in which very detailed points are at issue, comparisons between 1971 and 1976 will be impossible to make. Comparability has been retained, however, for the major items of behavior related to fertility.

The Data: Procedures, Cost, Quality

The two national surveys reported on in this volume were carried out according to the canons and procedures of scientific survey sampling. Households in randomly selected areas were visited by interviewers who enumerated the persons living in them. If a young woman of the right age for the study was found in a particular household and if that household happened to be one designated for sampling according to our selection procedures, she was then informed about the study and solicited for interview. Relatively few refused at this stage.[13]

In both 1971 and 1976 female interviewers were used for locating eligible respondents and for conducting the interview. Because in 1971 there had never been a survey of this age group on such a scale on a subject of such intimacy and which also obeyed the uncompromising dictates of scientific sampling, there was much concern about the likelihood of success, especially with respect to the more personal parts of the interview. This led us to design a self-administered questionnaire, which was introduced following the main background interview so that questions regarding sex and contraception could be answered with maximum privacy. This way of doing it required a very simple questionnaire, devoid of the devices available to an interviewer in the standard interview situation which make it possible to lead the respondent through a complex maze of

Introduction

questions. It worked. But it became clear also that we had underestimated the forthrightness of our respondents. This, after all, was a less inhibited generation in such matters certainly than that of the investigators and even, it seems, of their younger associates on the project, whose views of verbal proprieties were formed before young people were enjoined to "let it all hang out." Emboldened by success in 1971 and by the willingness of respondents to answer intimate questions, we abandoned the self-administered questionnaire in 1976 in order to obtain more detailed information about contraceptive use, that is, information pertaining to specific occasions of use, which is hard to pinpoint in the necessarily simple flow of a self-administered questionnaire.[14]

The major difficulties and much of the expense of field surveys such as these come well before the moment when the interviewer, successfully in the house, leads off with, "First, I'd like to ask you some questions about yourself." To arrive at that point means that the household must appear on a list of addresses of housing units and its human occupants must be listed. The 1971 survey was conducted eleven years after the 1960 census, at the time the only widely available source of information on the whereabouts of the population. But by 1971 the 1960 census information was badly out of date, whole areas having been transformed due to the natural mobility of the population, the transfiguring housing and urban development policies of public agencies, and the metastatic invasions of private developers. Many of the areas selected for the survey had been changed radically, making it necessary for the interviewers to first list neighborhoods and find out who lived there.

Extensive neighborhood changes not only meant that the listing of households took longer than would otherwise have been the case, but also that the possibility of missing certain housing units was increased.[15] The most troublesome questions concerning the representativeness of the sample arise at this stage of the operation. If households cannot be listed and screened (for example, as in the case of an apartment building to which the interviewer is denied access), it is likely in many instances that young women will be missed. They will not have a chance to fall into the sample, thereby undermining the assumption of random selection which underlies scientific sampling and the calculation of estimates of sampling error.[16]

Drawing a sample in 1976 was handicapped again by the lack of up-to-date information, although the 1970 census data were somewhat more helpful than the 1960 data had been in 1971. The listing and screening was handled somewhat more economically due to the availability of better information about the location and composition of households. In addition, the availability of more recent data made possible a more precise allocation of sampling points to the different strata developed for the oversampling of blacks. In 1971, 81,000 households were listed, or about 18 for every respondent subsequently interviewed. In 1976, 26,000 households were listed, or 12 per every successful interview.[17] It is this search for scattered respondents of a particular description, in contrast to surveys (for example, political opinion surveys), in which almost every household is likely to have an eligible respondent, that accounts in large measure for the high cost of acquiring these data.

At that, our costs per case have been substantially below those incurred by surveys essentially of married women 18 years of age and over conducted by private investigators and by the National Center for Health Statistics of the Department of Health, Education, and Welfare. The total field cost per completed interview in the 1971 survey was $84, and in the 1976 survey, the cost was $100 per completed interview (although, as indicated, this does not represent all actual field costs). The 1973 National Family Growth Study conducted for the National Center for Health Statistics reports figures that imply a cost per case of $220, even though a much larger sample and the greater general availability of married women covering an age range of some 30 years should have made the locating of eligible respondents much more efficient.

Even though expensive to acquire, the question must be asked: "Are the data any good?" If blemished, how seriously? These are difficult questions to answer. In Appendix B, we take up in some detail the questions of the reliability, validity, and completeness of the data, concluding therefrom that the data, while imperfect, are of usable quality. That is, the errors they contain are probably not severe enough to invalidate the major trends and relationships that can be discerned in them. To admit that the data are not free of error is not to say they are of lesser quality than survey data in general but rather to caution the reader against overinterpreting the findings. We will be able to discern the animal; the mites and fleas on it could be confused, if seen at all.

To be more specific, the various tests of the data detailed in Appendix B lead us to conclude:

(1) Reporting about intimate events, specifically whether or not the respondent has had sexual intercourse, appears to be valid, at least in the aggregate. While we were able to test this explicitly only in 1976, the results confirm our belief based on experience with the data from 1971 that concealment and distortion with respect to sensitive items are not serious problems. It seems reasonable to assume that if sexual intercourse is admitted to,[18] the respondent is likely to be candid about other aspects of sexual behavior: contraception, whether ever pregnant, and so on. At the same time, respondents may not report certain aspects of sexual behavior as openly and candidly as they report sex itself; abortion appears

Introduction

to be less completely reported, particularly by black respondents, than other forms of behavior.

(2) Reporting on vital events, births as well as abortions, appears to be reasonably complete for white respondents; blacks, in 1976 at least, underreported abortions and slightly overreported births.[19] These errors appear to be independent of one another—that is, it does not appear that black women who in fact had abortions reported live births instead. While underreporting of abortions by black respondents is perhaps not unexpected, we have no explanation for what appears to be an overreporting of births. We also are left uncertain regarding the effect of these two types of error on reports by black respondents of premarital pregnancies.

(3) The reliability of information as determined by analysis of reinterview information gathered in 1971 is about the same as has been reported for surveys dealing with the fertility of older, married women. In this respect, see Ryder and Westoff (1971) and Knodel and Piampiti (1977). At the individual level, data on attitudes are much less reliable, that is, more changeable, than data which refer to more factual matters, such as completed education. Partly for this reason (and partly because of inherent temporal ambiguities) little use is made of attitudinal data in attempting to explain individual behavior. However, such data are probably fairly valid in the aggregate and useful in giving a sense of the world as young women see it.

Beyond the question of how good (or defective) the data may be are broader questions: Did we ask the right questions and did we ask them in the right way? The answer, of course, depends on what we are trying to do. As demographers and as sociologists we are interested in behavior that has demographic consequences and in the demographic and social antecedents ("causes") of that behavior. The high fertility of young American females, the high fraction of that fertility that is unintended and outside of marriage—these were and are the concerns behind this study. We are not interested in "human sexuality" for its own sake, but rather matter-offactly in sex as a gateway to pregnancy and childbearing. Nor are we professionally interested in the psychodynamics of sex and reproduction unless there is some way that such knowledge might be practically useful. If, for example, it happens that a young woman is following a convoluted Freudian script in which her sexual and reproductive life are implicated in settling long suppressed psychic insults, there is not much in such knowledge that is readily translatable into policy or action. The example is perhaps somewhat strained; the point, however, is that at the present state of knowledge about teenage fertility the obvious and pressing gaps are of a social epidemiological kind: What is the prevalence of sex, pregnancy, abortion, and childbirth, and what seems to account for variations in prevalence? The areas of behavior we do examine are most readily surveyed by paging through the questionnaires (available from the authors).

Before the first survey went into the field, a substantial amount of preliminary work was undertaken to determine whether such a study was feasible. One of these preliminary efforts involved 24 videotaped group discussions held in 4 scattered locations. The participants, 166 in all, were black females of reproductive age living in or near Philadelphia, New Orleans, Raleigh, and Winston County, North Carolina. It was expected that these loosely structured discussions would reveal areas of linguistic or semantic confusion, as indeed they did, and also that from them we would be able to learn how situations involving sex, birth control, abortion, marriage, and children are defined by the participants—what distinctions they make, what issues are salient, what is common parlance for the technical and euphemistic terms in professional use.[20] There were an average of 7 participants per session, with sessions being differentiated by the age and economic status of the participants. In general, these discussions indicated that, while the universe of discourse of professionals and nonprofessionals differs in a number of interesting and important respects, and while some areas, such as abortion, require careful handling to avoid a break in communication, there is nevertheless enough commonality in language and outlook to make the use of a standard household questionnaire a workable proposition.

When a draft of the questionnaire was put together, it was tested and modified in 3 waves which, altogether, yielded 406 interviews with young women 15-19 years of age.[21] Simultaneously with this testing of the questionnaire, which allowed for redesign and then a further testing of changes, 2 experiments related to the use of incentives and the effect of interviewer characteristics on completion rates were carried out (see Appendix A). The final version of this pretest questionnaire was used for the 1971 survey and in great part was retained for the 1976 survey. As noted earlier, some items were dropped in 1976—particularly those dealing with selected attitudes, certain aspects of family background, and leisure activities—in favor of items that would provide more precise delineation of the timing and setting of sexual and contraceptive behavior. We aimed for an interview lasting no longer than an hour both because of cost and because of concern with declining quality if questioning continued much beyond this limit.

A major shortcoming in the studies to date has been the failure to investigate males in the same way that females have been studied. It is patent that to overlook the males' role in sex, contraception, and reproduction is to attempt a puzzle without all of the pieces. The 1971 survey does contain information as to the number of partners with whom the young woman has been sexually involved; in 1976 we again obtained

Introduction

information about the number of partners and, in addition, asked about the partner's age at first and last intercourse. This is important information to have, but far short of what is needed. We have since interviewed a national sample of males aged 17 to 21, the age range which, according to the findings from the 1976 survey, includes most of the consorts of sexually active females aged 15 to 19. Simultaneous with this interviewing of males, we interviewed a third round of young women.

Perspective

The bulk of discussion and of published output on adolescent fertility has seen it as a social problem rather than as a subject for scientific study. Not surprisingly, this perspective has given much attention to the consequences of early sex and pregnancy: illegitimacy and its long-term effects, venereal disease, child abuse, welfare costs, and so on. Some good research dealing with the consequences of early sex and reproduction has been produced, but the social problems perspective leads, often prematurely, to calls for action. This is inevitable when dealing with matters of such vital importance as these. By contrast, our concern here is with the determinants rather than the consequences of adolescent fertility, in the belief that better knowledge in this respect is crucial for more effective action. The reader looking for explicit prescriptions for social action will be disappointed. If it is true that social action is generally too important to be left to sociologists, action in this realm is certainly better left to the combined experience and talents of the many dedicated professionals in this field than to us. We think, however, that what we have learned will be useful to them. The results of these studies may also serve the purpose of those who oppose organized publicly supported programs to limit pregnancy and childbirth among the young, since the problem has proven to be resistent to intervention. Often overlooked is the likelihood that without the interventions things would have been a good deal worse.

Proclaiming a scientific interest in the roots of the problem, rather than taking a position of advocacy, does not allow us to escape concern with the normative context in which the behavior occurs. It obviously makes a great difference in understanding either the determinants or consequences of any item of behavior if it is licit or illicit, prescribed or proscribed, negatively or positively sanctioned.

How This Book Is Organized

Because of the large volume of published material dealing with the sex and fertility of married women, we focus here on premarital sex and fertility. The great majority of our respondents have never married; for the young women in our sample who have ever married, it is their premarital experiences with which we shall be concerned.

In Chapter 2 we present an overview of the world inhabited by young women, as it relates to reproductive behavior and as they see it. In doing so we introduce the variables that will be employed and further described in Chapters 3, 4, and 5. These three chapters deal in succession with premarital sex, the use of contraception, and pregnancy. The analysis is usually carried out separately for blacks and whites since, in general, there are large and not easily dissolvable differences by race in reproductive behavior. Chapter 6 provides a summary of the findings as well as a discussion of their implications. The sampling procedures, differences between the two surveys, evaluation of the survey results, the consent procedures, and the preliminary efforts undertaken in 1969-1970 prior to the 1971 survey are dealt with in the appendices.

Each of the analytical chapters (Chapters 3, 4, and 5) begins with a description of the behavior that is to be analyzed. The analysis then goes on to take account of the association between a fairly uniform set of variables which in general can be presumed to be antecedent to the behavior in question. To be sure, this does not settle the matter of causation, but it does bring us closer to an explanation of the behavior we are examining than if that condition were relaxed.

Although there is a considerable body of literature dealing with the sexual, contraceptive, and pregnancy-related behavior of young American women, there is very little that attempts to determine the causal significance of sociological variables. Much of the extant analysis involves psychological variables or sociological measures that are questionable on temporal grounds as causal variables. As a result, we have little to go on in positing the manner in which our variables presumably affect the various forms of behavior we are examining.

Whatever it may be that ultimately accounts for variation in premarital sexual behavior, contraceptive use, and the resolution of pregnancy, it seemed to us, a priori, that in addition to age and race we should look at the effects of such things as family background, social status, and religion. These are major structural elements of our system of social organization which, in theory at least, help to channel individual behavior along certain lines. Besides, it is of some real interest, in view of popular notions about the reproductive behavior of our teenage population, to know whether their behavior is homogeneous or sharply differentiated in terms of basic social differences. This is not the whole of the story by any means, since behavior is shaped by other influences, in particular by one's friends and

Introduction

associates. The trouble is that one picks one's friends and forms associations often as the result of behaving in certain ways or having certain experiences. Because of this inevitable circularity, we have deliberately avoided variables in which this issue appeared to be especially hard to resolve. We do, on occasion, depart from our self-imposed rule of avoiding intermixed contemporaneity between variables, as, for example, in the analysis of frequency of intercourse, when we introduce a consideration of marriage plans and type of contraception being used. For the most part, however, we stick to our resolve to respect a fairly evident time ordering among the independent and dependent variables.

Our ability to explain the behavior under observation is dependent on how well we have been able to identify and measure the appropriate variables. The short answer to that is "approximately—at best." What we call "family stability" is measured by how stable and how close to cultural prescription the young person's family situation was while she was being raised. Obviously, there is lots of room here for qualitative differences to which our measure is insensitive. As we treat it, socioeconomic status is simply an adjusted index based on the educational achievement of the person or persons who raised the young woman. Socioeconomic status is much more than that. Religion is perhaps a little better in that in addition to assigning the respondent to a religious group we also take account of how actively she observes her religion and how important it seemed to be for her and for her family while she was "growing up." Despite these disclaimers, it has been our observation that in social research important differences are usually revealed even by rough measures. Improved measurement sometimes sharpens a relationship but seldom alters broad lines of interpretation based on cruder assays.

As the analysis proceeds from a consideration of questions that are applicable to the entire sample (such as, "Have you ever had sexual intercourse?") to more restricted groups (such as those who have ever been pregnant) it necessarily becomes more coarse grained. This is true a fortiori in 1976, where in addition we are limited by a smaller sample.

There is need for much more research on the premarital behavior of young women. Our findings at best hold for only one society at one short interval in time. However, in spite of the various limitations of our analysis—sample size, quality of data, choice of variables, crudeness of measurement, and so on—we are convinced that we have made a reasonable start in separating the wheat from the chaff—a separation of fact from speculation—in regard to behavior that has important personal, familial, and societal consequences.

NOTES

1. In absolute terms; the birthrate peaked four years earlier, in 1957.
2. The average birthrate for the period 1942-1951 was 22.7, for 1952-1961, 24.4, and for the period 1962-1971, 19.2.
3. Reiss (1967), a leading student of attitudes about sexual behavior, maintains that attitudes toward premarital sex underwent a gradual shift toward greater permissiveness between 1920 and 1960 even though the prevalence of premarital sex remained fairly stable. Yankelovich (1974), comparing two national sample surveys, one conducted in 1969 and the other in 1973, reports a loosening of attitudes toward sex. Chilman (1978), in a comprehensive review of admittedly fragmentary and diverse research studies, concludes that by the late sixties sexual intercourse was becoming more common among young unmarried women.
4. If sociologists rediscovered the family during this period, the family came into prominence for other groups as well. Economists subsequently discovered the family and its relationship to fertility, as exemplified by the writings of the "new home economists." A "pro-family" movement recently has emerged as a significant political force dedicated to the defeat of any and all governmental actions such as ERA, payments for abortion, even the White House Conference on Families, which might interpose public policy between parents and children.
5. We use the phrase, "childbearing of young, unmarried women," to include the common phenomenon among adolescents of premarital pregnancies that subsequently are legitimated by marriage.
6. Whether the upsurge in the prevalence of casual unions is more of a prelude to marriage than a substitute for it, or whether the decline in the proportion of young women marrying represents a delay in marriage or an increase in the proportion who will never marry are questions still unanswered by recent research. It should be noted, however, that the demographic conditions for a bullish recovery in the marriage market (for young women) are better today than they have been for years. Beginning in the mid-sixties, much was heard about the "marriage squeeze" produced by rising numbers of births: females from the growing postwar cohorts looking for husbands in the smaller cohorts that preceded them. As the number of births have fallen, as they have since 1961, the marriage market for those cohorts is expected to improve. The young women in this study, however, must contend with an adverse marriage market (barring, of course, a radical shift in the traditional pattern of grooms being, on the average, a few years older than their brides).
7. There are, of course, problems involved in matching controls to cases and in determining whether the two groups are in fact from the "same population."
8. The 1971 baseline study also included a national sample survey of young women 15-19 living in college dormitories. These young women are excluded from the comparative parts of the analysis with the 1976 survey since it did not include a college dormitory sample.
9. Contact sufficient to confirm current address was made with 90 percent of the panel of respondents one year after the initial survey in 1971. The decision not to allow us to follow the respondents over a 5-year period as originally planned was not due to the technical problems of doing so, but rather to the expense. This is ironic in view of the much larger sums spent to follow cohorts of married women, many of whom have ended their childbearing careers.

Introduction

10. The overall cost of the 1976 survey was substantially reduced below what it otherwise would have been through the use of existing listings and screenings. Even so, the survey could not have been completed without additional funds from the Ford Foundation, subsidization by Johns Hopkins University, and some involuntary underwriting of costs by the subcontracting survey organization. Sacrificed in the 1976 survey were a reinterview to determine the reliability of selected items of information and a special sample of the college dormitory population, both of which were part of the first survey.

11. While material from both surveys has appeared in print, very little has been published which attempts to isolate variables which could explain the basic events in the behavioral chain: sex, contraception, pregnancy, and its outcome.

12. In addition, see the appendices.

13. See Appendix A for a detailed description of the sample designs and sample protocols, as well as a discussion of completion rates. The consent procedures followed in the two surveys are described in Appendix B.

14. We stubbornly avoid the fashion and the scientific pretentiousness of calling our questionnaires "instruments." This should not lead the reader to conclude that we slighted this aspect of the investigation. However, since we had to cover a lot of behavior and specify, as best we could, the context in which it occurred and the background from which it came, there was little warrant for using complicated scales and measurements of selected aspects of behavior or attitude which might indeed have merited the term "instrument." Our task was exploratory and extensive rather than probingly intensive.

15. Both the 1971 and 1976 surveys involved oversampling of blacks to ensure adequate numbers for analysis. The oversampling was most efficiently carried out by stratifying sampling points by race; the changes that had occurred in neighborhoods, however, meant that areas assigned to the strata were sometimes assigned to the wrong stratum; for fuller discussion, see Appendix A.

16. We use the term random, as in "random selection," as shorthand for "with known probability," as in selection with known probability. Failure to meet these requirements does not deter some investigators, especially the opinion polling fraternity, from solemnly reporting confidence limits or error ranges for their figures. We place little stock in such calculations and the ritualistic interpretations that accompany them when the basic data are of the rough and ready sort generally obtained from turning interviewers loose on the population no matter how careful the planning or conscientious the fieldwork. True random selection is seldom possible outside of controlled experimental conditions. Nevertheless, we cannot avoid the issue of chance as a factor in the differences we observe among our respondents. Therefore we make little of small differences (unless they display highly consistent patterns of difference), commenting instead only on those differences that are both relatively and absolutely large. We avoid also putting bounds on single parameter estimates.

17. We are indebted to Dr. Jeanne Claire Ridley of Georgetown University, who generously allowed us to use household listing and screening information which had been developed for the selection of an equally rare respondent: ever-married women age 65 and above. Without this assistance the cost of the 1976 survey would have been considerably larger and as a result probably would not have been carried out. Dr. Ridley's research was supported also by the Center for Population Research of

the National Institute of Child Health and Human Development, the primary source of funding for both the 1971 and 1976 surveys of young women.

18. Both the results of our test of validity in 1976 and the detailed flow of questions following the direct question on whether or not the respondent had had sexual intercourse suggest few, if any, instances of virgins reporting themselves as having had intercourse.

19. Data from the two surveys on "whites" refer to whites and nonwhites other than blacks.

20. A more complete description of how these sessions were organized and what was learned from them can be found in Kantner and Zelnik (1969) and Zelnik and Kantner (1970). The sessions were confined to black participants because at the time our intention was to undertake a national survey of black women, a group that up to then had not been well covered in national studies. This was rectified by the launching, in 1970, of the National Fertility Study, which included a generous oversampling of blacks. The group discussions were supported by Grant 10-P-56012/3 (originally CRD-470-C1) from the Social and Rehabilitation Service, U.S. DHEW. Also investigated under this grant were the relative advantages of using black or white, youthful or older interviewers (since by this time the focus had shifted to studying young women of all races), the usefulness of offering incentives to respondents, and, since a longitudinal study was then planned, the feasibility of relocating young respondents one year after initial contact (see Appendix A).

21. An analysis of pretest results as they relate to substantive rather than methodological issues has been published (Zelnik and Kantner, 1972a).

CHAPTER 2

THE WORLD OF THE TEENAGER

The chapters to follow are concerned with an explanation of sex, contraception, and pregnancy among young American women. Necessarily, they become quite technical as we seek to disentangle the overlapping factors that are involved. The overlap is not one that is neatly peeled away, like leaves of an artichoke, but more that of a plate of spaghetti, the unscrambling of which requires elaborate techniques. In the process of this unscrambling, the young woman and her world may become blurred, as can happen in inspecting a painting up close. So, before moving in for a closer look at circumscribed pieces of behavior, let us see what our subjects look like: their backgrounds, some of their attitudes, aspirations, their views of the world and of their own futures. Where possible, we compare information from both surveys, since the world of the teenager is a changing one. Whether the changes we can observe are the salient ones or, if they are, whether they can be captured in a short time segment we cannot say. Nevertheless, the pervasiveness of change in certain fundamental social relationships is undoubtedly an important influence on the changing behavior that this study attempts to interpret.

Family Background: Structure and Stability

It is axiomatic among behavioral scientists that one's upbringing is an important determinant of later behavior or, conversely, that clues to the interpretation of behavior are to be found in early family relationships. Other influences, such as friends, come into play subsequently, but these are necessarily refracted through the material that is there and that was shaped at an early age. We cannot, on the basis of coarse information such as results from a field survey, delve into the psychodynamic nuances that would be required for a thorough explication of the behavior of individual teenagers. But since we are observing gross changes and differences in behavior, such as broad changes in sexual activity, in contraceptive behavior, in the tendency to marry, to sustain, or abort a pregnancy, it is relevant to ask whether basic family relationships are also changing and, if so, in what manner. In addition to changes in behavior, we are interested also in differentials in behavior, especially as between whites and blacks, and thus we give attention to racial differences in family background.

The first question one might ask about a young woman's family background is who primarily raised her. We asked that question about the woman who was primarily responsible for the young woman's upbringing as well as about the male who stood in that same relationship to her. Overwhelmingly it is the biological mother who takes on this responsibility, although the grandmother or other female relative assumes this role for up to 10 percent of young black women. The young woman and the woman who raised her are found together in the same household with little change over the young woman's life course until she turns 18, after which there is some falling off in the percentage of households in which both are present. This situation is similar for whites and blacks and does not change appreciably between the two surveys.

As most readers would anticipate, things are different with respect to the male raiser. The father is the man responsible for the young woman's upbringing in about 9 out of 10 cases among young white women but among only 2 out of 3 young black women, 14 percent of whom in 1976 reported no male whatsoever involved in their raising. This difference can be seen also in whether the male raiser is presently in the household: For 4 out of 5 young white women, he is; whereas for only about half of the blacks is the male raiser a member of the household. These latter comparisons refer, as they should, only to young women who remain unmarried.

Focusing on the critical years between ages 10 and 15, when biological, psychological, and social changes are all occurring apace, sharp differences by race in the family setting are again clearly evident (see Table 2.1). A young black girl, as the figures in Table 2.1 show, is much more likely than her white counterpart during these years to be living in a family headed either by one parent only or by grandparents or other relatives. This difference is constant in the sense that the family situation for each birth cohort, from those born in 1952 to the births of 1961, looks essentially the same. The data are for the total samples, not just the never married. (When dealing with events or situations that refer to a time that generally predates marriage, we customarily consider the entire samples. Later on, when we consider current attitudes and perceptions or views about the future, matters which are likely to be influenced by marriage, we deal only with the never married.)

TABLE 2.1 Family Composition (in percentages)

Family Composition* Between Ages 10 and 15	1971			1976		
	Total	White	Black	Total	White	Black
Mother and father	79.7	83.9	52.7	76.5	81.1	47.9
Mother and stepfather	7.7	7.1	12.0	7.2	7.1	7.8
Mother or father only	10.3	7.7	26.7	13.7	10.0	36.2
Grandparents/aunt/uncle	1.7	0.8	7.3	1.2	0.6	5.3
Other	0.6	0.5	1.3	1.4	1.2	2.8
Total	100.0	100.0	100.0	100.0	100.0	100.0
n**	4392	2958	1434	2193	1491	702

*Each classification admits of the presence or absence of sibs.
**All percentages in this chapter are based on weighted sample cases.

In an effort to examine the stability of the family of orientation over a longer period, we have constructed, in greatly simplified fashion, a classification that distinguishes those who were raised in a sociologically, if not necessarily psychologically, "ideal" family from those raised in presumably less ideal circumstances. By "ideal" we mean that the natural (or adoptive) mother and father were both present in the household for at least the first 15 years of the respondent's life and that there was no prior marital dissolution due to separation, divorce, or death—a stable family situation so far as these criteria are concerned. A "less than ideal" or less stable family background is one in which the natural (or adoptive) parents raised the respondent, but one of the other conditions for the ideal situation has not been met. In the "least ideal" situation the respondent was not raised by natural (or adoptive) father and mother, that is, she was raised by a single parent, in a foster home, or by various parent surrogates. While the last category represents many different situations, attempts at further subdivision were frustrated both by logic and number of cases. There are "good" and "bad" families among all these types as anyone knows, although we would expect the more ideal type on average to have certain advantages in the difficult, demanding, time-consuming business of raising children.

The contrasts by race in family background seen from this perspective are sharp (see Table 2.2). By 1976 nearly as many blacks grew up in "least ideal" circumstances as belonged to "ideal families"; for whites the ideal situation predominated by a 7 to 1 margin.

There is a tendency toward the "ideal" type as the average education of the raisers increases. Table 2.3 shows the way the percentage living in the

TABLE 2.2 Family Type (in percentages)

Family Type	1971			1976		
	Total	White	Black	Total	White	Black
Ideal	70.1	74.8	40.2	66.0	70.9	36.1
Less ideal	17.1	15.6	26.5	20.9	19.5	29.7
Least ideal*	12.8	9.6	33.3	13.1	9.6	34.2
Total	100.0	100.0	100.0	100.0	100.0	100.0
n	4392	2958	1434	2193	1491	702

*Includes a small number of nonspecified cases.

TABLE 2.3 Percentage of Respondents in "Ideal" Family Type

Education of Raisers	1971		1976	
	%	n	%	n
Elementary school	64.8	825	56.7	379
Some high school	67.6	1497	64.3	700
High school graduate	75.3	986	69.2	576
Some college	73.4	757	71.8	363
College graduate	82.7	207	76.3	109

NOTE: Both races combined.

"ideal" family is distributed according to the education of the persons or person who raised the young woman.

Familism

The affectional side of family life is real, but how to capture its significance in a field survey is not obvious. Our attempt in this direction consists of several questions which we thought might reflect differences in how a young woman feels about her family and its importance to her. We assumed that, other things being equal, those who enjoyed a good relationship with their parents would tend to want to be around them after leaving home. It is easy to fault such a measure, but lacking the opportunity to go into this question in depth, we decided to see what we might learn from it.

Most young women believe it is important or "somewhat" important to live close to their parents after they leave home. Over 70 percent feel this way. Interestingly, those who say that proximity to those who brought them up is "not important" come disproportionately from the "least ideal" background, which tends to confirm that this classification, however broad it may be, does tap differences in familistic sentiment. Over 1 in 3 of young women from the "least ideal" background say that it is not important to be near those who raised them; less than 1 in 4 of those from "ideal" families profess to be indifferent on this score.

We made another stab at measuring familistic sentiment, this time attempting to get at the "tone" of the relationship—on whether, as we say, they "get along" with their parents. In 1971 the question was put directly, by asking whether they found it difficult to "keep pleasant around their parents." In 1976 we made the question more projective by asking whether they agreed or disagreed with the view that "most people" find it a chore to remain pleasant around their parents. The way the question is phrased appears to make some difference and therefore, in order to be as current as possible, we examine the less personalized form used in the more recent survey.

Young women, regardless of race or age, are about equally divided on the question of whether "most people" find it difficult to "keep pleasant around their parents." Agreement with the view that intrafamily cordiality is hard to maintain diminishes with increasing parental education, ranging from 60 percent for those whose parents had an elementary education down to 42 percent for those whose parents were college graduates.[1] Interestingly, this general view of the affectional tone of family life bears no relationship to the type of family of orientation: Young women from "ideal" families see this in about the same way as those from less stable backgrounds.

Family and Friends

A young woman's attitudes and behavior are strongly influenced, one way or the other, by her family. She is also influenced by the views and behavior of her friends. If these influences pull in the same direction, she will ordinarily be clear about the pressures she experiences; if they oppose each other, the young woman is faced with ambiguity and conflict in the pressures she feels. And, for most young women, there is often divergence in the views of her family and those of her friends. When asked, in 1976, "To what extent would you say that the things your friends wanted you to do and the things your parents wanted you to do were similar?" one-third responded that they were "not at all" similar; only 12 percent

TABLE 2.4 Similarity of Views of Family and Friends (in percentages)

Education of Parents	Very Similar	Somewhat Similar	Not at All Similar	Total	n
Elementary school	7.8	49.7	42.5	100.0	306
Some high school	12.5	51.3	36.2	100.0	597
High school graduate	11.8	58.5	29.7	100.0	498
Some college	13.9	64.9	21.2	100.0	330
College graduate	25.3	55.4	19.3	100.0	104

NOTE: 1976 data, never married only; both races combined.

said they were very similar. These percentages merely quantify the common observation that parents and peers represent two important influences in a young person's life which may be at times and on particular issues poles apart. The greatest divergence between the views of family and friends is found among those from the most deprived educational backgrounds. Table 2.4 presents the way the similarity of views of family and friends looks according to the education of the parents.

The young woman from a poorly educated family, on average, faces more ambiguity in the behavioral and attitudinal signals she receives from these two centers of influence than does the young woman from a well-educated family. This is true for both races. What this means precisely in terms of her sexual and reproductive behavior is not obvious, although there is theory to suggest that conflicting pressures of this sort can lead to indecision, to putting things off, to drifting into situations rather than moving by design.

Family and friends are heard differently depending on the issue. For life course decisions having to do with going to college, choosing a career, making money, the family appears dominant. Less than 1 in 5 young women, black or white, have views consistent with those of their friends on these issues (see Table 2.5). There is, however, a striking shift in reference groups when it comes to vital questions such as abortion and sex. On these matters, particularly sex, friends become relatively much more important. With respect to abortion, a sizable percentage hold views that are not like those of either family or friends.

We have seen that a young white woman is more likely to have parents around than is a young black woman. In theory, then, a white teenager would find it easier to consult with parents on difficult life course decisions. To see how this might work, we put to our 1976 respondents the following hypothetical question: In whom would you be most likely

TABLE 2.5 Similarity of Respondents' Views to Those of Family and Friends (in percentages)

R's Views Like:	Going to College	Choosing a Career	Making Money	Having an Abortion	Having Sex
Family	36.0	39.6	30.9	24.6	18.2
Friends	15.9	15.7	17.6	24.9	45.2
Both	32.7	32.9	33.2	21.3	15.5
Neither	15.0	11.2	17.1	27.1	20.1
Don't know	0.4	0.6	1.2	2.1	1.0
Total	100.0	100.0	100.0	100.0	100.0
n	1899	1899	1899	1899	1898

NOTE: 1976 data, never married only; both races combined.

TABLE 2.6 Person Respondent Would Consult if Pregnant (in percentages)

Would Consult:	Total	White	Black
Mother (or female guardian)	44.3	41.8	59.3
Friend*	38.0	40.1	25.5
Other relative	8.4	8.5	8.2
Physician	3.1	3.2	2.7
Other professional*	2.4	2.7	0.5
Father	1.5	1.4	1.8
Other	1.2	1.2	0.8
No one	1.1	1.1	1.2
Total	100.0	100.0	100.0
n	1891	1233	658

NOTE: 1976 data, never married only.
*"Friend" consists of girl friend, boy friend, or other friend; "other professional" consists of clergy, school counselor, teacher, in that order.

to confide if as an unmarried woman you found you were pregnant? The results are surprising. Blacks are more inclined than whites to consult their mothers; consulting one's peers is a more characteristic white response (see Table 2.6). Such crisis situations are matters for family or friends to advise on. Very few would seek professional counsel, and almost no one would go it alone. Whether fathers are as insignificant as these figures portray them is open to question. It does not appear that they would be the prime source of advice, but undoubtedly many young women in contacting their mothers on serious matters feel that they are seeking and getting a joint opinion. Responses to our question bore no relationship to type of family background—again, a somewhat surprising finding.

Religion

Most young American women profess some type of religious affiliation. Most are Protestants of some variety, principally main line Protestant churches. Fundamentalist Protestants, while increasing disproportionately between the two surveys, are nevertheless a small group amounting to less than 10 percent of the samples. The fastest-growing group, about the same size as the Fundamentalist Christians, are those who say they have no religious affiliation. About one-third of whites are Roman Catholics, a faith which claims very few blacks. Overall, young women, at least nominally, tend to be religious adherents with a distribution by faith and denomination similar to that of the larger population.

A more interesting question is how much adhesion there is to these nominal adherences. Aside from religious identification or affiliation, individuals differ in their sense of the importance of religion and the degree to which religion influences and affects their lives and their conception of the world around them. Even those who profess no affiliation with a formal religious organization or body may simultaneously believe themselves to be "religious," and believe that religion is important to their being and their conception and interpretation of reality. Conversely, many who are formal members of a religious body find little need or scope for a religious viewpoint in the ordering of their lives or in considering their surroundings and the daily flow of events. This sense of the importance of a religious orientation we have called religiosity.

We have created an index of religiosity from three separate items. The first asked: "(aside from attending religious services) how important would you say religion is to you?" Those answering "fairly unimportant" or "not important at all" were scored 0, those answering "fairly important" were scored 1, and those answering "very important" were scored 2. The second item, scored the same way as the first, asked about the importance of religion (aside from attendance at religious services) in the life of the respondent's family while she was growing up.

The third item was frequency of attendance at a religious service in the four weeks prior to the interview. Since frequency of religious services

TABLE 2.7 Religiosity of Respondents (in percentages)

Religiosity	1971		1976	
	White	Black	White	Black
Low	29.2	13.9	34.8	19.5
Medium	37.7	32.6	36.3	40.1
High	33.1	53.5	28.9	40.4
Total	100.0	100.0	100.0	100.0
n	2941	1420	1472	691

varies among the several religious denominations, the scoring of frequency was done separately for each of the religious categories, that is, the scoring was relative to the attendance of other persons in that category. An attempt was made to split the distribution by frequency into approximate thirds. This was not possible for the categories of Non-Christian and None since the majority in each of these categories reported zero attendance. Low frequency was scored 0, moderate frequency was scored 1, and high frequency was scored 2. Thus the total range of scores ran from 0 to 6; the final index is based on combining scores 0-2 to represent low religiosity, scores 3 and 4 to represent medium religiosity, and scores 5 and 6 to represent high religiosity.

According to our index, religiosity among young American women declined between 1971 and 1976 for both races (see Table 2.7). The figures in Table 2.7 are for both ever and never married. The trend is consistent with the large relative increase in those professing no religion and is quite pervasive. For example, the change is found at each age and, for whites at any rate, has no association with the parents' educational level. There is, however, an association between religiosity and family stability which is somewhat more evident among whites than among blacks. The decline in religiosity, while evident at either the low or high end of the family stability scale, was least among young women from "ideal" families.

Some readers may be tempted to see in this decline of the apparent influence of religion among young women a root cause of the rise in sexual activity, pregnancy, abortion, and the decline in marriage, all of which we document and analyze in subsequent chapters. Before reaching such a conclusion, one should wait to see to what extent religiosity, either alone or in combination with family stability, is a factor in these things and, where it is, to consider whether there may not be other factors that underlie both changes in sex and reproductive behavior and the decline in religiosity.

Social Life

To a casual observer of contemporary teenage social behavior in the United States, it may seem that anything as structured and planned as a "date" would be an anachronism. Certainly the Norman Rockwell version of a dandified, front porch caller, if he ever made it out of small-town America, is now on the list of extinct species. A more realistic model for adolescent social behavior might seem to be that of Brownian movement—constant, random movement, chance collision of particles, decipherable only in the aggregate. Nonetheless, our respondents did respond to a question about "Saturday dates" in such fashion as to suggest that the term, however quaint or archaic, still has meaning for them.

The frequency of dating increases rapidly with age. At age 15 about half report having no dates in the last month. This figure declines to less than one-third by age 19. Those who are fully booked, that is, 4 or more dates per month, rises from around 15 percent at age 15 to 35 percent at age 19. There is very little association between dating and either parents' educational background or residence among blacks; among whites there may be a somewhat greater degree of circulation by young women who live in urban areas but outside of the central city. The pattern of dating in 1976 looks essentially the same as in 1971. Family stability has no effect on the amount of dating—a finding that will be surprising to some.

The time available for social activities and the resources available to pursue them no doubt are affected by whether a young woman has a job for which she is paid. Is a young woman without financial resources of her own handicapped in sexual negotiations? Does her partner assert a greater claim on her? Or does income provide independence from parental control, with the result on balance that these considerations become irrelevant as factors in heterosexual dealings? We can't answer these questions. Nevertheless, it is interesting to note that regardless of the educational level of parents, whites are much more likely to be economically active than are blacks, and they appear to be somewhat more active in 1976 than earlier (see Table 2.8). We leave it to the reader to reflect on these figures and to our professional colleagues to discover what, if any, relationship there may be between economic activity and other facets of a young person's social existence.

TABLE 2.8 Percentage of Young Women with Paid Employment

| | 1971 | | | | 1976 | | | |
| | White | | Black | | White | | Black | |
Education of Parents	%	n	%	n	%	n	%	n
Elementary school	34.4	349	15.5	389	40.2	143	14.0	163
Some high school	35.1	821	20.6	540	42.6	363	20.0	237
High school graduate	37.5	707	16.0	205	44.7	352	23.9	146
Some college	37.2	597	20.3	122	49.6	278	40.2	54
College graduate	35.5	172	22.2	29	53.0	85	19.8	20

NOTE: Never married only.

Perceptions of Society

The sexual and reproductive behavior with which this book is concerned occurs in a normative context. Such behavior may be in conformity with or in defiance of recognized norms but is always carried out with respect to them. In this section, we consider the perceptions young women have of what is permissible and what is forbidden in this realm of behavior and the extent to which society is seen to enforce sanctions against transgressors.

As a general proposition one might suppose that the more serious the consequences of a normative transgression the more explicit and severe the collective condemnation of it, and vice versa. Such matters are, of course, highly relative. Premarital intercourse among some groups is as much of a moral transgression and as severely condemned as illegitimacy is among others. Nevertheless, the bearing of a child out of wedlock ordinarily provokes the greater concern and comment. For this reason we give most attention to the views young women have of the way their neighbors and society generally respond to illegitimacy. On the way we have a brief look at how young women regard premarital sex in moral terms and under what conditions they would approve of abortion. Both are obviously gateway events affecting the prevalence of illegitimacy.

Premarital sex: Most young women think that sex before marriage is all right. Some add the provision that the young couple must be serious about getting married. There are large differences by race, with blacks being much less inclined to disapprove. Attitudes about the permissibility of premarital sex alter rapidly in a more permissive direction as the young woman advances through adolescence toward adulthood (see Table 2.9).

TABLE 2.9 Attitudes Toward Premarital Sex (in percentages)

Age Group and Race	Sex Always All Right	All Right if Planning to Marry	Never All Right	Total	n
White					
15-17	18.9	33.6	47.5	100.0	857
18-19	27.9	40.3	31.8	100.0	380
Black					
15-17	43.4	30.1	26.5	100.0	408
18-19	59.9	23.9	16.2	100.0	247

NOTE: 1976 data, never married only.

Views about the permissibility of sex before marriage vary by family stability as well as by age and race. Young women from "ideal" families are somewhat more conservative. For 1976 the data are presented in Table 2.10. Overall there is little difference in attitude between those raised in the two relatively "unstable" family situations; the young woman from a stable family background, on the other hand, is much less inclined to give blanket approval to premarital sex and much more likely to say that sex before marriage is never permissible. However, overwhelming the differences by family type are the differences in attitude toward premarital sex by race. The most common view among blacks, regardless of family background, is that sex before marriage is always all right; either an outright prohibition or approval on condition that there be the prospect of marriage is the attitude of most whites. As we shall see later, these attitudinal differences are matched by corresponding differences in sexual behavior.

There is an interesting interaction by race in the association between parents' education and the attitude toward premarital sex. Among blacks, those from the most educated homes are the most conservative: one-third of those whose parents went to college (half of those whose parents were college graduates) disapprove of premarital sex; approximately one-fifth of those whose parents failed to make it through high school take this view. Whites exhibit the opposite tendency. For each race and at each age, the attitude regarding premarital sex attributed by respondents to their "girl friends" is more liberal still. This is particularly true if the young woman is from an "unstable" family: half of such young women report that their girl friends think premarital sex is always all right; this is the case for only

TABLE 2.10 Attitudes Toward Premarital Sex, by Family Type and Race (in percentages)

Family Type and Race	Sex Always All Right	All Right if Planning to Marry	Never All Right	Total	n
White					
Ideal	18.9	35.2	45.9	100.0	899
Less ideal	30.6	37.2	32.2	100.0	229
Least ideal	30.5	39.4	30.1	100.0	107
Black					
Ideal	45.2	28.2	26.6	100.0	238
Less ideal	50.9	30.3	18.8	100.0	199
Least ideal	52.8	25.5	21.7	100.0	217

NOTE: Never married only.

one-quarter of young women from "ideal" families. All of this would seem to mean that although some young women do not approve of premarital sex, it is not difficult to find a contrary opinion held either by a friend or someone a little older. Nothing so undermines a normative prescription as exceptions to it. Indeed, if statistical evidence can be entertained as relevant to a normative question, it would seem reasonable to conclude that in the United States, as of the mid-1970s, premarital chastity was effectively defunct as a widely held behavioral norm.

Illegitimacy: Traditionally, the bearing of a child outside of a sanctioned marital union has been condemned the world around.[2] It is a threat to the integrity of the family system and therefore to the larger system of which the family is an integral part. This view of the basis for the near universal disapproval of illegitimacy represents the accumulated social wisdom which recognizes the dysfunctional effects of extramarital childbirth. How do young women see it? To what extent would they anticipate condemnation from their neighbors and from society at large should they fall from social grace in this manner?

Since we are interested in whether young women anticipate that there would be condemnation, we confine ourselves in this instance to the never married, proportionately fewer of whom have experienced premarital pregnancy and the direct effect of collective disapproval. Table 2.11 presents the responses to a question concerning the degree to which society condemns an unwed mother. Relatively few see society as noncon-

TABLE 2.11 Respondents' Perceptions of Societal Condemnation of Unwed Mother (in percentages)

Society Condemns Unwed Mother	1971 White	1971 Black	1976 White	1976 Black
Very strongly	23.5	30.6	18.9	23.1
Strongly	38.8	29.7	36.3	29.7
Somewhat	34.5	30.2	38.8	30.6
Not at all	2.6	8.6	4.8	13.6
Don't know	0.6	0.9	1.2	3.1
Total	100.0	100.0	100.0	100.0
n	2666	1355	1241	658

NOTE: Never married only.

TABLE 2.12 Respondents' Perceptions of Neighborhood Condemnation of Unwed Mother (in percentages)

Neighborhood Condemns Unwed Mother	1971 White	1971 Black	1976 White	1976 Black
Very strongly	35.2	21.3	31.2	17.7
Strongly	29.8	20.8	27.6	18.6
Somewhat	25.7	30.8	28.5	26.4
Not at all	6.4	23.9	10.1	32.7
Don't know	2.9	3.2	2.6	4.6
Total	100.0	100.0	100.0	100.0
n	2664	1356	1241	658

NOTE: Never married only.

demnatory; even fewer say they don't know what the reaction would be. These figures vary only a little by age (whites are less inclined in 1976 toward "very strongly" as age increases), scarcely at all by parents' education or family stability, and are not greatly dissimilar by race. A brute social fact would seem to be reflected in these responses; yet it cannot be ignored that approximately 2 out of 5 young women do not feel that social disapprobation of illegitimacy is strong. This strikes us as a significant breach in our social defenses.

A similar question was asked about the way the neighborhood would react to an unwed mother. The data in Table 2.12 show an interesting racial division. Whites tend to see their neighborhoods as strict as society

TABLE 2.13 Respondents' Perceptions of Attitudes Toward Illegitimate Child (in percentages)

People Look Down On Illegitimate Child	1971 White	1971 Black	1976 White	1976 Black
Very much	20.8	30.6	17.5	26.4
Somewhat	51.6	33.3	49.9	36.2
Very little	20.7	26.0	25.3	25.2
Not at all	6.9	10.1	7.3	12.2
Total	100.0	100.0	100.0	100.0
n	2656	1349	1234	658

NOTE: Never married only.

at large. One might say that for whites the neighborhood is society or a reasonable surrogate (although when society is the reference, respondents shy away from the extremes of very strong condemnation or unconcern). Blacks, on the other hand, see their neighbors as holding much less stringent views than those they project for society at large. Between one-fourth and one-third of blacks say either that their neighbors would not condemn an unmarried mother or that they are not sure what their attitudes would be. There are also relatively fewer at the other extreme, who expect their neighbors' attitudes to be as strongly negative as those found generally in society. Again, there are no consistent or strong trends in these data by the respondent's age whether she be black or white. If, as is often alleged without much data, young unmarried women are having babies to establish themselves as autonomous adults, most would have to expect a poor reception from society. The black neighborhood, while also seen as generally against this kind of behavior, does appear to be accepting of it by a significant minority of the young women who live there. It is interesting to note that between 1971 and 1976 both "society" and "neighborhood" were perceived as having softened their objections slightly. The change is not great, but it is consistent for both races.

What about the child? The mother of an illegitimate child must be concerned not only about her reception but also that accorded her child. In the aggregate, the responses to the question, "To what extent do people look down on an illegitimate child?" resemble those for the earlier question relating to society's view of an unwed mother (see Table 2.13). The dispersion of views among blacks is greater than among whites, but the primary message in these data is that the majority of young women of either race expect the child in such a situation to suffer more than a little discrimination. There is virtually no change in this regard between surveys nor are there strong or consistent trends by parents' education or family stability. This is, in short, a relatively stable, pervasive perception. Differences by the age of the respondent lack consistency between the two surveys.

In response to a separate question that asked whether the respondent thought an illegitimate child was disadvantaged by the fact of social disapproval, whites answered very much as they did with respect to the previous question. That these are taken as different questions is suggested by the different way blacks answered the two questions. There is lack of agreement among blacks about the handicaps resulting from illegitimacy. About the same proportion of blacks say a child is "very much" disadvantaged through bastardy as say a child is "not at all" disadvantaged by this circumstance.

Taking all these questions together, one might summarize by saying that whites see illegitimacy and the reaction to it in somewhat harsher terms than blacks. Both groups have a similar perception of the general position of society toward the unwed mother and her child. Blacks, however, find a somewhat greater vein of tolerance running through their neighbors and are less inclined to feel that the illegitimate child is disadvantaged.

These are interesting differences which could have something to do with some of the difference we report later on the racial differences in the resolution of pregnancy, and perhaps also of sexual activity. None of this, however, should cause us to lose sight of the larger fact that the great majority of young women, black or white, see illegitimacy as deviant behavior, condemned by society and neighbors and handicapping for the innocent party—the child.

What should the role of society be? Should it help the unwed mother or should it remain sternly aloof and let her learn her lesson the hard way? Or, as the women we talked with in preparing for these studies often maintained without apparent contradiction, is "everyone entitled to one mistake," after which, presumably, forgiveness fades? On this point our respondents are in broad agreement (see Table 2.14).

Very few would deny help to the unwed mother, although whites are consistently less openhanded than blacks. There is some suggestion that both groups have become a bit more willing to see help extended beyond the initial transgression. Views on this subject among blacks are unvarying by age or parents' education and lack consistency between the surveys relative to the association with family stability; among whites, generosity

TABLE 2.14 Responses Concerning Societal Help for Unwed Mother (in percentages)

| Society Should Help | 1971 | | 1976 | |
Unwed Mother	White	Black	White	Black
Never	5.8	3.0	7.9	4.4
First time only	53.4	48.7	41.3	33.2
Each time	40.8	48.3	50.8	62.4
Total	100.0	100.0	100.0	100.0
n	2660	1353	1231	656

NOTE: Never married only.

(giving help each time) is negatively associated with age. As with blacks, there is no consistent association with parents' education or with family stability.

In these various responses concerning the perceptions of the normative climate surrounding illegitimacy, the evidence consistently signals a trend toward more tolerant, accepting attitudes. As is the case of the relaxation of attitudes toward premarital sex, the loosening of attitudes toward illegitimacy and some of its consequences is matched by changes in the corresponding behavior.

Abortion: Premarital sexual activity has been rising steadily in recent years and has been responsible in large part for rising pregnancy rates. At the same time, the shotgun marriage is becoming a cultural relic. Thus, it is only an increase in abortion more or less paralleling the rise in pregnancy that has prevented runaway illegitimacy rates (Zelnik and Kantner, 1980).

With abortion becoming more common as part of the defense system against premarital births, the expectation would be that attitudes toward it would become more definite and possibly also more liberal. Conventional practice in measuring attitudes toward abortion is to use a set of questions defining different conditions under which abortion might be acceptable. Attitudes are then arrayed from those who would accept abortion under no circumstances at one extreme to those who would approve it to save a life or in case of rape, on down the list to those whose conditions are less demanding. We followed this practice in the two surveys.

Comparison of responses between the surveys is difficult because of differences in the way the questions were handled. In the first survey the questions on abortion attitude were included as part of a self-administered questionnaire, with three possible response categories provided, including

TABLE 2.15 Percentage of Respondents Approving Abortion for Young, Unmarried Woman

Would be All Right if:	1971 White	1971 Black	1976 White	1976 Black
Health endangered	88.9	76.9	86.6	75.8
Case of rape	86.3	80.3	81.0	76.7
Child likely to be deformed	71.1	50.4	61.5	48.8
Mother very young	59.6	39.1	57.9	50.8
Can't afford	32.4	33.1	28.3	31.4
Any reason, i.e., on demand	32.4	32.4	39.0	41.4
n*	2621	1317	1239	657

NOTE: Never married only.

*n is same for each of the conditions.

"don't know" as one. In 1976, on the other hand, the same questions were asked by the interviewer, who also read out the possible positive and negative responses but omitted the "don't know" response, although it was available on the questionnaire as a response. For this reason, perhaps, there was a substantial drop in the "don't know" category in 1976 for both races. The change might, of course, represent a real reduction in the ambiguity surrounding this issue during a time when abortion was becoming more common and a salient national issue. But the possibility that the change is traceable to the change in the way the question was presented is equally plausible. For the sake of comparison, we have resorted to a proportional reallocation of "don't know" responses on the assumption that if forced to reply one way or the other those who were uncertain of their opinions would distribute themselves in the same fashion as those who stated a definite view.[3] Table 2.15 shows percentages who would approve of abortion for a young, unmarried woman (with "don't know" proportionately allocated) relative to six different conditions.

The results are not unlike those from surveys of adults. Danger to the mother's health or rape are widely acknowledged as reasons justifying abortion. Opinions on this score have remained steady from one survey to the next. The likelihood that a child would be born with a congenital defect is less compelling, but nevertheless most whites see it as sufficient justification for abortion, although fewer do so in 1976 than in 1971; blacks are more nearly divided on this one. The case of a "very young" mother is accorded about the same measure of sympathy in 1976 as the young woman faced with the prospect of a defective child; we are not inclined to make much of the differences between the responses to these two questions in 1971 because of the ambiguity referred to earlier. There is, however, a decided drop in approval when the reason given is one in which the ratio of victimization to indulgence appears to be low. Somewhere around a third or less of the respondents are persuaded by economic reasons that abortion would be an acceptable resolution of a teenager's premarital pregnancy. Abortion on demand gets about the same reception, although it may have gained some adherents between the two surveys. Generally, however, the pattern of responses has remained fairly stable, there being little or no evidence of a shift toward a more liberal position on the issue of abortion. Most teenagers feel that abortion is justified only under circumstances involving conditions beyond the mother's control. Although a substantial minority would disagree, the majority of young women appears to dismiss as valid grounds for the termination of a premarital pregnancy economic reasons or unspecified reasons which seem important to the mother.

The proportion approving abortion under any of these conditions varies positively with parents' education among whites; among blacks the relationship is more erratic but shows a positive inclination (Figures 2.1 and 2.2). Beyond that it is hard to generalize. Whites are more liberal than blacks except where the "softer" reasons are concerned, but there are exceptions. It is worth noting that 85 percent or more of teenagers of either race whose parents had at least a high school education would approve of abortion for a young unmarried woman if she had been raped or if her health would be endangered by continuing the pregnancy. At the other extreme, approval of abortion on demand approximates 50 percent among children of white college graduates, more than 20 percentage points higher than among white children whose parents had only an elementary education. Curiously, the educational background of parents has no clear relationship among blacks to their attitude toward abortion on demand.

In the national debate on abortion that has become an unfortunate part of the political process in the United States, a liberal position has come to be one that would agree to public payment for an abortion to preserve the health of the mother or in the case of rape or incest. As we have seen, young women have little trouble approving abortion under these conditions. Whether they would agree to using public funds for this purpose is a separate issue on which we have no information.

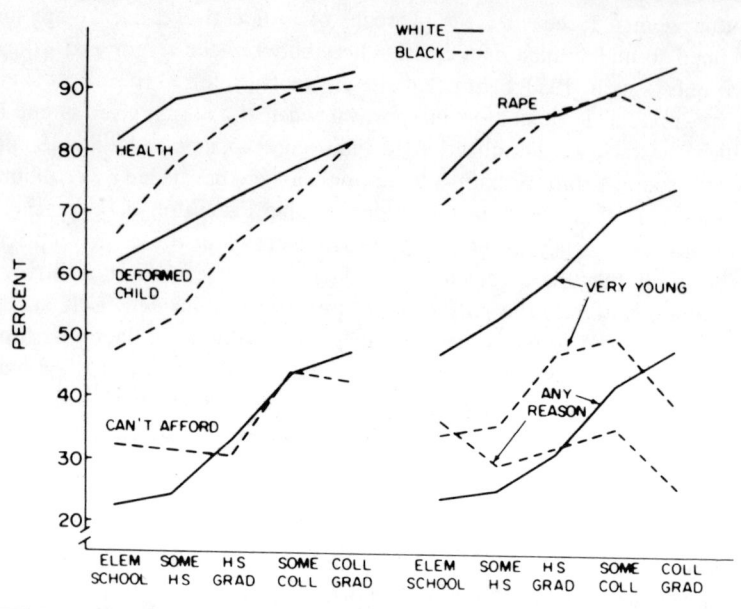

Figure 2.1 Percentage of Never-Married Women 15-19 Years of Age Approving Abortion for Stated Reasons, by Education of Parents and Race: 1971

The Future

Among the "explanations" frequently encountered for early pregnancy and premarital childbirth is that many young women either have no notion of where they are heading or have such bleak prospects that they seek some kind of fulfillment in the present. They are said to center their lives around "a baby," finding in this absorbing activity meaning, contentment, affection, and sometimes a new identity. We have never seen anything more than selected anecdotal evidence for this interpretation, but it is persistent and much loved by those who espouse it since it is at once an explanation and a social indictment—a social indictment because "society" has failed to offer these young people a vision of a satisfying and realizable future. However true or untrue this view, it does suggest that a young woman's future orientation is relevant to the way she behaves in the present.

Another, less romantic view, to which many seasoned service providers attest, is one of the teenager as inarticulate, befuddled, directionless, and indecisive, with no view at all of the future. As such, they exhibit certain

The World of the Teenager

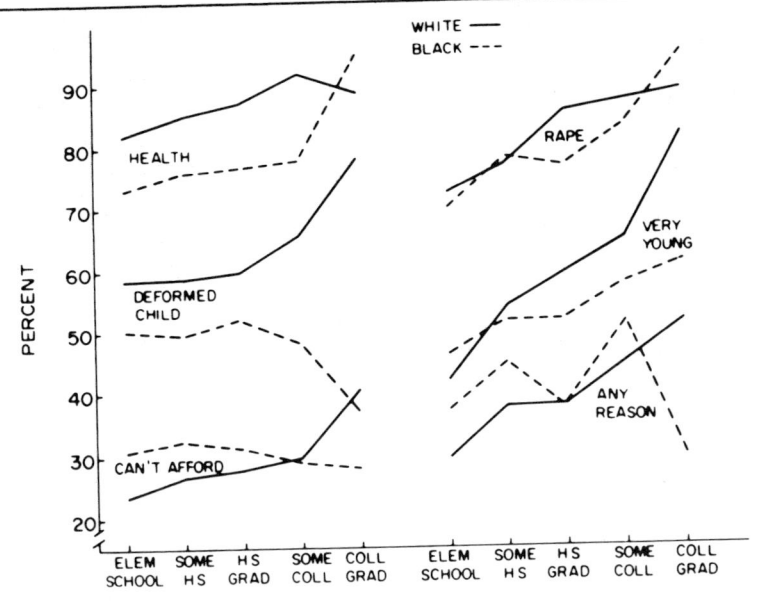

Figure 2.2 Percentage of Never-Married Women 15-19 Years of Age Approving Abortion for Stated Reasons, by Education of Parents and Race: 1976

tropistic forms of behavior, are subject to urges and subcortical promptings, and have a planning horizon which stretches barely beyond the next weekend. They are propelled by a vague serendipity and display an amazing sense of immunity and of displaced responsibility for their actions. This unflattering view is no more supported by hard fact than the romantic version. No doubt it also fits many teenagers; the question, as with the first depiction, is its generality.

Familiar also is the achievement-oriented young woman, who knows exactly what she wants from life and will often sacrifice immediate gratification on the altar of her long-term ambitions. Or, if gratification is not totally denied, then care is taken to avoid derailing consequences. Many paths are taken, and young people have developed their own incisive, sometimes derisive, stereotypes for those who take them: the "preppy," who sees herself becoming a young matron; a conforming "goody two shoes," who follows her good reputation like the grail; an achiever with visions of the laboratory, the executive suite, the courtroom, the theater—either operating or thespianic—and on and on. Many pathways, the point being that there are paths and the future has form.

TABLE 2.16 Educational Aspirations (in percentages)

Educational Aspirations*	1971 White	1971 Black	1976 White	1976 Black
Beyond high school	60.7	52.7	61.3	59.7
Finish college or beyond	42.2	37.9	40.7	39.3
n	2644	1341	1226	654

NOTE: Never married only.

*Don't knows were classified in terms of education already completed.

There is no reason to stop here. Other models of behavior are available. Our aim, however, is not to catalogue behavior—we don't have the data to do so properly in any case—but to see in general how the young women in our samples view certain aspects of the future.

Educational aspirations: A place to start, perhaps, is with educational aspirations. Education is the gateway to the future. It defines the range of future opportunity and also conditions current behavior, since the present becomes the prelude to what comes after. It is also a mechanism highly vulnerable to damage from early childbearing, which is the main reason such an event is handicapping.

The question regarding educational aspirations or, more accurately, educational expectations, was asked the same way in the two surveys, both with respect to wording and its place in the sequence of questions. This is important to note because there has been essentially no change in the expected level of completed education, as seen from the percentage who expect to go beyond high school and those who aim to finish college (see Table 2.16). Educational aspirations, as might be expected, are positively associated with parents' education. In 1976, for example, 24 percent of those whose parents had less than a high school education expected to complete college; 88 percent of the children of college graduates had such expectations. Young women from stable family backgrounds were also more likely to aspire to a college education.

Career and family: The overwhelming majority of young women intend to work after marriage, an expectation that differs little by age or by race. We limited our question to those who were seriously intent on marriage to their current "boy friend" in order to force as much realism as possible. In recent years, women of all ages have entered the labor force in unprecedented numbers and proportions. Those in our survey expect to join their ranks, and marriage is no bar.

TABLE 2.17 Attitudes Toward Family and Career, by Parents' Education (in percentages)

Having a Family Should Not Interfere With Career	Elementary School	Some High School	High School Graduate	Some College	College Graduate
1971					
Strongly agree	11.7	8.1	10.2	11.6	14.5
Agree	29.3	29.5	25.2	33.6	35.0
Disagree	40.9	41.5	44.6	39.7	29.2
Strongly disagree	18.1	20.9	20.0	15.1	21.3
Total	100.0	100.0	100.0	100.0	100.0
n	728	1337	896	709	199
1976					
Strongly agree	14.6	18.7	22.8	30.5	36.3
Agree	46.8	43.6	45.1	39.7	41.9
Disagree	31.7	30.2	26.8	25.2	13.3
Strongly disagree	6.9	7.5	5.3	4.6	8.5
Total	100.0	100.0	100.0	100.0	100.0
n	305	595	495	331	104

NOTE: Never married only; both races combined.

A more interesting question, perhaps, is whether having a family should be allowed to interfere with a career. In 1971, young women whose parents were college educated were almost equally divided on this issue. Support for the idea that "having a family should not interfere with one's career" was only slightly less strong among young women from less educated backgrounds. By 1976, something significant seems to have happened to increase the resolve of young women that careers should not be sacrificed to family responsibilities. A solid majority, of both blacks and whites, feels this way, and agreement goes up with parents' education, sharply so with respect to strong agreement on this point. Table 2.17 presents the figures by parents' education for the two surveys.

In putting questions to respondents, there is the risk that one might precipitate answers on matters that previously had been given little

TABLE 2.18 Concern with the Future, by Parents' Education (in percentages)

Have Thought About the Future	Elementary School	Some High School	High School Graduate	Some College	College Graduate
A lot	35.9	39.5	43.8	46.5	55.5
Some	35.7	39.0	35.5	36.5	34.8
Very little/not at all	28.4	21.5	20.7	17.0	9.7
Total	100.0	100.0	100.0	100.0	100.0
n	306	598	498	331	104

NOTE: 1976 data, never married only; both races combined.

thought. From general observation, our impression is that many young people do give a lot of thought to what they will be doing a few years hence. However, we thought we might better ask them, and so in 1976 we asked our respondents how much they had thought about what they would be doing at age 25. Most had given some thought to the question; some had given it "a lot" of thought. Differences in this regard by race or by family stability were negligible, but for both blacks and whites, concern with the future, if that is the correct term, was greatest among those whose parents had the most education (Table 2.18).

The question, of course, was without specific content. Not having the luxury of probing what it was they thought they might be doing, we settled for merely finding out to what extent they had the future in view. Most expect to work. Beyond that are the questions of marriage and family.

Having some children figures in the future of these young women. In response to a question regarding the number of children they intend to have, less than 1 in 10 said they did not plan to have children. Nor were many attracted by a one-child family. The most common reply in 1976 was 2 children; more than 2 out of 5 of blacks and whites gave this response. More surprising, perhaps, given all we hear about replacement fertility, is the continued popularity of families with 3 or more children: 55 percent of blacks and 46 percent of whites gave that as their answer. Replacement fertility, of course, does not rule out families with 3 or more children. These responses have little or no consistent association with family stability or parents' education. Although not strictly comparable because of the coding categories used, a comparison of responses for 1971

TABLE 2.19 Ideal Age to Have First Baby

Ideal Age for First Baby	1971		1976	
	White	Black	White	Black
Modal age	23-25	18	23-25	18
Percentage less than age 20	5.2	34.1	6.5	35.2
Percentage greater than age 25	9.0	5.8	15.1	6.6
Percentage nonnumeric	18.6	11.5	18.8	18.5
n	2667	1356	1241	660

NOTE: Never married only.

and 1976 provides little evidence of change with respect to family size intentions; certainly no indication of a downward revision of family size goals (Hirsch et al., 1981).

What is the best age for a young woman to start a family, to have her first baby? In both surveys there were some who did not specify an age, but gave instead a qualitative reply, such as, "whenever she is old enough" or "whenever she is ready." Among the more than 80 percent who provided a quantitative answer, responses were more or less the same in the two surveys, with allowances for minor differences in the coding of responses. There are major differences, however, by race, as can be seen from the statistics presented in Table 2.19. Blacks clearly favor earlier childbearing: Approximately one-third put the ideal age under 20, with age 18 the preferred age. Whites, on the other hand, place the ideal age in the early 20s; relatively few would pick an age under 20.

The education of parents has the effect of deferring childbearing, at least in this idealized version of when it should begin. This is consistent with the findings reported earlier on the association between parents' education and educational aspirations: The more educated the parents, the more likely are their children to aim high educationally and therefore to push the ideal age for the start of family building into the early to mid-20s. This is true for both blacks and whites, and so we show (Table 2.20) the median ideal age to have[4] first baby for both races combined according to parents' education.

Marriage and childbearing are not always perceived in synchrony; indeed, that is the nub of the problem of premarital childbirth. But behavior is one thing; what should be is another. We show in Table 2.20

TABLE 2.20. Ideal Age to Marry and Have First Child, by Parents' Education

	1971			1976		
Education of Parents	Median Ideal Age to Marry	Median Ideal Age First Child	Difference	Median Ideal Age to Marry	Median Ideal Age First Child	Difference
Elementary	20.8	21.9	1.1	21.1	21.6	0.5
Some High School	20.9	22.3	1.4	21.3	22.5	1.2
High School Graduate	21.5	23.3	1.8	22.1	23.8	1.7
Some College	21.9	23.8	1.9	22.7	24.5	1.8
College Graduate	22.2	24.4	2.2	23.6	25.3	1.7

NOTE: Never married only; both races combined.

the median ideal age at marriage. Overall, the ideal age to marry increased between 1971 and 1976 by a fraction of a year, except among children of college graduates, where there was a more substantial increase. In general, the more the parents' education, the higher the ideal age for marriage. The spread between marriage and the first child also tends to widen with increased parental education, although more uniformly so in 1971 than in 1976 (see Table 2.20). The difference between the ideal age to marry and to have the first child implies approval of premarital conception or something close to it in those cases in which the parents have less than a high school education; a year or two beyond marriage is the implied interval preferred by young women from more educated backgrounds. If, on average, the first child is born when a mother of unimpaired fecundity is aged 24 or younger, she will have no difficulty in completing her family by the time she is 30. Childbearing, therefore, as ideally viewed, is confined to a relatively limited period. Child rearing extends well beyond, but in most instances would be completed, coincidentally, around the age of menopause.

If historical trends continue, this group of young women, the "baby boom" children, will enter the labor force in unprecedented numbers, form and dissolve marriages at rates that will raise doubts about the survival of the family, but, withal, they will have some children. Most students and commentators predict their road will be rough because, if for no other reason, there are so many of them. This study sees them off.

NOTES

1. Most "raisers" are parents. Because of the awkwardness of continually referring to "those who raised the young woman," we adopt the slightly inaccurate shorthand, "parents," in place of the ear-offending, but more accurate, "raisers."

2. This is not to deny that pregnancy or sometimes stillbirth before marriage may be valued in some societies as proof of fecundity. So long as this occurs as a recognized prelude to a marriage that is scheduled to follow if the issue of gravidity is settled to everyone's satisfaction, we would not regard that as inconsistent with our proposition.

3. In all instances, reallocation of "don't knows" was greatest in 1971, substantially greater for blacks than for whites; least uncertainty was registered for "health endangered" and greatest for "any reason." Average proportions allocated were: 1971–black 23 percent, white 14 percent; 1976–black 5 percent, white 3 percent.

4. To "have" a baby is an unfortunately ambiguous expression. The intended meaning was childbirth; for some it may have meant the beginning of the process, that is, pregnancy.

CHAPTER 3

PREMARITAL INTERCOURSE

Efforts to study and explain the fertility of young women heretofore have been handicapped by an inability to focus on those young women who are exposed to the risk of becoming pregnant.[1] When we read that fertility has either gone up or down among young women, we cannot be certain whether this is because there is a change in the level of sexual activity, or in the likelihood of pregnancy among the sexually active, or some of each. National data on fertility that relate childbearing among women in a given age group to women of that age do so regardless of the extent of sexual activity among them. The problem is particularly troublesome among young women, proportionately fewer of whom are married or sexually active if unmarried. Fertility data for older women are less problematic in this respect since exposure to the risk of pregnancy, that is, sexual activity, is much more pervasive among them than among younger women. It is a matter, in short, of how appropriate the denominator of the fertility rate is with respect to the numerator. Among older women the fit is good enough for most analytical purposes; among younger women, say, those under age 20, it is necessary to take account of sexual activity in order to avoid misinterpreting what the data mean.

One could, of course, deal only with the fertility of married women, for whom the assumption of exposure to the risk of pregnancy is generally valid. However, for young women this would exclude a substantial portion of those who are having babies since much of their childbearing and an even greater fraction of their pregnancies occur outside of marriage. There is thus an unavoidable methodological problem in attempting to analyze the fertility of young women on the basis of data in which the events (the numerator) are related to all women (the denominator) rather than to just the women exposed to the events. It is impossible with such data to separate the effect of different or changing levels of sexual activity from differences or changes in the risk of pregnancy among those who are sexually active.

At the other extreme are studies conducted with pregnant or recently delivered women. These tell us nothing about those women who have been sexually active but have not become pregnant. A study involving pregnant women that fails to utilize a "control group" of women who are not pregnant may lead to important and fruitful insights but it cannot be expected to isolate or determine the factors that "cause" or "explain" pregnancy. Whereas the first type of study fails to identify and exclude those who are not exposed to the risk of pregnancy, the second type fails to include all of those who are so exposed. Neither of these approaches, alone or together, is capable of explaining fertility.

Complicating matters further is the question not only of what group to study but how the study should be designed. In order to "explain" an item of behavior—for example, the initiation of sexual activity or the seeking of an abortion—it is necessary, but not sufficient, that the factors one suspects are operative—the causes—be clearly antecedent to the behavior to be explained—the effect. In principle this means following cases from a time prior to the behavior in question to the time of its onset, in short, a longitudinal study. Most studies attempting to explain fertility, including the two reported on here, are deficient in this respect. By imposing certain restrictions on our choice of explanatory variables and by winnowing their effects statistically, we can make a useful approach to the problem of explanation. To settle the question more conclusively requires a longitudinal study. It is too late to capture in this fashion the cohorts of young women who were the teenagers of the 70s. That would have been the preferred way of doing it, even though some of the sample would have been lost to adulthood at each successive follow-up interview.

A major advantage of the two studies reported on here is that they allow us to consider pregnancy in the appropriate context, that is, among the sexually active. Since engaging in sex is a necessary (but not sufficient) condition for pregnancy, a further virtue of these studies is that we can take our quest for an understanding of teenage premarital pregnancy back to a consideration of who does and who does not have premarital intercourse—a task we undertake in this chapter. In addition, we shall look at certain characteristics associated with premarital sex: age at first premarital intercourse, the number of premarital sexual partners, and the frequency of intercourse.

The Prevalence of Premarital Sexual Activity

In 1971, 30 percent of young women 15-19 years of age had experienced premarital intercourse; by 1976, the proportion of premaritally

TABLE 3.1 Percentage of Women 15-19 Years of Age Who Had Premarital Intercourse, by Race, Current Age, Marital Status, and Educational Aspirations

Variable	1971			1976		
	Total	White	Black	Total	White	Black
Current Age	(4341)	(2924)	(1417)	(2178)	(1482)	(696)
15	14.2	11.4	32.1	18.5	15.2	38.5
16	22.3	18.3	48.7	27.9	24.0	53.0
17	28.6	24.3	56.8	43.6	39.3	69.3
18	40.7	37.1	62.0	54.0	50.3	76.8
19	49.5	45.3	77.9	60.4	56.6	84.2
15-19	30.1	26.3	54.1	40.9	37.2	64.3
Marital Status	(4341)	(2924)	(1417)	(2178)	(1482)	(696)
Never married	26.8	22.7	52.4	36.1	31.7	62.3
Ever married	57.9	55.9	78.3	80.2	79.2	90.5
Educational Aspirations	(4301)	(2899)	(1402)	(2154)	(1465)	(689)
≤11 years	50.5	42.8	86.9	71.1	67.0	93.0
12 "	35.1	30.7	61.0	45.9	42.1	69.7
13-15 "	28.9	24.9	58.5	43.8	39.2	72.0
≥16 "	21.6	19.5	36.6	30.5	27.4	49.9

NOTE: Numbers in parentheses refer to the number of sample cases for which both pieces of information in the cross-tabulation were provided; n's for each cell are not shown to simplify the presentation but are, unless otherwise indicated, equal to or greater than 20. Estimates are based on weighted sample cases.

sexually experienced young women had increased to 41 percent (Table 3.1). Not surprisingly, the proportion of sexually experienced increases with current age.[2] The level of prevalence among those 19 years of age reached 50 percent in 1971 and 60 percent in 1976. Blacks are much more prone to have premarital sex than are whites but the increase in the level between the two surveys was greater for whites than for blacks. While blacks in 1971 were twice as likely as whites to have had premarital intercourse, in 1976 they were 1.7 times as likely to have done so.

Premarital sex is more common among those who have married (Table 3.1). The differences between the never married and the ever married exist at each age (data not shown) and always to a greater degree for whites than for blacks. Part of the reason for this—an important part—is the tendency for pregnancy to trigger marriage, a tendency which is more pronounced among whites. Consistent with this observation is the fact that young women, black or white, who are planning to marry are more likely to have had intercourse than those with no definite plans to marry. It seems clear that sex often engenders marriage, especially where a pregnancy is involved; at the same time the anticipation of marriage acts to facilitate sex. From these data we cannot in a given case tell whether the prospect of marriage leads to sex or vice versa. For the sample as a whole we can be confident that it works both ways.

In Table 3.1 we do not show figures on sexual activity for different regions of the United States. Since we are asked about this frequently, we note here that except for whites living in the West there is little variation in the level of sexual activity by region of residence. Young white women living in Western states have substantially higher levels of premarital sexual activity than the national average for white women—15 percent higher in 1971 and 42 percent higher in 1976.

A similar lack of variation is found with respect to place of residence, that is, central city or suburban areas of metropolitan areas or places outside of metropolitan areas. There are small differences, but these are not consistent between the surveys. For example, in 1971 those living in suburban areas of Standard Metropolitan Statistical Areas (SMSAs) were less likely to have had intercourse than either those living in central cities or those living outside the boundaries of SMSAs. In 1976 below-average rates were still found in nonmetropolitan areas but among the SMSA population suburban rates remained relatively low for blacks and, in a switch from 1971, were higher than average for whites. On the whole, however, where a young woman lives appears to make relatively little difference in whether she is sexually active. A longitudinal study might yield different results.

If geography makes little or no difference, the same cannot be said for certain social characteristics. Dramatic differences in prevalence appear when young women are classified by their educational aspirations, or if they report no aspirations for additional schooling, by the level of their completed education. These differences exist for each race at each date (Table 3.1). In both periods the level of sexual activity for those expecting to finish college was less than half (43 percent) as great as for those who do not expect to complete the twelfth grade (including those who had dropped out of school previously with no intention of returning).

This strong relationship between expressed educational goals and the likelihood of premarital sex is not a simple one. Beyond the question of whether the goals are realizable or firmly pursued, there is the question of cause and effect. For some young women it is no doubt true that there is some sacrifice of immediate gratification on the altar of future ambition; or it may be that the pursuit of future goals channels activities and associations in such ways that opportunities for sex are reduced. However, it is equally evident that sex and the consequences stemming from it, the most significant being pregnancy, can alter the prospects for further education. Because of this circularity, we have not included educational aspirations among the "explanatory" variables in subsequent analyses even though for some young women this is no doubt an important consideration in whether or not to have sex.[3]

The figures presented above on the prevalence of sexual intercourse are based on whether or not a young woman ever had premarital intercourse. Included among the sexually active are those who had intercourse only once as well as those who had it many times. Undoubtedly there are differences, at least at the extremes, in terms both of "causes" and consequences. No information was obtained in either survey on the total or "lifetime" number of events of intercourse, with the exception that in 1976 we identified those who had intercourse only once. These one-timers, 13 percent of all premaritally sexually active women in 1976, were not homogeneous with respect to the recency of that event or the likelihood of continued sexual activity. To maintain comparability with 1971, the one-timers are generally included in the analysis of data from the 1976 survey; exceptions are noted.

Variables and Analysis

By now, perhaps, the reader has been exposed to enough caveats concerning the design of these studies and the data derived from them and does not need to be continually reminded that our quest for explanation proceeds under certain handicaps. Nevertheless, there is considerable interest in finding out whether such basic social facts as socioeconomic status (SES), religion, and the stability of the family have any bearing on premarital sex, contraceptive use, or pregnancy and its resolution.

The analyses in this as well as the following two chapters involve a relatively small number of explanatory variables. Although each analysis may involve a different set of variables, common to all of them is a subset consisting of SES, family stability, religion, and religiosity. There are several reasons for the limited number of explanatory variables, in addition to the desirability of keeping explanation as simple as possible. First, we sought variables of apparent sociological importance that were common to both surveys. Our focus on the premarital behavior of all young women, married or single, put some added restrictions on our choice of variables. Further, we confined the list of variables to those that, as best we can determine, temporally preceded sexual activity (and, therefore, the other items of behavior we examine).

With respect to this latter criterion it must be obvious that there is some chance of retrospective bias in obtaining information about an earlier period. Thus, for example, considering whether religious affiliation contributes to the explanation of premarital sex, we implicitly treat information on a young woman's "current" religion, the only information we have about her religious preference, as if it were a valid basis for classification when she was several years younger. People, even young ones, do occasionally change their religions, and it is not inconceivable that a few young women might have done so because of new experiences, including sexual intercourse. We doubt whether such instances of retrospective bias are frequent enough to be troublesome for those aspects of behavior we have selected for analysis. It was our concern, however, with temporal ordering that kept us from considering as explanatory variables items such as educational aspirations or place of residence, even though these and other temporally ambiguous items have some currency in the literature and may indeed be important determinants.

In the following sections we consider separately each of our explanatory variables as it relates to the prevalence of premarital intercourse, and then all variables together with the aid of multivariate analysis.[4]

Socioeconomic status: We have used as our measure of socioeconomic status (SES) the mean number of years of completed education of the persons identified by the respondent as the female who raised her and the male who helped to raise her. In most instances these persons are the natural parents. To avoid ambiguity and confusion, we use the term "raisers" in setting forth our definitions and discussions of SES and family stability (below); in discussing the effects of these variables, we shall substitute the term "parents." The respondent not only provided the information on who the raisers were but also on their years of completed education. If the respondent identified only one raiser, that person's years of completed education was used alone.

Over time, the level of completed education has been increasing; respondents raised by grandparents would be penalized in terms of this measure because of the long-term upward trend in years of completed education. As a result, where a raiser was a grandparent we made an adjustment to account for generational differences in education. The adjustment, carried out separately for each race and sex, consisted of adding to a grandparent's years of completed education the difference between the mean years of completed education for all grandparents who were raisers and the mean years of completed education for all other raisers (essentially the parental generation). It did not seem necessary to be concerned about the small number of instances where the raiser was of the parental generation but more elderly than might be expected, such as an elderly parent or an elderly uncle.

While our measure of SES is uni- rather than multidimensional, we believe it is satisfactory: It captures a significant portion of SES; comparable information is available from the two surveys; there is little ambiguity about the temporal ordering of this measure in relation to premarital sex; and it is applicable to the entire sample(s).[5]

There is no sociological basis for predicting the direction of relationship between SES and premarital sex. Most readers, we suspect, would be surprised if it were not inverse, but the reasons that this should be the expectation are far from clear. Our measure of SES does, in fact, show an inverse relationship with prevalence of premarital sexual activity—the lower the level of SES, the higher the prevalence (Table 3.2). An apparent anomaly appears for whites both in 1971 and 1976 in that the highest prevalence of intercourse is not found in the lowest SES group. However, as we have seen in Chapter 2, there is a positive association among whites between parents' education and approval of premarital sex; for blacks the association is negative. It is not surprising, therefore, to find that the decline in prevalence of premarital sexual activity with increasing SES is much steeper for blacks than for whites. As a result, differences by race are least pronounced at the highest level of SES.[6] Among both races, the category of upper-status blacks, those with college-educated parents, is the only one that shows no increase in sexual activity between the two surveys.

Family stability: In the belief that the character and stability of the family of origin are important factors in the development and behavior of adolescents, we developed an index that attempts to reflect those conditions. (See Chapter 2 for a description of the family stability index.) One would expect a greater measure of effective social control over the adolescent in the "ideal" or stable family situation. In our society, however much it appears to be changing, we would expect that situation to be somewhat less permissive toward premarital sexual involvement than the other two. Obviously, our index cannot embody all of the subtleties and affectional nuances of the parent-child relationship.

TABLE 3.2 Percentage of Women 15-19 Years of Age Who Had Premarital Intercourse, by Race, SES, Family Stability, Religion, Religiosity, and Age at Menarche

Variable	1971			1976		
	Total	White	Black	Total	White	Black
SES (years)	(4247)	(2900)	(1347)	(2116)	(1466)	(650)
<9	34.4	27.0	61.0	45.6	38.2	70.3
9-11	33.4	29.0	55.8	45.5	41.9	64.0
12	26.9	25.0	47.7	39.4	35.9	67.2
13-15	26.2	24.8	42.8	33.7	32.6	50.6
≥16	23.5	22.8	33.7	30.2	29.9	33.8
Family Stability	(4315)	(2912)	(1403)	(2175)	(1480)	(695)
Ideal	25.5	23.5	48.9	33.7	32.2	52.3
Less ideal	37.7	33.1	55.0	53.0	48.0	73.3
Least ideal	45.2	37.6	59.2	58.3	51.8	69.5
Religion	(4335)	(2921)	(1414)	(2173)	(1480)	(693)
Fundamentalist Protestant	28.8	24.6	48.0	44.2	40.2	60.6
Other Protestant	31.8	26.7	54.6	42.4	37.5	63.6
Catholic	24.4	23.4	51.5	33.6	33.0	53.0
Non-Christian	22.0	22.0	}60.8	38.4	36.6	}79.0
None	49.0	46.7		57.7	52.5	
Religiosity	(4311)	(2907)	(1404)	(2149)	(1463)	(686)
Low	38.4	37.0	56.1	53.8	52.2	71.0
Medium	32.8	28.5	65.0	43.2	38.2	71.4
High	20.8	14.2	47.1	24.2	17.4	54.5
Age at Menarche	(4291)	(2898)	(1393)	(2161)	(1473)	(668)
≤11	34.6	31.8	52.5	50.1	47.3	63.8
12-13	30.3	26.4	56.4	39.3	35.8	64.4
14-15	23.8	20.2	45.9	33.3	28.0	64.3
≥16	35.4	18.4	69.6	69.9	68.5*	73.3*

NOTE: Estimates are based on weighted sample cases; in addition, see Table 3.1.
*n <20

Premarital Intercourse

In 1971 there is a strong association, for blacks and whites, between family stability and prevalence of premarital intercourse (Table 3.2). This association also holds for whites in 1976 but not for blacks, although even then prevalence in the "ideal" situation is lower than for the other two situations. Premarital sex in both years is less than 60 percent as likely in the "ideal" situation as in the "least ideal" case.

Religion: Respondents were asked to name their religions, if any. Those identifying themselves as Protestants were asked for their denomination, which subsequently was categorized either as Fundamentalist or Other Protestant. For whites the other categories represented in this variable are Catholic, Non-Christian, and None. The Non-Christian category consists mainly, but not completely, of Jews. For blacks, Non-Christians and young women with no religious affiliation have been combined in one category. Since most of the cases in this category had no religious affiliation, we refer to it as "None."

Here again there is little sociological basis for predicting the association between premarital sex and the independent variable, in this instance, religion. The highest levels of premarital intercourse in both 1971 and 1976 are found among those reporting no religious affiliation; this holds for blacks and for whites (Table 3.2). Differences in prevalence of premarital sex among the other religious categories are fairly small at both dates and for both races. With the exception already noted, even the ordering of prevalence by religious categories shows little consistency.

Religiosity: Aside from religious identification or affiliation, individuals differ in their sense of the importance of religion, the degree to which religion influences and affects their lives and their conception of the world around them. Even those who profess no affiliation with a formal religious organization or body may simultaneously believe themselves to be "religious," and believe that religion is important to their being and their conception and interpretation of reality. Conversely, many who are formal members of a religious body find little need or scope for a religious viewpoint in the ordering of their lives or in considering their surroundings and the daily flow of events. This sense of the importance of a religious orientation we have called religiosity. (See Chapter 2 for a description of the index of religiosity.)

As was the case with our other variables, we have no theoretical or empirical basis for predicting the relationship between religiosity and premarital intercourse. Whites at both dates show a strong association between religiosity and prevalence of premarital intercourse, high religiosity showing low prevalence and low religiosity, high prevalence (Table

3.2). Interestingly, there is little change between 1971 and 1976 in prevalence among whites of high religiosity. For blacks, the high religiosity category has the lowest level of prevalence at both dates, but there is little or no difference between the other two categories.

Age at menarche: Age at menarche has been declining in the United States (and elsewhere) and now stands at about 12.5 years on the average. Intercourse can and sometimes does precede menarche but usually occurs after it. In spite of much popular discussion of the sexual involvement or sexual "problems" of early "maturers," there is little in the scientific literature to indicate what the relationship might be between age at menarche and prevalence of sexual activity. Thus, while we might expect those who mature early to exhibit a high level of sexual activity, it is conceivable that there is essentially no relationship between age at menarche and prevalence of premarital intercourse. A more sensitive test of the notion that biological precosity might be conducive to the early initiation of sex would be to examine the relationship between age at menarche and age at first intercourse, something we do later in this chapter. At this point we are interested in the question of prevalence— whether a young woman's chances of having sex while under age 20 have anything to do with the age at which, as the saying goes, she "becomes a young lady."

Blacks show no clear relationship, at either date, between age at menarche and prevalence of premarital sexual activity—the level in 1976 is, in fact, horizontal across the age at menarche categories (ignoring the highest age category which involves a small number of cases).[7] Whites, on the other hand, show an inverse relationship between the two (again, ignoring the highest age category in 1976).

MULTIVARIATE ANALYSIS
OF THE PREVALENCE OF SEX

To consider the simultaneous effect of all of these variables and to assist in determining the (statistical) significance of each of them, we have used a technique known as multiple classification analysis (MCA). In MCA all of the explanatory or independent variables are handled in a categorical manner. This is necessary since, for variables like religion, race, or family stability, respondents fall into particular categories which are not aligned along a recognized scale or continuum. Techniques of analysis that assume an underlying continuum are thus of no help. For each category of an explanatory variable, MCA provides the mean value of the dependent variable for that subgroup adjusted for the effects of all other explanatory variables Thus we see (for example, see Appendix C, Table C.1) that when allowance is made statistically for the effects of current age, SES, family stability, religion, religiosity, and age at menarche, the proportion of whites who have had intercourse is .26, and of blacks, .51. In other words, a consideration of the adjusted proportions (or in some cases, means) for the categories of a variable shows the effect of that variable "independent" of all other variables.

The procedure might be thought of as analogous to a laboratory experiment in which the experimenter is able to control or eliminate all factors other than the one being tested. By contrast, the figures in Tables 3.1 and 3.2, for example, show the effect of each explanatory variable on the prevalence of sexual activity—without adjusting for or controlling the effects of the other explanatory variables. It is as if we were examining the effect of temperature (or changes in temperature) on some substance without controlling for the effect of pressure.

Since continuous variables are not used as such in MCA, but are converted to discontinuous or categorical variables, some information is lost. In addition, the categories of the explanatory or "predictor" variables used in MCA should include at least 50 observations to avoid large sampling errors. In the several analyses presented in this and subsequent chapters, some categories of some variables do on occasion contain less than 50 observations; the results for those categories should be interpreted with some caution.

The data in Tables 3.1 and 3.2 (and similar tables) are based on weighted sample cases. Since blacks were oversampled in each survey, weighted data make it possible to show distributions for the total population which reflect the actual proportions of whites and blacks in the population; unweighted sample data would not permit this. MCA, however, *requires* unweighted sample cases. In the MCA analysis of the total population, the oversampling of blacks does not represent a problem since race is used as a control variable. MCA also excludes cases with missing data for any of the variables involved, whereas the simple tabulations in Tables 3.1 and 3.2 exclude cases only when data are missing on the variable of interest.

The multivariate analysis (MCA) of the effects of seven demographic and social variables, including race and current age, on prevalence of premarital sexual intercourse is presented in Table C.1 for 1971 and Table C.2 for 1976 (both tables appear in Appendix C). There are large and statistically significant differences at each date between blacks and whites in prevalence even after controlling for the effects of the other variables.[8] Because of these highly significant differences by race, our discussion will center on the separate analyses for whites and blacks. Before moving to that, however, some general comments are in order regarding the overall relationships, that is, irrespective of race, in the 1971 and 1976 samples.

The extent to which the seven variables used in the analyses account for the variation in prevalence of intercourse is not such as to permit us to conclude that we have identified or adequately measured all of the factors that "explain" why some young women become sexually active and others do not. Most of the variance remains unexplained even when such seemingly powerful predictors as race, age, SES, family background, religion, and religiosity are brought to bear. Certainly much popular and scientific discussion revolves around the alleged action of such variables as these. However, without denying the fact that demographic and social variables of the type used here tell only part of the story, it is worth noting that even with this short list of variables we are significantly beyond a chance interpretation of the prevalence of sexual activity. Moreover, technical considerations suggest that it is possible that more has been achieved by way of explanation than the R^2s (.19 for 1971, .25 for 1976) suggest.[9] When one is faced with a dependent variable that registers only two readings—yes or no, on or off—the amount of variation that even a fully specified and appropriate model can explain is limited. Under such conditions, R^2s in the range of .15 to .20 or greater can be regarded as exceptionally high. It also needs to be noted that the categories of the independent variables used here are in some cases unavoidably broad, a fact, again, that tends to attenuate a statistical relationship. These points are made, not defensively, but to caution against underestimating the explanatory power of demographic and social variables. This has sometimes led to overstating the extent to which other factors, such as personality and situational variables, must be called upon.

More fundamentally, it is to be expected that many young women essentially alike in basic characteristics will differ in the timing of their first intercourse in response to a host of chance factors. The girl who has just passed over the threshold to sex and one just like her who is on the verge of doing so may have essentially the same propensity toward sex, but, when frozen in place by a cross-sectional survey, they appear as diametrically different.

The first thing to notice in Tables C.1 and C.2 (Appendix C) about the analysis for each race in the two periods is that while the extent of variance explained is similar in each period there are some interesting differences in the relative importance of the variables, that is, in the structure of explanation for each race. Apart from current age, which is by far the most potent single factor, accounting generally for over half of the explained variance, family stability and religiosity are associated with large and statistically significant differences in prevalence for both races in both periods. In the case of family stability the "ideal" situation shows a below-average level of prevalence (8 percent to 18 percent, depending on race) with little difference between the two other situations; high religiosity also shows a relatively low level of prevalence (12 percent to 46 percent below average, depending on race), with no difference between the other two categories for blacks but consistent differences for whites.

On the other hand, age at menarche, which is important for whites, makes much less of a difference among blacks. For whites, the earlier the age at menarche the higher the prevalence of premarital sexual intercourse; for blacks in 1976, prevalence is essentially uniform for the different categories of age at menarche, and in 1971, the relationship, while statistically significant due to the below-average prevalence for those who first menstruate at ages 14 or 15, is inconsistent. SES is not associated with large differences in prevalence among whites in 1971, but is in 1976. It is among blacks, however, that the inverse relationship between SES and prevalence of sex is most clearly evident. Among blacks at both dates, the higher the level of SES, the lower the prevalence of premarital sexual intercourse. Differences in prevalence between religious groupings are insignificant among blacks and, except for relatively low prevalence among the small group of Non-Christians, the same is generally the case for whites.[10]

The Initiation of Premarital Intercourse

Among those young women 15-19 years of age who have had premarital intercourse, the mean age at first intercourse can be expected to be, and is, fairly young—16.4 years in 1971 and 16.1 years in 1976 (Table 3.3). Obviously, these figures apply only in cross section; as these cohorts of women become older and more of them engage in sex, mean age at first intercourse will increase. The decline over the five-year period in the age of initiation of sex, although less than 4 months on average, is nevertheless part of the reason that the premarital pregnancy rate has remained high despite the spread of contraceptive use. We look more at this in Chapter 5. In both surveys, blacks have a younger mean age at first intercourse than whites—a difference of 0.6 years in 1971 and 0.7 years in 1976. Again anticipating the story, this is a difference to which we shall return when we analyze racial differences in premarital pregnancy.

TABLE 3.3 Mean Age at First Premarital Intercourse for Women 15-19 Years of Age

Variable	1971			1976		
	Total	White	Black	Total	White	Black
All Women	(1443)	(715)	(728)	(1016)	(575)	(441)
	16.4	16.5	15.9	16.1	16.3	15.6
SES (Years)	(1400)	(710)	(690)	(979)	(566)	(413)
<9	16.0	16.2	15.7	15.8	16.0	15.4
9-11	16.2	16.3	16.0	16.0	16.1	15.5
12	16.5	16.6	15.8	16.4	16.5	15.7
≥13	16.8	16.8	16.2	16.3	16.4	15.9
Family Stability	(1433)	(712)	(721)	(1015)	(574)	(441)
Ideal	16.6	16.7	16.1	16.4	16.5	15.9
Less ideal	16.0	16.1	15.6	15.9	16.0	15.5
Least ideal	16.1	16.2	15.9	15.6	15.8	15.3
Religion	(1442)	(715)	(727)	(1014)	(574)	(440)
Fundamentalist Protestant	15.9	16.1	15.6	15.8	16.0	15.3
Other Protestant	16.4	16.6	15.9	16.1	16.3	15.7
Catholic	16.6	16.7	15.9	16.4	16.5	15.4
Other	16.0	16.1	15.6	15.8	16.0	15.0
Religiosity	(1432)	(710)	(722)	(1003)	(567)	(436)
Low	16.3	16.3	16.1	16.1	16.2	15.2
Medium	16.4	16.6	15.8	16.1	16.3	15.6
High	16.3	16.8	15.8	16.2	16.6	15.7
Age at Menarche	(1432)	(713)	(719)	(1008)	(570)	(438)
≤11	15.9	16.1	15.4	15.6	15.8	15.0
12-13	16.4	16.6	15.9	16.2	16.4	15.6
≥14	16.9	17.1	16.2	16.4	16.5	16.2

NOTE: Estimates are based on weighted sample cases; in addition, see Table 3.1.

The 1976 survey provides information on two interesting aspects of the initiation of sex: the age of the male partner, and where it occurred. Among blacks the mean age of the initial partner was 18.1 years (median age was 17.9), whereas among whites it was 19.3 years (median age was 18.6 years). Thus, on average, the partner at first intercourse was 2.5

(blacks) or 3.0 (whites) years older. The closeness of the mean and median values reflects the fact that there were relatively few cases in which the first partner was a much older male, although somewhat more for whites than for blacks. Just as a young white woman tended to be older at the time of her first intercourse than her black counterpart, so was her partner older than the partner of the young black woman. The age difference between the partners was greater than the difference in age between the young women themselves.

More than 75 percent of the premaritally sexually active in 1976 reported that the initial event occurred at their partners' homes, their homes, or the home of a friend or relative. There was little difference in this respect between blacks and whites. Among those who did not have intercourse "at home," blacks were most likely to have it at a motel or hotel, whereas whites were most likely to have it in an automobile. The fact that only 12 percent had their first full experience with sex in an automobile does not mean, of course, that the motor vehicle is not instrumental in various ways. A common view has been that the availability of "wheels" enables young people to escape parental and other nonpermissive types of supervision. The fact that so much sex occurs "at home" (admittedly, we are able to speak only of the initial experience) suggests that the nature of the "home" environment is equally important. Our society is experiencing remarkable changes in living arrangements—more single persons, single parents—and in the labor force activity of women with children. Unfortunately, we do not know whether there has been a change in "situs" of the first intercourse; all we can say with certainty is that for most sexually active teenage women, the home, whatever it is, is not effectively off limits for sex. Those who initiated sex at a very young age (under age 13) were most likely to have it at their homes, while those who started at age 14 or over were most likely to have it at their partners' homes. We remind the reader that these comparisons leave out young women living in college dormitories (and other kinds of institutions).

Our analysis of mean age at first premarital intercourse involves the same set of variables as were used in considering the prevalence of premarital intercourse. However, since we are dealing here with only the subset of those sexually active, it has been necessary to combine categories for some variables: age at menarche (in 1971), SES, and religion.[11] As with the prevalence of sex, there is little or no basis on which to predict the direction of relationship between these variables and the mean age at first premarital intercourse.

In both surveys, early age at first intercourse is most clearly associated with age at menarche; other variables appear to make little difference

(Table 3.3). There is, as would be expected, a very marked positive association with current age, which, because of truncation bias, holds little theoretical or practical interest and therefore is not shown. The positive association with age at menarche is not in any sense a necessary relationship but suggests, not unexpectedly perhaps, that physical maturity helps to touch off sexual involvement. For the rest we are left with little consistency in regard to the timing of first intercourse. It is somewhat retarded in the "ideal" family situation; high religiosity, except for blacks in 1971, also is associated with a delay of 5 to 6 months. SES is positively associated with mean age but, again, not for blacks in 1971. For both blacks and whites, Fundamentalist Protestants and the Other category have the lowest mean age of first intercourse. For a closer look at the dynamics of these relationships, it is useful to turn to the multivariate analysis, particularly since current age may have a confounding effect on the data as they appear in simple classification.

MULTIVARIATE ANALYSIS OF AGE AT FIRST INTERCOURSE

The strong racial differences in age at first intercourse are relatively unaffected by adjustments made for other variables—blacks have a younger mean age than whites (Tables C.3 and C.4, Appendix C). Our comments, therefore, are confined to the relationships within racial categories. For both races and for both dates, age at menarche remains highly significant after adjustment for the effects of the other variables: The earlier the age at menarche, the earlier the initiation of sex. Differences over both surveys average about 7 months for whites and 10 months for blacks between the lowest and the highest menarchial ages. Parents generally have an intuitive appreciation of this relationship.

Among whites, family stability and SES also retain their importance; in the case of the former, the "ideal" situation retards the timing of first intercourse as compared to the "least ideal" case by an average difference for both periods of just over 5 months, whereas low SES leads to initiating sex about 5 months earlier than high SES. Blacks present a different situation; with the exception of current age and age at menarche, none of the other variables are consistently significant at both dates.

The proportion of variation in the mean age at first intercourse explained by these variables (R^2) ranges from .27 for blacks in 1971 to .35 for whites at the same date. However, these values are due in large part to the very strong effect of current age, which, depending on race and survey

TABLE 3.4 Percentage Distribution of Premaritally Sexually Active Women 15-19 Years of Age, by Number of Partners

Number of Partners	1971			1976		
	Total	White	Black	Total	White	Black
	(1409)	(705)	(704)	(1000)	(567)	(433)
1	60.9	60.6	61.6	54.3	57.3	43.2
2-3	25.8	24.9	28.9	27.8	24.5	39.9
4-5	7.6	8.1	5.9	8.5	7.8	11.2
≥6	5.7	6.4	3.6	9.4	10.4	5.7
Total	100.0	100.0	100.0	100.0	100.0	100.0

NOTE: Estimates are based on weighted sample cases.

year, accounts for from half to more than three-quarters of the explained variance.

Total Number of Premarital Sexual Partners

Aside from intrinsic interest in the number of sexual partners young women have, this aspect of behavior is of interest because of its possible implications inter alia for contraceptive practice. Ideally we should like to know, for each young woman who has been premaritally sexually active, the number of sexual partners she has had prior to marriage. There are some minor complications in achieving this seemingly simple goal. The 1976 survey provides the needed information in straightforward fashion. However, in the 1971 survey, a more timorous operation on the whole, information on number of partners was collected by means of a precoded question with grouped response categories: 1, 2-3, 4-5, and 6 or more. In addition, the majority of young women at both dates reported having had only one partner (Table 3.4). As a result, the median number of partners would have an artifactual quality, and for that reason we have avoided it as a dependent variable. We also have refrained from computing the mean number of partners, since for 1971 that would have involved assigning an arbitrary value to the open class "6 or more." The possibility of closing the interval based on the 1976 data was rejected because of the differences in the distributions by broad categories for the two dates, which suggested to us that there could have been a shift as well within categories. Thus, we use as our summary measure of the total number of premarital sexual partners the proportion who have had two or more partners.[12]

Before examining the data on premarital partnerships, one other important difference between the 1971 and 1976 surveys needs to be mentioned. In 1976, separate questionnaires were used for never-married and ever-married respondents. Never-married respondents who reported having had intercourse were asked how many partners they had ever had intercourse with; ever-married respondents who reported having had intercourse prior to marriage were asked how many partners they had intercourse with *before marriage*. In 1971, information on number of partners (and other aspects of sexual behavior) was collected via a self-administered questionnaire—with the same form and the same questions being used for all women regardless of marital history, and for the ever married regardless of whether intercourse preceded or followed marriage. Thus, in that survey, all women who reported that they had intercourse were asked to indicate how many partners had ever been involved. This poses no problem for us in connection with the never married; for the ever married who were premaritally sexually active, the reported number of partners includes postmarital partners. An examination of the number of partners reported by ever-married women who had intercourse only after marriage indicates few postmarital partners among these women. Further, a comparison of the number of partners reported by ever-married women who had intercourse prior to marriage with the number of partners reported by never-married women suggests a relatively small number of postmarital partners among the former. We have used, therefore, for 1971, the number of partners reported by the ever married who were premaritally sexually active. Relative to 1976, these reports are undoubtedly biased upward, but we believe the bias is small.

Our consideration of the number of premarital sexual partners involves the same set of explanatory variables used previously, with two exceptions: age at menarche and current age (a "control" variable) are both dropped and replaced by the variable "years at risk," which is the interval in years between first premarital intercourse and marriage or survey, whichever comes first. More precisely, "years at risk" is the difference between age at first intercourse and the earlier of age at marriage or the survey. Thus, if a woman had premarital intercourse, for instance, at age 15 and married at age 16, she is classified as "1 year at risk," even though in some instances possibly only a few months may separate intercourse and marriage. In effect, we are assuming that an event occurs at the midpoint of the age interval. This procedure reflects the constraints of the available data.

TABLE 3.5 Percentage of Women 15-19 Years of Age Having Two or More Premarital Sexual Partners

Variable	1971 Total	1971 White	1971 Black	1976 Total	1976 White	1976 Black
SES (Years)	(1369)	(701)	(668)	(964)	(558)	(406)
<9	37.2	38.5	34.9	52.5	51.1	55.2
9-11	37.0	36.2	39.2	44.2	40.6	56.4
12	38.6	37.2	46.2	41.8	38.0	57.6
≥13	44.2	46.1	28.9	48.3	47.4	57.2
Family Stability	(1400)	(702)	(698)	(999)	(566)	(433)
Ideal	35.3	34.7	38.6	38.6	37.2	48.8
Less ideal	48.9	52.3	40.8	49.2	46.2	57.1
Least ideal	40.7	43.5	37.4	61.4	60.3	62.9
Religion	(1408)	(705)	(703)	(998)	(566)	(432)
Fundamentalist Protestant	36.7	35.1	40.9	58.0	58.4	57.0
Other Protestant	37.9	38.1	37.5	43.8	38.5	57.5
Catholic	38.3	38.1	40.7	42.8	42.8	40.8
Other	50.2	51.2	44.7	52.3	49.7	59.9
Religiosity	(1398)	(700)	(698)	(989)	(561)	(428)
Low	48.3	49.4	38.0	49.7	47.9	64.3
Medium	35.5	34.7	38.2	42.9	38.9	55.0
High	31.1	25.2	38.4	43.2	34.6	55.8
Years at Risk	(1402)	(703)	(695)	(996)	(566)	(430)
0	12.7	11.9	17.3	12.4	12.4	12.4
1	38.4	40.5	30.0	36.1	35.0	42.1
2	53.0	58.1	42.7	67.5	67.6	67.4
3	69.1	74.8	57.7	69.7	68.0	73.8
≥4	71.5	74.6	66.1	80.4	78.0	84.6

NOTE: Estimates are based on weighted sample cases; in addition, see Table 3.1.

The proportion of premaritally sexually active women who have had two or more premarital sexual partners is presented for each variable by race, for 1971 and 1976, in Table 3.5. In examining this table, it strikes one immediately that the greatest influence determining whether a young woman has more than one partner is the length of time since she first became sexually active—her "years at risk." The majority of young women who have been sexually active for 2 or more years have had more than one partner; among those with the longest period of exposure, 4 or more years, multiple partnership generally is above 70 percent. By comparison, the influence of the other factors we have considered ranges from nil to weak, and, to the extent that they appear to have an association, may in fact operate through their association with length of exposure. For example, young women who were brought up in what we are calling the "ideal" family setting or those scoring high on the religiosity index tend to low proportions of multiple partnerships; however, as we have seen earlier, these categories of young women also tend to delay first intercourse, thereby shortening the duration of exposure. To suggest a mechanism by which these variables may have their effect does not, of course, diminish their importance. On the other hand, white women at the highest SES level also tend to delay first intercourse, but they have the highest proportion with two or more partners among the SES categories in 1971 and the second highest proportion in 1976. In general, the association between number of partners and variables other than years at risk is more pronounced and systematic among whites than among blacks. With few exceptions, the range of differences found in Table 3.5 are greater in 1976 than in 1971. The importance of the number of years at risk for the number of partners helps to explain the increase in partnerships that can be observed in Table 3.4. As we saw earlier, the age at first intercourse has declined, thus increasing the years at risk and so the number of partnerships.

MULTIVARIATE ANALYSIS OF PARTNERSHIP

The results of the multivariate analysis of partnership are shown in Table C.5 for 1971 and in Table C.6 for 1976 (both tables appear in Appendix C.). Race, which is weakly significant in 1971 ($p < .1$) is not significant in 1976—a very different situation from that encountered with prevalence of premarital intercourse or mean age at first premarital intercourse, where race is highly significant at both dates. Since race failed to be statistically significant in 1976, we do not show in Table C.6 results for whites and blacks. In the next section of this chapter, we reanalyze the 1976 data, using as our dependent variable mean number of premarital partners. In that analysis race again manifests itself as a highly significant variable, with whites having more partners on the average than blacks. This result is consistent with the analysis of the 1971 data, which indicates a higher proportion of whites with two or more partners (Table C.5).

In the analysis of the total population based on the proportion having two or more partners, only years at risk and family stability are significant in both 1971 and 1976. The "ideal" category of family stability shows a lower proportion having two or more premarital sexual partners than the other two categories. There is a clear positive relationship between years at risk and the proportion having two or more premarital sexual partners, with the most rapid change coming in the first two years after sex begins. In terms of amount of variance explained, very little is attributable to any variable other than duration of exposure.

REANALYSIS OF 1976 DATA ON PARTNERSHIP

The choice of the proportion having two or more partners as our measure of the number of premarital sexual partners was, as we have noted above, a choice imposed on the analysis by the open-ended nature of the 1971 data. The 1976 survey, on the other hand, provides data which allow us to compute in a straightforward manner the mean number of premarital sexual partners and to use that mean as the summary measure of our dependent variable. In addition, we are enabled by the greater detail available from the 1976 survey to introduce a variable called "years sexually active" in place of the less satisfactory "years at risk." The new variable measures the number of years between first premarital intercourse and last premarital intercourse, rather than the interval from first premarital intercourse to the survey (for never married) or date of marriage (for ever married).

Table 3.6 gives the mean number of premarital partners for each independent variable. The figures shown include young women who had premarital intercourse only once, the one-timers; these young women, by definition, could have only one sexual partner. Multivariate analysis was carried out on the 1976 data including and excluding the one-timers; the results were essentially identical.

If a young woman in 1976 came from a family with above-average education (high SES), or from a somewhat irregular family setting ("least ideal" family situation), or if she was fairly indifferent to religion (low religiosity and categorized religiously as "Other"), or had been sexually active for two or more years, she exhibits a relatively high degree of what we may call, nonpejoratively, promiscuity. Blacks, who generally appear less promiscuous, are more homogeneous with respect to this aspect of sexual behavior and are less inclined than whites to take on additional partners with the passage of time. We remind the reader again against reading these figures as if they validly represent the course taken by a cohort of sexually active young women. The group that has had, for

TABLE 3.6 Mean Number of Premarital Sexual Partners for Women 15-19 Years of Age in 1976

Variable	Total	White	Black
All Women	(991)	(562)	(429)
	2.7	2.8	2.4
SES (Years)	(964)	(558)	(406)
<9	2.4	2.4	2.5
9-11	2.4	2.5	2.3
12	2.5	2.5	2.6
≥13	3.6	3.7	2.2
Family Stability	(999)	(566)	(433)
Ideal	2.4	2.4	2.3
Less ideal	2.8	2.9	2.5
Least ideal	3.3	3.9	2.6
Religion	(998)	(566)	(432)
Fundamentalist Protestant	2.4	2.4	2.4
Other Protestant	2.4	2.4	2.4
Catholic	2.9	2.9	1.9
Other	3.9	4.3	2.9
Religiosity	(989)	(561)	(428)
Low	3.3	3.3	3.2
Medium	2.4	2.5	2.2
High	2.0	1.7	2.4
Years Sexually Active	(994)	(566)	(428)
0	1.2	1.3	1.2
1	1.9	1.8	1.9
2	3.1	3.2	2.8
3	4.7	5.4	3.3
≥4	7.6	10.1	3.7

NOTE: Estimates are based on weighted sample cases; in addition, see Table 3.1.

example, an average of 3.1 partners by the end of 2 years of sexual activity (Table 3.6) will not necessarily run that number up to 4.7 by the end of their third year; nor did the group that averaged 4.7 necessarily average 3.1 at the end of their second year. These are different groups in cross section. Nevertheless, the rise in the mean number of partners in relatively short time intervals suggested by the figures, especially for whites, is remarkable.

When the data in Table 3.6 are submitted to multivariate analysis, it turns out that years of sexual activity and race are the dominant factors (Table C.7). Differences by SES, family stability, and religiosity are reduced to the point of statistical insignificance. The main difference in these results from those obtained when the analysis is performed on 1976 data, in terms of the proportion having two or more partners, is that racial differences assert themselves—whites with, on the average, a shorter duration of exposure average 2.8 partners, blacks 2.2—as do religious differences, and family stability appears less important. A comparison of the 1971 data in Table C.5 with the 1976 data in Table C.7 (both in Appendix C) shows that other than race only years of exposure to sexual activity is consistently significant, a result holding for whites and blacks as well as for the total population.

Frequency of Intercourse

Our consideration of frequency of intercourse involves only nevermarried respondents. The surveys asked the number of times intercourse occurred in the "last month" (1971) or in the "last four weeks" (1976). With such data we can examine this aspect of premarital sexual behavior only among the sexually active never-married women, that is, the comparable premarital behavior of the ever married is not covered. In 1976, a unique number was obtained from the respondent in reference to frequency; in 1971, the question on frequency was precoded (0, 1-2, 3-5, 6-10, 11-15, and 16 times or more). In calculating mean frequency for 1971 the midpoint of each closed interval was used; the last category was "closed" using the mean for that interval based on the 1976 distribution. The "closing" was done separately for blacks and whites.

In spite of the increase between 1971 and 1976 in the prevalence of premarital intercourse, a small decrease in mean age at first intercourse, and an apparent increase in the number of premarital sexual partners, there does not appear to have been an increase in frequency of intercourse.

TABLE 3.7 Mean Frequency of Intercourse in Period Preceding Survey for Never-Married Women 15-19 Years of Age

Variable	1971 Total	1971 White	1971 Black	1976 Total	1976 White	1976 Black
Never Married Women	(1169)	(528)	(641)	(782)	(378)	(404)
	2.9	3.1	2.1	2.6	3.0	1.7
SES (years)	(1133)	(525)	(608)	(751)	(371)	(380)
<9	3.1	3.8	2.2	2.2	2.6	1.6
9-11	2.5	2.7	2.2	2.5	2.7	1.8
12	2.1	2.1	2.1	2.7	3.0	1.6
≥13	3.7	4.0	1.4	3.1	3.2	1.3
Family Stability	(1162)	(526)	(636)	(781)	(377)	(404)
Ideal	2.8	2.9	2.4	2.3	2.4	2.0
Less ideal	3.0	3.6	1.8	3.1	3.7	1.8
Least ideal	2.9	3.8	2.0	2.6	3.6	1.5
Religion	(1168)	(528)	(640)	(781)	(378)	(403)
Fundamentalist Protestant	1.8	2.0	1.4	2.5	3.1	1.2
Other Protestant	2.6	2.8	2.2	2.2	2.4	1.7
Catholic	3.0	3.2	1.6	2.9	3.0	2.5
Other	4.5	4.9	2.7	4.0	4.7	2.0
Religiosity	(1160)	(523)	(637)	(772)	(373)	(399)
Low	3.6	3.8	1.9	3.4	3.5	2.5
Medium	2.6	2.8	2.3	2.4	2.7	1.6
High	2.2	2.4	2.0	1.3	1.2	1.4
Marriage Plans	(1167)	(527)	(640)	(781)	(378)	(403)
Yes	4.0	4.5	2.3	4.2	4.7	2.2
No	2.2	2.3	2.0	1.8	1.8	1.6
Contraceptive Use Last Intercourse	(1113)	(511)	(602)	(781)	(377)	(404)
Medical method	6.0	7.2	2.6	3.9	4.6	1.8
Nonmedical method	1.9	2.0	1.6	1.7	1.9	0.9
None	2.3	2.4	2.0	2.1	2.2	2.0

TABLE 3.7 Continued

Number of Partners	(1135)	(518)	(617)	(767)	(372)	(395)
1	2.4	2.6	1.8	1.7	1.9	1.1
2-3	3.7	4.4	2.3	2.2	2.4	1.8
≥4	3.8	3.9	3.5	5.8	6.6	3.0

NOTE: Estimates are based on weighted sample cases; in addition, see Table 3.1.

There was, in fact, a decrease from 2.9 times per month in 1971 to 2.6 times per month in 1976 (Table 3.7). Interestingly, whites had higher mean frequencies than blacks at both dates, although the modal frequency during the reference period for each race in both surveys was zero. The relatively low frequency of intercourse among never-married women has been cited as one factor contributing to their relatively high levels of contraceptively unprotected intercourse. This is not to suggest that encouraging higher frequencies of intercourse is the way to improve consistency of contraceptive use, but rather that currently available contraceptive methods, especially medical methods, are not wholly suitable for sporadic, episodic sex.

In analyzing the factors associated with the frequency of intercourse, we depart somewhat from our standard procedure. We will again take account of race, SES, family stability, religion, and religiosity, but, since we are dealing with young women who are unmarried, in fact who have never married, it seems important to distinguish among them by whether or not they have reasonably definite plans to marry. Two other variables which seem likely to have something to do with the frequency of intercourse—method of contraception and total number of partners—also were added to the analysis. With respect to method of contraception, in this instance the method used at the last intercourse, the supposition is that medical methods either lower the inhibition to have sex, possibly by reducing the fear of pregnancy, or, and this may be more often the case, are part of a complex of behaviors associated with the establishment of sex on a more or less regular basis. The case for using the total number of partners perhaps is less immediately apparent. It is likely that the duration of sexual experience may be related to frequency. As we have seen in the previous section, the number of partners is highly correlated with both "years at risk" and "years of sexual activity." We could have used either of those, but for convenience have chosen to use total partnerships as a satisfactory proxy.

Marriage plans and use of contraception at last intercourse pose a special problem in that the temporal ordering vis-à-vis frequency is less clear or certain than in the case of the other variables. Conjecturally, high frequency of intercourse could lead to the use of contraception as well as have some influence on the likelihood of marriage. Presumably that influence could go in either direction, that is, of increasing the likelihood of marriage or of decreasing it. Although these possibilities exist, in using marriage plans and use of contraception as variables we are assuming that the direction of causality is from them to frequency of intercourse rather than the other way around.

Table 3.7 gives mean frequency by each of the variables, while Tables C.8 and C.9 (Appendix C) give the MCA results. Earlier in the chapter we observed that blacks were more likely to be sexually active than whites. Among the sexually active, however, whites report a greater rate of activity, differing, on average, by 1 or more encounters per month—a considerable difference when the mean frequency is less than 3 times per month (Table 3.7).

Partly because there is greater variation in intercourse frequency among whites, relationships to other variables are much more discernible among them than among blacks. For all variables except total number of partners—which, as we have noted, picks up the effect of duration of exposure and to some extent current age as well—the relationship for blacks is either inconsequential, inconsistent from one period to the other, or both. Among whites, on the other hand, consistent and sometimes quite large differences can be observed for several of the variables: high frequencies in excess of 1 per week for those out of the religious mainstream, for those planning to marry, for those using medical contraception, or for those who have had more than a single partner, and low frequencies for those who use nonmedical contraception (or no contraception) and for those who do not have plans to marry. To sort these relationships out more clearly, we turn to the multivariate analysis.

MULTIVARIATE ANALYSIS OF FREQUENCY OF INTERCOURSE

The MCA results tell essentially the same story. There is a significant racial difference in frequency amounting to almost 1 encounter per month more for whites than for blacks (Tables C.8 and C.9, Appendix C). For blacks very little of the variance is explained; the only variable that shows a statistically significant association with frequency among blacks at both dates is total number of partners—perhaps the most difficult of all the variables to interpret. In any case, as measured by its contribution to R^2 it explains very little.

The independent variables included in the analysis do a better job of explaining differences in frequency of intercourse of whites. Particularly important are variables that possibly reflect the maturity of the relationship: plans to marry and the choice of contraceptive method. Frequency is high when marriage is in prospect or when medical methods of contraception are used. Whether having more than the average number of partners is in some way related to the maturity of the current relationship can be argued—it certainly represents more than that. Whatever we take it to mean, the total number of partners is the third most important variable that operates in consistent fashion in both periods. However, most of the explained variance is accounted for by whether there are marriage plans.[13]

Summary

Four facets of premarital sexual behavior among young women 15-19 years of age—prevalence of premarital intercourse, mean age at first intercourse, number of premarital sexual partners, and current frequency of intercourse among the never married—have been analyzed in relation to a limited number of variables, a subset of which—SES, family stability, religion, and religiosity—has been used throughout. For each of the four areas of behavior, we have proceeded by first considering the effect of each variable in the presence of others and then by considering their effect when the operation of other variables is statistically controlled. In a number of instances a variable that appeared to have some explanatory value was found in the multivariate analysis to have no effect.

The multivariate analysis of each of these four areas of behavior has been done for the total population and for each race, since the sexual behavior of blacks and whites shows important differences. As compared to whites, blacks have a higher prevalence of premarital intercourse and a lower mean age at first intercourse; whites have a larger number of premarital sexual partners and (at least among the never married) a higher frequency of intercourse. Sex thus is more extensive among blacks but, as measured here, more intensive among whites.

Since race is uniformly a significant variable, our concern is with what part the other variables play in explaining the behavior of each race and how consistently they do so in the two surveyed populations. Only a few variables, in any of the four areas of sexual behavior, are significant at both dates for each race. If we summarize the preceding analyses, taking account only of relationships that are both statistically significant when adjusted for other variables and consistent in the way they operate in the two surveys (Table 3.8), three broad conclusions emerge:

(1) Variables that reflect biological or social readiness for sex (current age, age at menarche) and/or the duration of exposure (years at risk, number of premarital partners) are significantly related to the several facets of premarital sexual behavior and tend to account for a large part of the explained variance.
(2) Social variables associated with the initiation (and thus the prevalence or extensiveness) of sex explain nothing about the intensiveness of sex—number of premarital partners and frequency of sex—among the sexually active.
(3) The "structure of explanation" varies by race: Except in conjunction with prevalence, the social variables considered here play no part in the explanation of black sexual behavior; among whites the initiation (and prevalence) of sex and the frequency of sex are partly explained by some of these same social determinants.

Although the social variables we have employed play some part among whites in explaining prevalence of premarital intercourse and mean age at first intercourse, the only social variable of significance for both areas of behavior is family stability. A similar lack of overlap in significant variables occurs in the racial analyses of prevalence of premarital intercourse, where only family stability and religiosity are important for both races.

In two of the four areas—number of premarital partners and frequency of intercourse—our analyses of the 1976 data have been carried out both including the one-timers, so as to be comparable with the 1971 data, and excluding them. The results, in terms of significant variables and explained variance, have been essentially identical. The same cannot be said for our two analyses of the 1976 data with regard to number of premarital partners, one analysis based on the proportion having two or more partners and the other based on the mean number of partners. The significance of race, family stability, and, to a lesser extent, religion, for promiscuity depends on how the promiscuity is measured.

To require statistical significance and consistency of relationship in both surveys may be unduly stringent, as it overlooks the occasional relationship found in one survey but not the other. In insisting on this stringency we implicitly are taking the position that while there were changes between the two surveys in each of the aspects of sexual behavior

TABLE 3.8 Summary of Significance and Consistency of Relationship of Explanatory Variables for Four Aspects of Premarital Sexual Behavior

Variable	Prevalence of Intercourse			Mean Age at First Intercourse			Number of Premarital Partners[a]			Frequency of Intercourse[b]		
	Total	White	Black	Total	White	Black	Total	White	Black	Total	White	Black
Race	x	—	—	x	—	—	x	—	—	x	—	—
Current age	x	x	x	x	x	x	—	—	—	—	—	—
Age at menarche	x	x	0	x	x	x	—	—	—	—	—	—
Years at risk/ years sexually active	—	—	—	—	—	—	x	x	x	—	—	—
Number of premarital partners	—	—	—	—	—	—	—	—	—	x	x	x
SES	x	0	x	x	x	0	0	0	0	0	0	0
Family stability	x	x	x	x	x	0	0	0	0	0	0	0
Religion	0	x	0	x	0	0	0	0	0	0	0	0
Religiosity	x	x	x	x	0	0	0	0	0	0	0	0
Marriage plans	—	—	—	—	—	—	—	—	—	x	x	0
Contraceptive use last intercourse	—	—	—	—	—	—	—	—	—	x	x	0

x = significant at $p < .10$ and consistent in direction in both surveys; 0 = not significant and/or not consistent; dashes = not applicable.

a. Proportion 2 or more partners in 1971 and mean number of partners in 1976; see text.
b. Refers to never-married women.

we have examined, we doubt that the manner in which the underlying social forces operate altered in such a short period. A similar requirement might be less warranted in regard, for example, to pregnancy resolution when changes in the underlying social forces or the manner in which they operate did occur between 1971 and 1976. It is, of course, axiomatic that significant associations can turn up quite by chance and thus we are not inclined to make too much of evanescent findings. It should be borne in mind throughout that we are dealing here with a relatively brief and rapidly changing part of a young woman's life cycle. Some social scientists will no doubt be surprised that we are able to uncover any robust findings, especially in those instances where we are attempting to explain an item of behavior that is apt to change suddenly or be highly vulnerable to chance circumstances.

In another sense, our summary of findings occasionally overstates the case. Total variance explained is generally modest, although no more so than in most social science research. However, a significant and consistent finding sometimes does not "signify." For example, the attempt to account for variation among whites or blacks in the number of premarital sexual partners can be said to have failed even though we are able to report a consistent and significant association with years at risk. What strikes us most forcefully about these data is the relative homogeneity across presumably significant social divides in the nature and extent of premarital sexual behavior. The occasional small hillock revealed through our statistical binoculars does not belie the fact that the behavioral plain is relatively flat.

NOTES

1. To simplify the discussion at this juncture we take pregnancy to be synonymous with childbirth, ignoring for the moment any form of fetal loss.

2. For estimates of the (cumulative) probability of having premarital intercourse at individual ages, see Zelnik et al. (1979).

3. The same applies to the analysis of contraceptive behavior, pregnancy, and childbirth. A fairly dependable declamation at conferences or workshops on teenage fertility is the one that posits, usually in tones of moral indignation, an overwhelmingly strong relationship between future prospects and fertility. If prospects are bright, fertility is postponed; if they are dim, one takes pleasure where it can be found—so the argument goes.

4. Current age and race, which are included in the multivariate analysis as "control" variables, have been discussed previously.

5. For a discussion of alternative attempts at developing a measure of SES and the reasons for rejecting those efforts, see the second section of Appendix B.

6. Since our intention is to include each of the independent variables in the multivariate analysis, we have not tested differences for each variable.

7. The age at menarche categories shown in Table 3.2 are the precoded categories used in the 1971 survey. In the 1976 survey, data on age at menarche were collected by single years of age; see Table C.2, Appendix C.

8. Ordinary least squares regression, which gives approximately the same R^2 as MCA, has been used to determine the statistical significance of the explanatory variables. In judging whether a variable is statistically significant, we have used three levels of significance: $< .1, < .05$, and $< .01$.

9. The apparent increase in the overall explanatory power of these variables in 1976 is not readily interpretable. R^2 measures the amount of variation in a dependent variable, in this case sexual activity, that is accounted for by an independent variable or variables.

10. We should note that we have not tested for interaction between our independent variables either in this or the subsequent analyses. To have dealt with it in each case would have made the analysis quite complex and very costly to perform. We have dealt with the issue partially by always examining relationships separately by race, which, in our experience, is the greatest source of interaction one finds. Moreover, and anticipating the results of the subsequent analyses, since a major conclusion of the book is that the background variables we study generally make little difference—a finding we find fascinating—we did not feel the need to embark on a long and tedious search for interaction. If we were claiming to have found strong relationships in these variables, then it would have been incumbent on us to test for interaction to see how much of the association might derive from this source. If there is strong interaction, it is possible to overstate and misinterpret the importance of a relationship. We generally have not had to face that situation.

11. Among whites, Non-Christian and None have been combined into a category called "Other"; for the sake of consistency, the black category of "None" also is referred to as "Other."

12. However, see below where the 1976 data are reanalyzed using the mean number of partners, including and excluding the respondents who had intercourse only once and therefore could have only one partner.

13. Excluding one-timers from the analysis, as well as young women who during the reference period were in the last two months of pregnancy or had recently terminated a pregnancy, has no effect on the results.

CHAPTER 4

CONTRACEPTIVE USE

Patterns of sexual activity among teenage women changed rapidly during the 1970s. The previous chapter on sexual experience indicated that the proportion of young women who had experienced premarital intercourse increased between 1971 and 1976 and that among the sexually active first intercourse was occurring at younger ages. This chapter is concerned with the extent of contraceptive use among sexually active young women.

Previous publications from the 1971 and 1976 surveys have helped to define the extent of use and nonuse of contraceptives. In general, it was found that contraception, though widely used by young women, is often neglected. A fairly substantial proportion of the sexually active never use it, while others who have used contraception report one or more incidents of unprotected intercourse. However, a small but growing group has always used some method of contraception. By 1976 this group amounted to slightly under 30 percent of all sexually active young women, or about 40 percent of those who had ever used contraception. Between 1971 and 1976 there was a shift among users toward better methods of contraception, that is, toward oral contraception. Blacks and whites appear to differ somewhat in extent of use, with whites being more likely to always use and less likely to never use. Differences also emerge with respect to the methods used. For example, withdrawal was about as common as condom use among whites but was seldom used by blacks; blacks, on the other hand, were somewhat more partial to oral contraception (although by 1976 more whites had used this method than any other). There is no evidence that blacks who use contraception consistently are any less efficient about it than whites. Even though sexually active blacks have a much higher pregnancy rate than whites, this is due entirely to more pregnancy among those blacks who never use contraception and those who use it only occasionally (Zelnik and Kantner, 1978b). This in turn appears to be due to the greater exposure of blacks to pregnancy because of their earlier initiation of sex. Our task here is not just to describe contraceptive practice, but also, continuing the type of analysis in the previous chapter, to determine the degree to which variables such as race, socioeconomic status, family stability, and religion influence the use of contraception.

In designing questionnaires for surveys that inquire about past behavior, researchers are usually torn between asking questions in the detail that they would like and being concerned about the quality of the information gathered when the questioning becomes complicated or puts unusual demand on recollection. At the time the 1971 questionnaire was designed, our research on adolescent childbearing was in an exploratory phase, and we included only a few questions on contraceptive use in the interview. However, with that experience behind us, we included many more questions on contraceptive use in the 1976 survey. As a result, we can say much more about contraceptive practice and say it more precisely for 1976 than for 1971. For this reason, many of the tables in this chapter show data from only the 1976 survey. Comparisons between the two surveys are made when possible.

Several aspects of contraceptive use are discussed in this chapter: use at first intercourse, use at last intercourse, regularity of contraceptive use, methods ever used, sources of methods, and reasons for nonuse. We did not attempt a complete contraceptive history, which, even if it could be done, would pose formidable problems of condensation and analysis.

Use at First Intercourse

The majority of American teenagers begin their sexual careers without using a contraceptive method. About 60 percent of the young women with premarital sexual experience interviewed in 1976 were not protected against pregnancy the first time they had intercourse (Table 4.1). The percentage using a method was marginally higher for white than for black teenagers.

Whether contraception is used at first intercourse depends to a considerable extent on the age of the young woman at the time. Less than 1 in 5 who were under age 14 used contraception on their first sexual encounter; over half of those who waited until they were aged 18 or 19 to have sex started off as contraceptors. The relationship is what might be expected; the precise numbers would have been difficult to predict. It is worth noting that we accept a broad definition of use. As we shall see later, much of the contraception that was used at first intercourse consisted of nonmedical methods, which are less effective in preventing pregnancy than more modern ones. The young woman who at her initiation to sex is protected against pregnancy by highly effective contraception is the exception at any age under 20 and decidedly in the minority below age 18.

The sociological variables also appear to have some bearing on whether a young woman seeks to avoid pregnancy on her first exposure (Table 4.1). Coming from what popularly would be called a "good" background—high status, stable family, inclined toward a religious outlook—is associated with an above-average tendency to use contraception. It will be recalled that these same factors were negatively associated with the tendency to have sex. Thus, their joint effect on exposure to risk is not fully appreciated by examining either sex or contraception alone. Note, however, that among the sexually active there are no sociologically defined subgroups in which a majority used contraception. Irrespective of background, as we have measured it, contraception is more the exception than the rule. In most instances whites are more likely to be careful than blacks, but this is not always the case, and where it is, the differences are often small. Whether these general observations hold up under more rigorous analysis, in which each variable is examined for its effect on contraceptive use independent of the effect of all the other variables, is the irresistible question to which we now turn.

MULTIVARIATE ANALYSIS
OF USE AT FIRST INTERCOURSE

Continuing the analysis begun in Chapter 3, we again use MCA to consider the simultaneous effect of all of these variables—religion, religiosity, socioeconomic status, family stability, race, current age, and age at first intercourse—and to assist in determining their statistical significance (Table C.10, Appendix C). We include age at first intercourse as an independent variable since it is an indicator, undoubtedly an imperfect one, of the maturity of the young woman at her first experience. Current age also is included as a cohort indicator. If, over time, contraceptives are becoming more available to teenagers, then for any given age at first intercourse the more recent cohorts (that is, younger current age) should be more likely to use contraceptives, other things equal.

The picture resulting from the MCA is essentially unchanged. With allowance for the operation of other variables, especially age at first intercourse, the uncertain difference between blacks and whites now virtually disappears.[1] Age at the time of first intercourse is clearly the dominant variable and the only one to attain unquestioned statistical significance. The sociological variables look about the same as before, but through the combined effect of small differences and the way the cases fall

TABLE 4.1 Percentage of Premaritally Sexually Active Women 15-19 Years of Age in 1976 Who Used a Contraceptive Method at First Intercourse

		1976	
Variable	Total	White	Black
Current Age	(1021)	(576)	(445)
15	38.3	39.9	34.5
16	36.6	33.8	45.0
17	33.8	34.4	31.7
18	42.7	43.3	40.4
19	40.4	43.9	25.3
15-19	38.9	40.0	34.9
SES (years)	(983)	(567)	(416)
<9	29.5	30.5	27.7
9-11	39.2	39.1	39.3
12	39.7	40.8	34.6
≥13	45.8	45.5	49.4
Family Stability	(1020)	(575)	(445)
Ideal	43.3	43.9	38.7
Less ideal	36.6	35.4	40.1
Least ideal	28.9	30.2	27.2
Religion	(1019)	(575)	(444)
Fundamentalist Protestant	43.4	47.3	32.6
Other Protestant	39.0	40.1	36.3
Catholic	40.0	40.0	39.7
Other	33.2	35.1	27.3
Religiosity	(1008)	(568)	(440)
Low	34.2	35.1	27.4
Medium	41.3	43.7	34.1
High	43.6	45.8	40.5
Age First Intercourse	(1013)	(574)	(439)
≤13	18.0	18.6	17.1
14	29.5	28.8	31.2
15	38.0	40.4	29.1
16	36.9	34.1	47.6
17	48.8	50.3	40.5
≥18	56.9	56.2	63.7

NOTE: Estimates are based on weighted sample cases; in addition, see Table 3.1.

numerically, only socioeconomic status and family stability approach statistical significance. Some cohort effect is evident, although it appears most convincingly at the extremes: Those who are currently age 15 are 50 percent more likely to have used contraception at first intercourse than those who are currently age 19. We see this as indicative of a pervasive trend toward increasing use of contraception among younger women. Overall, however, we are only modestly successful in accounting for the fact that some young women start off as contraceptors and others do not. Age at first intercourse, social position, family stability, and current age all have something to do with it and perhaps with better measures of these variables they would explain more than they do. But the inescapable conclusion would seem to be that the essential answer has eluded us.

USE OF A MEDICAL METHOD AT FIRST INTERCOURSE: 1976

As we have cautioned previously, our definition of what constitutes contraception is a generous one, including as it does some methods of dubious effectiveness. From one point of view, a broad definition is appropriate as an indication of the desire to avoid pregnancy. But from the point of view of pregnancy prevention, the kind of method used is obviously important. The questions we raise next, therefore, relate to the methods used at first intercourse, specifically what proportion used the most effective methods, that is, medical methods, and whether the choice is in any way differentiated by the demographic and social variables we have been looking to for explanation.

Use of a medical method (the pill, the IUD, or the diaphragm) at first intercourse involves planning for intercourse ahead of time. The young woman must visit a physician or a clinic before first intercourse and tacitly acknowledge her planned sexual activity to the medical personnel. Furthermore, the use of medical methods requires some income, either from the young woman's own resources or from a program such as Medicaid.

Perhaps the major findings in Table 4.2 are the much greater use of medical methods by blacks and by young women whose first intercourse is delayed to age 18 or above. Nothing else makes much difference, though it is interesting to observe that use of medical methods is extremely low among Fundamentalist Protestants and above average for young women from the least stable family background. It is tempting to see this as all of a piece: These are young women who, because of age or loosened family ties, are more inclined to find their own way in the world. In the case of

TABLE 4.2 Percentage of Premaritally Sexually Active Women 15-19 Years of Age in 1976 Using a Contraceptive Method at First Intercourse Who Used Medical Method

Variable	1976 Total	1976 White	1976 Black
Current Age	(383)	(228)	(155)
15-16	20.3	}13.0	}41.1
17	20.1		
18	22.7	}22.7	}43.8
19	29.7		
15-19	23.7	19.1	42.4
SES (years)	(372)	(224)	(148)
<9	24.8	}16.2	}41.7
9-11	21.8		
12	24.1	}22.1	}45.8
≥13	26.5		
Family Stability	(382)	(227)	(155)
Ideal	20.2	17.2	45.4
Less ideal	26.5	}23.4	}41.0
Least ideal	34.5		
Religion	(382)	(228)	(154)
Fundamentalist Protestant	11.3	}22.0	}38.8
Other Protestant	29.0		
Catholic	15.9	}14.9	}57.6
Other	25.5		
Religiosity	(376)	(223)	(153)
Low	21.8	20.2	38.6
Medium	22.0	16.0	45.5
High	29.4	23.7	38.7
Age First Intercourse	(381)	(227)	(154)
≤14	20.0	}10.8	}33.4
15	13.6		
16	25.0	15.9	50.8
17	22.5	}27.6	}46.7
≥18	39.0		

NOTE: Estimates are based on weighted sample cases; in addition, see Table 3.1.

contraception, this will often mean reliance on publically provided services with their emphasis on medical methods.

The greater tendency for younger women, for example, those currently age 16 and under, to use contraception at first intercourse than those who are currently age 19—the cohort effect seen in Table C.10—does not hold for the use of medical methods. Thus, the increase in initial use among the younger cohorts is attributable to increased use of traditional methods, which in turn suggests that this upward trend has not come from organized programs.

MULTIVARIATE ANALYSIS OF USE OF A MEDICAL METHOD AT FIRST INTERCOURSE

Multiple Classification Analysis, the results of which are provided in Table C.11 (Appendix C), confirms the importance of age at first intercourse and race independent of social status, family stability, religion, or cohort effects. Even after adjustment for these variables, the differences by race are striking: 19 percent of whites who used contraception at first intercourse used a medical method; 42 percent of blacks did so. Large differences also are encountered by age at first intercourse: 23 percent for those under age 15; 48 percent for those who were aged 18 or 19.

Use at Last Intercourse

Use of contraception at the time of the last intercourse brings us closer to current practice, even though among our respondents this event will have occurred at various times in the past. For some, the one-timers, who represent about 13 percent of the premaritally sexually active in 1976, the last intercourse is also the first intercourse.

Nevertheless, an examination of contraception at the last intercourse is the best approximation of current use we have. In analyzing the factors associated with use at last intercourse, we confine ourselves to the never married. The reason for this is purely technical. The 1971 data do not permit us to identify the last premarital intercourse for the ever-married respondent. Since other information on use at last intercourse is common to both surveys and affords an opportunity to compare premarital contraceptive practice in the two periods, we limit the analysis to those who have never been married, thus guaranteeing that the last intercourse will have been premarital. We again take into account the familiar set of demographic and sociological variables. In addition, we consider the prospect of marriage, since having plans to marry changes the character of a couple's relationship and possibly, too, the nature of their contraceptive behavior. It is difficult to predict how plans for marriage should affect contraceptive use. If such plans signify a stable relationship, then one might expect more regular use, in line with findings reported by some investigators (for example, Foreit and Foreit, 1978; Furstenberg, 1976). On the other hand, there may be less concern about pregnancy and thus less done to prevent it if marriage is contemplated. We do not know precisely when the last intercourse occurred and thus we cannot be sure whether the marriage plans were in force at that time. This constitutes a violation of our self-imposed rule regarding the temporal ordering of variables.

Probably the most important finding in these data is the strong and pervasive increase between 1971 and 1976 in the use of contraception at last intercourse (Table 4.3). We find it at each age, for blacks and whites, and among all sociologically defined subgroups. In the earlier survey, reflecting conditions around the beginning of the decade, less than half of sexually active never-married women were current users. There were no differences in definition or survey procedures that could have accounted for this very marked upturn in pregnancy prevention.

Before examining the way "current" use is associated with selected demographic and social differences, a comment is in order concerning the retention of age at first intercourse among the "explanatory" variables. At first glance it might seem to have no possible bearing on current use. However, when taken together with current age, as we are able to do with multivariate analysis, it becomes part of a measure of duration of exposure—the interval from first to last intercourse. We present data on current use and age at first intercourse in Table 4.3, but its interpretation should be deferred until later.

Uniformity is as evident as differences in Table 4.3. Differences in current use do appear in positive relationship with age—current age or age at first intercourse. This relationship holds for whites in both years and for blacks in 1971; for blacks in 1976, current age shows no relationship. Other than age there are few high (or low) spots. Above-average current use is found in the highest SES category. Use among Catholics is average or above, depending on the year. Fundamentalist Protestants are well below average in 1971 but slightly above in 1976; indeed, it appears that differences by religion and religiosity among whites all but disappear in the upsurge of contraception that occurred in those 5 years. Were we to observe a like convergence with respect to SES and family stability, one would be tempted to posit a pervasive change in contraceptive behavior sufficient to overwhelm social differences. If such a trend is indeed under

Contraceptive Use

TABLE 4.3 Percentage of Never-Married Women 15-19 Years of Age Who Used a Contraceptive Method at Last Intercourse

	1971			1976		
Variable	Total	White	Black	Total	White	Black
Current Age	(1174)	(536)	(638)	(786)	(378)	(408)
15	30.5	29.9	31.8	48.9	55.3	35.3
16	40.3	41.2	38.2	55.1	50.0	69.0
17	46.1	46.5	45.0	62.5	64.6	55.9
18	50.5	50.2	51.6	70.3	71.9	65.1
19	57.7	61.1	46.9	69.6	74.0	55.2
15-19	46.9	48.1	43.7	63.6	65.5	57.8
SES (years)	(1137)	(533)	(604)	(756)	(372)	(384)
<9	42.4	39.6	46.2	51.7	50.2	53.5
9-11	42.7	43.7	40.3	63.5	62.3	58.7
12	45.6	45.7	45.1	59.6	59.5	59.9
≥13	59.0	60.6	49.0	76.6	77.7	64.2
Family Stability	(1166)	(533)	(633)	(785)	(377)	(408)
Ideal	50.7	52.1	43.4	65.7	67.2	56.0
Less ideal	41.4	38.1	48.0	63.8	63.8	63.9
Least ideal	42.1	43.7	40.5	56.7	59.7	53.2
Religion	(1173)	(536)	(637)	(785)	(378)	(407)
Fundamentalist Protestant	29.2	27.1	33.6	67.1	69.0	63.3
Other Protestant	44.7	45.6	43.1	63.2	65.5	58.9
Catholic	53.7	53.2	58.7	64.1	64.3	59.6
Other	55.1	56.5	47.7	61.5	67.0	46.3
Religiosity	(1164)	(532)	(632)	(776)	(373)	(403)
Low	48.7	50.5	33.8	64.3	66.3	50.4
Medium	48.0	49.5	44.1	64.1	65.7	60.1
High	42.8	39.4	46.4	61.0	62.3	59.6
Age First Intercourse	(1160)	(532)	(628)	(782)	(377)	(405)
≤13	40.8	44.3	33.7	40.7	44.1	36.0
14	27.2	22.0	36.7	57.5	57.1	58.2
15	43.6	45.2	40.5	63.7	65.9	57.3
16	46.0	45.5	47.1	66.1	66.8	63.7
17	57.0	58.6	52.4	72.4	73.4	67.7
≥18	56.0	57.1	46.5	70.4	69.4	78.3
Marriage Plans	(1171)	(534)	(637)	(785)	(378)	(407)
Yes	49.2	52.2	40.1	65.3	67.8	54.2
No	45.6	45.6	45.5	62.6	64.1	58.9

NOTE: Estimates are based on weighted sample cases; in addition, see Table 3.1.

way, it had not yet run its course by 1976. Having plans to marry makes little if any difference in contraceptive behavior.

MULTIVARIATE ANALYSIS OF USE AT LAST INTERCOURSE

Table C.12 shows the multivariate analysis of the effects of race, current age, SES, family stability, religion, religiosity, age at first intercourse, and marriage plans on use at last intercourse in 1971 and in 1976. Race is not significant in either analysis: After the proportions are adjusted for the other independent variables, young black women are as likely as young white women to use contraception.

Relatively little of the variation in current use that is found among individual respondents is explained by the demographic and social variables employed in the analysis. The same weak tendencies already observed in the bivariate analysis show up in the multivariate analysis: a slight increase in use with age at first intercourse; above average use in the highest SES category; inconsistent differences by religion as between 1971 and 1976. In short, there are a few rather weak tendencies, but almost nothing other than age at first intercourse and SES that clearly and consistently sets the current user apart from the nonuser.

REANALYSIS OF 1976 DATA ON USE AT LAST INTERCOURSE

Part of the reason the foregoing analysis may provide so little insight into current use is that in the interest of making time comparisons we were able to refine the richer 1976 data only to the extent permitted by the type of information also available for 1971. Because of the importance of knowing more about the factors associated with current use, we have refined and extended the analysis of the 1976 data. First, we eliminate those who have had intercourse only once and those who were pregnant at last intercourse. Elimination of the one-timers leaves us with a more experienced group, one that has had greater opportunity to adopt a contraceptive regimen. Being pregnant, of course, obviates the need for contraception and thus could negate the action of factors that at other times might be associated with the use of contraception. Whether and to what extent these refinements will result in a population exhibiting greater use of contraception is uncertain before the fact, but the relationships under study should show up in sharper relief.

In addition, we have extended the analysis by adding three new variables which, a priori, would appear to have some relevance for the establishment of regular contraceptive habits. We expect that those who have used contraception in the past would be more likely to be current users than those who at times failed to do so. Moreover, those whose past use included medical methods might be expected to show up disproportionally among current users. Without a complete contraceptive history, the quickest way to go about this was to select a sexual episode that was already in the past and for which we knew whether contraception had been used and, if so, what kind. For this purpose, we chose the first intercourse—an event for which we have all the requisite information.

It seems possible also that establishing a contraceptive routine would be affected by whether the young woman had been involved with more than one partner, although it is hard to know what the direction of such an effect might be. Those who are prone to theorize about such matters might see the young woman who "plays the field" as having accepted sexual activity as an integral part of her self image. It is thought by some writers, without much evidence, that such coming to terms with sex helps to establish regular contraceptive use, especially of the type, such as the use of oral contraception, which implies the anticipation of sex. While that may be true, the same view of self and sex could develop out of a stable one-partner relationship. The variable available to us—the number of partners—cannot do justice to these behavioral and psychological subtleties, but commends itself as a possibly relevant consideration.

Finally, we take account of experience with pregnancy. From previous analysis (Zelnik and Kantner, 1978b; Zelnik, 1980) we know that pregnancy concentrates the mind wonderfully on the prevention of further conceptions. At this point we must again caution the reader concerning the underreporting of pregnancies by blacks in 1976. To the extent that pregnancy is conducive to the subsequent use of contraception, the underreporting of pregnancies would tend to obscure or at least diminish the relationship by including among the supposed "never pregnant" some who in fact have had such an experience. Fortunately, such cases, although we cannot identify them, make up only a small fraction of the never-pregnant category.

If anything, the standard set of demographic and social variables shows even less association with current use than before (Table 4.4). Young women who become sexually active at a very young age (under age 15) are less likely to be current users. As we have seen, age at first intercourse is positively associated with use of contraception at first intercourse. Thus, it is to be expected, and is the case in fact, that those who did not use contraception initially are much less likely to be current users. It is indeed striking that all or nearly all of those who used a medical method of contraception the first time they had intercourse are also current users. The number of partners has little association with current use; high status and experience with pregnancy contribute positively to current use among whites.

TABLE 4.4 Percentage of Never-Married Women 15-19 Years of Age in 1976 Who Used a Contraceptive Method at Last Intercourse

Variable	Total	White	Black
Current Age	(637)	(313)	(324)
15	64.1	75.0	40.6
16	60.3	56.9	69.0
17	67.4	69.0	62.2
18	73.2	74.1	70.3
19	73.2	75.7	63.8
15-19	69.0	70.7	63.8
SES (years)	(611)	(307)	(304)
<9	58.1	54.2	63.7
9-11	71.0	73.4	64.7
12	63.9	63.9	64.1
≥13	78.7	79.9	65.2
Family Stability	(636)	(312)	(324)
Ideal	71.6	72.3	67.0
Less ideal	66.6	67.4	65.0
Least ideal	64.4	68.2	59.8
Religion	(636)	(313)	(323)
Fundamentalist Protestant	71.5	71.6	71.2
Other Protestant	68.7	70.3	65.4
Catholic	70.4	70.4	68.4
Other	66.1	72.3	47.5
Religiosity	(630)	(309)	(321)
Low	69.7	71.4	56.4
Medium	70.0	71.0	67.5
High	64.5	65.7	63.4
Age First Intercourse	(634)	(312)	(322)
≤13	46.7	51.3	40.8
14	64.2	61.3	69.4
15	70.2	72.8	63.2
16	70.6	72.0	64.6
17	76.0	76.0	76.1
≥18	75.6	73.7	93.3*

TABLE 4.4 Continued

Variable	Total	White	Black
Marriage Plans	(637)	(313)	(324)
Yes	68.9	70.0	64.3
No	69.1	71.4	63.6
Contraceptive Use First Intercourse	(633)	(312)	(321)
Medical method	98.6	100.0	96.3
Nonmedical method	92.3	91.9	94.8
None	52.4	54.6	46.3
Number of Partners	(620)	(306)	(314)
1	71.4	72.2	67.8
2-3	65.5	65.0	66.7
≥4	71.1	76.4	51.7
Ever Pregnant	(635)	(312)	(323)
Yes	72.3	78.5	63.1
No	68.1	69.2	63.9

NOTE: Estimates are based on weighted sample cases; in addition, see Table 3.1. This table contains data for young women who had intercourse at least twice and were not pregnant at last intercourse.

* n < 20.

The first thing to note about the results of the multivariate analysis is the substantial increase in the extent to which current use is explained. Whereas we had been able previously to account for only 6 percent of the variance in current use in 1976 (Table C.12, Appendix C), the present analysis accounts for 26 percent (Table C.13, Appendix C). This increase in explanation may be due in some small part to the refinements introduced into the analysis, but in large part it is due to the inclusion of two additional variables—prior contraceptive use and experience with pregnancy. Neither the third variable added to this analysis—number of partners—nor the two variables that were significant in the initial analysis of the 1976 data—SES and age at first intercourse—are statistically significant.

Thus, to the extent we have succeeded in explaining current use, we are saying that it is determined to a significant degree by past use and by past failure to avoid pregnancy. As the reader will recall, the variable most responsible for use at first intercourse was age at that event. At this juncture, then, the conclusion regarding current use is the not very helpful one that it is influenced by past use, specifically by whether contraception was used at first intercourse, and that, in turn, is, in part at least, a matter of the young woman's age at that time.

USE OF A MEDICAL METHOD AT LAST INTERCOURSE

Among those young women who used a method at last intercourse, most used either the pill, the condom, or withdrawal. The dominant method in 1976 was the pill, followed by the condom and withdrawal (data not shown). This represents a substantial increase in the use of oral contraceptives since 1971, with a corresponding decrease in the relative popularity of other methods. Young women of 18 and 19 were more dependent on the pill than the younger women.

Although young black women were less likely than young white women to use a method at last intercourse (before adjusting for other factors), those who did were more likely to use oral contraceptives. Among black contraceptors in 1976, 62 percent used the pill at last intercourse, compared to 48 percent of white users. A further difference in choice of methods was less use of withdrawal and more use of douche by blacks as compared to whites.

To pursue our interest in how the four social variables plus current age, age at first intercourse, and marriage plans influence the choice of a method, we have constructed Table 4.5, which shows, for those who used contraception at last intercourse, the percentage who used a medical method. Although medical methods include the pill, the IUD, and the diaphragm, the pill predominates. Again in these data, the increase in the use of medical methods between 1971 and 1976 and the greater preference for these methods by blacks is evident. There are some large differences in the choice of methods by religion, which, because of the necessity for rather severe grouping of the data, are hard to interpret. Otherwise current age and an unstable family background appear to favor using effective contraception and, in 1976 primarily, whites who are relatively indifferent to religion (low in religiosity and "other" on religion) were most apt to use medical methods.

MULTIVARIATE ANALYSIS OF
USE OF A MEDICAL METHOD AT LAST INTERCOURSE

The analyses presented in Tables C.14 and C.15 (both in Appendix C) indicate the strong, positive effect of current age on the choice of medical methods. This is true for both 1971 and 1976, even though the range of

TABLE 4.5 Percentage of Never-Married Women 15-19 Years of Age Using a Method at Last Intercourse Who Used a Medical Method

	1971			1976		
Variable	Total	White	Black	Total	White	Black
Current Age	(525)	(247)	(278)	(478)	(245)	(233)
15-16	9.8	3.2	26.6	35.3	39.1	50.0
17	32.7	32.4	33.5	57.9	54.7	69.2
18	43.5	42.4	46.9	63.6	60.9	73.9
19	58.0	58.1	57.4	66.5	64.9	73.9
15-19	37.4	36.4	40.5	56.7	54.0	65.8
SES (years)	(508)	(245)	(263)	(460)	(240)	(220)
<9	37.4	}31.8	35.5	62.0	}45.2	64.3
9-11	35.1		50.3	46.6		63.4
12	32.5	32.1	}27.2	59.6	55.8	}70.6
≥13	42.1	44.9		62.1	62.0	
Family Stability	(522)	(247)	(275)	(477)	(244)	(233)
Ideal	33.6	34.1	30.5	51.2	48.8	68.9
Less ideal	41.0	40.1	42.5	59.6	58.5	61.8
Least ideal	48.4	46.0	50.8	69.9	71.5	67.9
Religion	(525)	(247)	(278)	(477)	(245)	(232)
Fundamentalist Protestant	15.1	}30.9	}38.3	}56.4	}53.0	}64.2
Other Protestant	34.6					
Catholic	34.9	32.7	}61.7	47.9	46.3	}73.2
Other	62.0	64.7		76.3	78.2	
Religiosity	(520)	(245)	(275)	(472)	(242)	(230)
Low	35.7	35.4	39.4	62.7	62.5	65.1
Medium	40.9	39.2	46.3	52.5	48.6	68.0
High	32.5	29.9	34.8	47.7	34.3	62.4
Age First Intercourse	(521)	(247)	(274)	(476)	(244)	(232)
≤14	49.3	19.2	49.3	57.9	51.3	69.3
15	39.7	20.9	39.7	57.0	56.7	58.0
16	34.6	30.7	34.6	52.2	48.9	64.4
17	33.6	}47.6	}38.6	58.5	}56.4	}70.3
≥18	52.6			58.6		

(Continued)

TABLE 4.5 Continued

Variable	1971			1976		
	Total	White	Black	Total	White	Black
Marriage Plans	(524)	(246)	(278)	(477)	(245)	(232)
Yes	41.1	39.7	46.5	58.2	56.1	69.9
No	35.4	34.4	37.8	55.7	52.6	64.3

NOTE: Estimates are based on weighted sample cases; in addition, see Table 3.1.

difference by age was reduced as proportionally more younger women adopted orals after 1971. Largely for this reason, that is, the fact that current age is a more powerful predictor in 1971, more of the variance in the use of medical methods can be explained in 1971. During the five-year period under review, blacks increased their use of orals somewhat more than whites so that differences in use by race sharpened. The only other variable that appears to have a non-chance effect on the use of medical methods in both years is religion, although it is a better predictor in 1971 than in 1976.

REANALYSIS OF 1976 DATA ON USE OF A MEDICAL METHOD AT LAST INTERCOURSE

As with use at last intercourse, we have exploited the greater supply of information available in the 1976 survey. Again, we eliminated the one-timers and those pregnant at last intercourse from the analysis. Furthermore, we added the three independent variables included in our earlier reanalysis of 1976 data: use at first intercourse, number of partners, and whether ever pregnant.

Elimination of the one-timers leaves us with a more sexually experienced population and one with a slightly greater use of medical methods. Table 4.6 shows for never-married women who used a method at last intercourse the percentage who used a medical method by race, current age, SES, religion, religiosity, age at first intercourse, marriage plans, contraceptive use at first intercourse, number of partners, and whether they were ever pregnant before their last intercourse. In general, although there is more use of medical methods, the data reveal about the same relationships between medical use and race, current age, the four social variables, age at first intercourse, and marriage plans, as we noted in the earlier analysis: current age, race, family background, and religion make a difference; the other variables make little or no difference.

TABLE 4.6 Percentage of Never-Married Women 15-19 Years of Age in 1976 Using a Method at Last Intercourse Who Used a Medical Method

Variable	Total	White	Black
Current Age	(424)	(220)	(204)
15-16	40.1	34.0	55.8
17	60.3	56.7	73.9
18	72.2	70.0	79.7
19	67.1	64.1	80.9
15-19	61.3	58.3	72.3
SES (years)	(408)	(215)	(193)
<9	64.9	}50.1	69.0
9-11	52.0		67.7
12	63.9	58.3	}79.9
≥13	66.6	66.4	
Family Stability	(423)	(219)	(204)
Ideal	55.9	53.7	72.8
Less ideal	65.7	62.8	72.0
Least ideal	71.8	71.5	72.1
Religion	(423)	(220)	(203)
Fundamentalist Protestant	62.7	}58.5	}70.3
Other Protestant	62.0		
Catholic	51.7	49.9	}81.5
Other	77.4	77.6	
Religiosity	(418)	(217)	(201)
Low	64.8	64.1	71.3
Medium	59.0	53.5	74.4
High	54.5	39.4	69.1
Age First Intercourse	(424)	(219)	(203)
≤14	62.9	56.1	73.6
15	63.2	63.6	61.8
16	54.8	50.4	75.9
17	62.8	}61.2	}78.2
≥18	65.4		

(Continued)

TABLE 4.6 Continued

Variable	Total	White	Black
Marriage Plans	(424)	(220)	(204)
Yes	61.8	59.5	75.7
No	61.1	57.4	71.2
Contraceptive Use First Intercourse	(421)	(219)	(202)
Medical method	88.4	88.3	88.6
Nonmedical method	37.9	38.5	34.8
None	72.8	69.2	85.1
Number of Partners	(414)	(215)	(199)
1	55.3	51.6	73.6
2-3	60.8	56.2	70.5
≥4	73.2	73.6	70.7
Ever Pregnant	(422)	(219)	(203)
Yes	82.7	80.1	87.7
No	55.9	53.6	65.7

NOTE: Estimates are based on weighted sample cases; in addition, see Table 3.1. This table contains data for young women who had intercourse at least twice and were not pregnant at last intercourse.

The first new variable, contraceptive use at first intercourse, shows a strong relationship with use of a medical method at last intercourse. If a young woman used a medical method or no method at her first intercourse, she was likely to use a medical method at last intercourse. If she used a nonmedical method at first intercourse, she was likely to continue with a nonmedical method. (Recall that these figures refer only to those who used some method of contraception at their last intercourse.) These patterns hold for both white and black women. Number of partners is directly related to use of a medical method at last intercourse (but not for blacks) and those who were ever pregnant were more likely to have used a medical method than the never pregnant.

The explained variance for the reanalysis of the use of a medical method at last intercourse is nearly twice as high as in the previous analysis of the 1976 data. Neither race nor religion are significant. Current age retains some significance, but is overshadowed by the effect on current medical use of the method used at first intercourse and experience with pregnancy (Table C.16, Appendix C). Over 90 percent of those who used a medical method at first intercourse and who used contraception at their last intercourse used a medical method. This figure is more than 50 percentage points above the comparable figure for those who began with a nonmedical method at their first intercourse. If one is interested in what promotes the use of medical methods as a current method, one has to ask what promoted their use at first intercourse. This, some will recall, was primarily a matter of race (blacks more likely to use medical methods) and age at first intercourse (the older the young woman at first intercourse, the more likely she is to start with a medical method). However, some will recall also that these variables plus the others we have customarily employed explain relatively little of the variance in choice of method at first intercourse. So we are left with a few clues to what remains essentially a puzzle.

Experience with pregnancy works as we thought it might. Having had a pregnancy encourages use as well as the use of the most effective methods. Whether they are used effectively is, of course, another question. Discontinuation of use is fairly high among those who adopt contraception subsequent to pregnancy.

Patterns of Contraceptive Use

To discuss use at first and last intercourse raises the inevitable question: What about the time in between (for those cases, that is, where the two events are not the same)? There is no simple answer to this for the simple reason that contraceptive histories vary tremendously as young women begin and interrupt contraception and change from one method to another, sometimes more than once. The only uncomplicated cases are those who have never used contraception. Even here there is the nagging problem of truncated histories, since most never-users will eventually become users. Despite these complications, it is important to have some measure of consistency of use, recognizing that consistency may be transitory. For this purpose we have classified the sexually active cases in the 1976 survey into three categories: those who always used contraception, those who used contraception but not every time, and, finally, those who never used it. This classification refers to contraceptive behavior up to the earliest of three cutoff events: marriage, first pregnancy, or, if neither of these obtain, the survey. In thus classifying the cases, it was necessary to drop those who did not have a contraceptive history, that is, those who up to the survey had intercourse only once. As previously noted, they represent about 13 percent of the sexually active, with little variation by race or marital status.

The less specific and detailed information collected in the 1971 survey did not permit us to classify the cases who had experienced a premarital pregnancy and who had ever used contraception by whether they had used it prior to the pregnancy or, where that could be determined, by whether they had always or irregularly used it before conception. Furthermore, the ever married who had intercourse before marriage could be classified only as premarital ever- or never-users.[2] These limitations, plus our inability to identify the one-timers in the 1971 survey, cause us to focus here on the data from the 1976 survey.

The data on the pattern of use as revealed in that survey are set forth in Table 4.7 for the total population. Differences by race show up for those who never used contraception or used it irregularly. The largest group of whites were those who had used contraception sometimes but not always; the largest group of blacks were the never-users. Looking ahead, however, to the multivariate analyses of always use and never use, race is not statistically significant in either case.

It appears, in addition, that consistency of use is favored by high status, by a normal ("ideal") family background, and by a relatively strong religious orientation. These are the factors which we found earlier to favor use at first intercourse. To a degree this similarity may be an artifact of our scheme of classification. To be an always-user one has to have used contraception at first intercourse; similarly, a never-user had to be a nonuser at first intercourse. The irregular user, of course, could have been either a user or a nonuser at that time.

The fact that these variables are less closely associated with use at last intercourse may be puzzling at first glance since the same identities might be expected to hold. However, in analyzing use at last intercourse we dealt only with the never married and those who were pregnant at that time were excluded in part of the analysis. The classification by time pattern of use, on the other hand, is made for both married and unmarried and is bounded by marriage or pregnancy if either of those events occurred. Therefore, it involves a somewhat different group from those whose last premarital intercourse was examined; more importantly, the partial identity that obtains for first intercourse does not hold for last intercourse. The use status at last intercourse of anyone who had ever married or had ever been pregnant has no necessary relationship to their pattern of use up to that time. This technical digression merely says that while we should expect some overlap between use at first intercourse and pattern of

TABLE 4.7 Percentage Distribution of Pattern of Contraceptive Use for Premaritally Sexually Active Women 15-19 Years of Age in 1976

Variable	n	Total	Always Used	Sometimes Used	Never Used
Race					
White	(497)	100.0	27.7	44.0	28.3
Black	(387)	100.0	24.0	33.2	42.8
Current Age					
15	(67)	100.0	28.2	40.3	31.6
16	(117)	100.0	30.2	38.7	31.0
17	(195)	100.0	28.3	41.2	30.5
18	(252)	100.0	25.8	41.7	32.5
19	(253)	100.0	25.2	43.6	41.7
15-19	(884)	100.0	26.9	41.7	31.4
SES (years)					
<9	(178)	100.0	21.9	34.9	43.2
9-11	(300)	100.0	28.1	36.8	35.1
12	(228)	100.0	24.8	46.2	29.0
≥13	(146)	100.0	31.8	51.5	16.7
Family Stability					
Ideal	(411)	100.0	31.1	44.7	24.2
Less ideal	(258)	100.0	23.3	41.2	35.5
Least ideal	(214)	100.0	19.5	34.4	46.1
Religion					
Fundamentalist Protestant	(86)	100.0	30.1	34.4	35.5
Other Protestant	(517)	100.0	26.1	42.9	31.0
Catholic	(162)	100.0	29.5	39.8	30.7
Other	(117)	100.0	23.1	44.8	32.1
Religiosity					
Low	(327)	100.0	25.5	42.4	32.1
Medium	(351)	100.0	26.9	46.8	32.3
High	(195)	100.0	28.8	42.9	28.3

(Continued)

TABLE 4.7   Continued

	n	Total	Always Used	Sometimes Used	Never Used
Age First Intercourse					
≤13	(97)	100.0	7.9	41.2	50.9
14	(138)	100.0	19.3	42.8	37.9
15	(209)	100.0	25.1	46.0	28.9
16	(212)	100.0	29.0	39.3	31.7
17	(142)	100.0	34.0	40.9	25.0
≥18	(80)	100.0	39.5	37.8	22.7

NOTE: Estimates are based on weighted sample cases. This table contains data for young women who had premarital intercourse at least twice.

subsequent use, such is not the case for use at last intercourse. It follows that similar factors might be expected to explain use at first intercourse and the pattern of use; these same factors need not, and in fact do not, relate to use at last intercourse.

The pronounced association between the pattern of use and age at first intercourse also requires some comment. With the passage of time both the always-users and never-users are subject to losses to the middle group—the irregular or "sometimes" users. The process cannot work any other way. Both current age and age at first intercourse are required to establish the time interval during which the always- and never-use categories are subject to such attrition. Apart from its role in defining the duration of sexual activity, age at first intercourse undoubtedly says something about persons which may have some bearing on their pattern of contraceptive use. Current age also may have meaning, in a cohort sense perhaps, in addition to its contribution to a measure of duration. Whatever these interpretations might be, they are inextricably bound up with duration of sexual experience. In any event, the bivariate distributions involving either measure of age and pattern of use cannot be clearly and simply interpreted.

MULTIVARIATE ANALYSIS
OF THE PATTERNS OF CONTRACEPTIVE USE

Unless the patterns of contraceptive use can be measured in some summary fashion, as by a score or index for example, the way to handle the multivariate analysis is not obvious. Our choice, after examining the bivariate distributions, is to perform separate analyses for always and never use. Both categories have clear substantive meaning and are associated with marked differences in the probability of premarital pregnancy. One could also look at the sometimes users, but the heterogeneity of that category makes its interpretation an even more daunting prospect.

Whether or not a young woman uses contraception consistently, that is, is an always-user, is explained for the most part by considerations of age (Table C.17, Appendix C). The younger she is, other things—including duration of sexual activity—equal, the more likely she is to be a regular user. This looks, in part at least, like a possible cohort effect. On the other hand, the younger she is when she first becomes sexually active, other things—including duration, again—equal, the less likely she is to have always used contraception. This could represent the operation of some unidentified factor which is responsible both for early initiation to sex and indifferent use of contraception. In both instances, however, whether we are concerned with current age or age at first intercourse, the effects of differences in duration are unavoidably present. Even though duration is "controlled for" in each age category, errors of composition can still arise with respect to comparisons between categories. It is most unlikely that the distribution by duration of sexual activity will look the same for young women aged 15 and those aged 19. It would not be surprising to find someone aged 19 who had been sexually active for 5 or 6 years; that would be phenomenal for a girl aged 15. The same point can be made in reverse for age at first intercourse. Thus we are left with the conclusion that current age and age at first intercourse are important in explaining a highly regular pattern of contraceptive use but we cannot say what it is about age that produces that effect. Whether it is a cohort phenomenon, reflection of the attritional effect of time on consistency of use, or some, as yet, undefined variable is moot. None of the other variables, including race, plays any part in explaining regular use of contraception.

The items of significance for never use (Table C.17) are somewhat different from those for always use. SES and family stability both have strong enough effects on never use to be highly significant, although neither was significant in the analysis of always use. The two age variables, age at first intercourse and current age, show the direction of relationship that might have been expected from the analysis of always use. Thus, whereas always use declines with current age and increases with age at first intercourse, never use increases with current age and decreases with age at first intercourse. In the case of never use, however, current age is not statistically significant. After adjusting for the effect of other variables, blacks are no more likely than whites to never use contraception (nor, as already noted, are they less likely to always use).

The part played by age in the never use of contraception is no less, and possibly more, difficult to determine than in the case of always use. The analysis of always use in conjunction with the analysis of never use suggests that while young women of high SES are no more likely to be always users of contraception than those lower on the SES scale, they do begin to use contraceptives earlier in their sexual careers. However, as we shall see in the next chapter, this earlier use does not lead (in 1976) to a statistically significant lower prevalence of premarital pregnancy.

Ever Use of Medical Contraception

Up to this point we have discussed whether contraception was used—at first intercourse, at last intercourse, and whether a medical method was used at each of these events—and how consistently contraception was used. In this section we examine methods ever used, which represents contraceptive experience in the widest sense, and changes between the first and last method used (1976 only). For those who used a method at last intercourse that method is, of course, the last method used. For irregular users whose last intercourse went unprotected, last use would have occurred some time earlier. The distribution by the last method is constrained by this overlap to resemble the distribution by method used at last intercourse.

If all methods of contraception ever used are considered, the pill stands out as the method that was used by young women in the 1976 survey more than any other (data not shown). Blacks had more experience with it than did whites and for both blacks and whites experience with the method increases with age. Next in apparent popularity was the condom, though whites favor this method more than do blacks. Withdrawal, distinctly a white method, stands third, its place among blacks being taken by the douche.

The mean number of methods used by whites who had ever used contraception was 1.8, whereas for blacks, who on average begin contraception later, the mean was 1.5. It is of interest to inquire more specifically about method shifts, although this can only be done with recourse to some simplification. To consider all changes in method, even those shifts for which we have information, would be complicated methodologically, and possibly more bewildering than enlightening in the result. Accordingly, we confine our attention to the three most popular initial methods—pill, condom, and withdrawal. What degree of method loyalty attaches to these as first methods—judging by whether they were also the last method

TABLE 4.8 Percentage Distribution of Contraceptive Method First Used, by Contraceptive Method Last Used, for Premaritally Sexually Active Women 15-19 Years of Age in 1976

Contraceptive Method First Used	n	Total	Pill	Foam, Cream, Jelly	IUD	Diaphragm	Condom	Douche	Withdrawal	Rhythm
All Women										
Pill	(299)	100.0	84.9	2.3	4.2	0.8	5.2	0.4	1.0	11.6
Condom	(191)	100.0	33.0	2.5	3.2	1.5	49.5	1.3	6.2	2.7
Withdrawal	(92)	100.0	15.8	0.0	0.0	0.0	9.7	2.2	70.2	2.1
White Women										
Pill	(121)	100.0	83.5	2.9	4.1	1.0	5.9	0.0	1.0	1.6
Condom	(135)	100.0	33.4	2.7	3.4	1.7	47.8	1.3	6.9	2.8
Withdrawal	(74)	100.0	14.3	0.0	0.0	0.0	10.1	1.4	72.4	1.7
Black Women										
Pill	(178)	100.0	87.8	1.1	4.4	0.6	3.9	1.1	1.1	0.0
Condom	(56)	100.0	30.5	1.8	1.7	0.0	60.9	1.7	1.8	1.7

NOTE: Estimates are based on weighted sample cases. This table contains data for young women who had premarital intercourse at least twice.

used? The data are presented in Table 4.8 (one-timers are not included, since to have done so would have overstated the extent of method loyalty). In examining Table 4.8, note that, given the tendency for some users to progress from nonmedical to medical methods, there is a somewhat greater opportunity for defections to arise in the case of the condom and withdrawal than of the pill. As might be expected, the median interval from first to last method is shorter for those who begin contraception with the pill than for those who start with a nonmedical method (data not shown).

Clearly, the pill holds its clientele better than the other two methods, although, as noted above, this may be due partly to the shorter interval involved. Defections are slight, mostly to the condom and IUD. By contrast, the condom loses a third of those who used it as a first method to the pill, retaining only half of its original clients. Withdrawal, among whites, is intermediate in staying power between the pill and the condom; more than 7 in 10 whose first method was withdrawal used it also as their last method. Racial differences are minimal for the methods shown.

By collapsing all methods into either medical or nonmedical, it becomes clear (Table 4.9) that the major shift is from nonmedical to medical. Almost 90 percent of those who start with a medical method were found to be using a method of that type as their most recent method. By contrast, one third of those who began with a nonmedical method shifted to a medical method. Once again, the racial differences are inconsequential.

Since the use of medical methods is associated with a greatly reduced risk of pregnancy as compared to the use of other methods (Zelnik and Kantner, 1978b; Zabin et al., 1979), it is relevant to ask what factors influence that choice. Table 4.10 shows the percentage of premaritally sexually active women ever using contraception who ever used a medical method. Irrespective of age or background, blacks are more apt to have used medical methods than whites. Among blacks as well as among whites, being 18 or older, or from an unstable family background, or relatively indifferent to religion are all seemingly conducive to above-average use of medical methods. There is a suggestion here that those who are somewhat independent, either by virtue of age or what they have seen of life, are the ones who find their way to oral contraception. It does not seem to be a matter of being disadvantaged socioeconomically. Even though the use of health services generally in the United States is positively related to socioeconomic status, this does not hold for the use of medical methods of contraception. Also surprising is the fact that age at first intercourse, which is related to most aspects of sexuality as well as to the use of contraception, has little bearing on the type of contraception ever used.

TABLE 4.9 Percentage Distribution of Type of Contraceptive Method First Used, by Type of Contraceptive Method Last Used, for Premaritally Sexually Active Women 15-19 Years of Age in 1976

Type of Contraceptive Method First Used	Type of Contraceptive Method Last Used											
	Total				White				Black			
	n	Total	Medical	Nonmedical	n	Total	Medical	Nonmedical	n	Total	Medical	Nonmedical
Medical	(313)	100.0	89.8	10.2	(127)	100.0	80.2	11.8	(186)	100.0	93.1	6.9
Nonmedical	(349)	100.0	33.2	66.8	(244)	100.0	33.6	66.4	(105)	100.0	30.2	69.8

NOTE: Estimates are based on weighted sample cases. This table contains data for young women who had premarital intercourse at least twice.

MULTIVARIATE ANALYSIS OF EVER USE OF MEDICAL CONTRACEPTION

The results of the multivariate analysis (Table C.18, Appendix C) confirm that young women who are black are much more likely to have used medical methods than whites of similar age and background. Current age and, among whites only, family instability and a low degree of religiosity also promote the use of the most effective methods. Age at first

TABLE 4.10 Percentage of Premaritally Sexually Active Ever-Contracepting Women 15-19 Years of Age in 1976 Who Ever Used a Medical Method

Variable	Total	White	Black
Current Age	(674)	(374)	(300)
15	38.5	}36.0	}60.9
16	45.2		
17	62.5	59.0	75.4
18	75.5	72.4	86.3
19	72.0	68.9	85.9
15-19	65.5	62.1	77.9
SES (years)	(648)	(369)	(279)
<9	66.2	61.5	73.9
9-11	60.4	53.8	81.3
12	62.5	59.0	78.4
≥13	72.6	72.5	74.1
Family Stability	(673)	(373)	(300)
Ideal	57.8	55.3	76.2
Less ideal	71.7	69.5	77.0
Least ideal	80.1	79.9	80.3
Religion	(672)	(373)	(299)
Fundamentalist Protestant	65.7	65.4	66.5
Other Protestant	65.1	59.8	78.3
Catholic	58.4	57.3	}82.3
Other	79.4	78.5	
Religiosity	(665)	(368)	(297)
Low	71.9	70.9	80.4
Medium	62.2	56.5	79.0
High	56.2	42.7	74.3

Contraceptive Use

TABLE 4.10   Continued

Variable	Total	White	Black
Age First Intercourse	(668)	(373)	(295)
≤13	79.8	}55.0	}82.0
14	57.5		
15	68.1	67.2	71.2
16	61.0	56.7	80.1
17	66.0	64.1	77.4
≥18	69.3	67.5	86.1

NOTE: Estimates are based on weighted sample cases; in addition, see Table 3.1. This table contains data for young women who had premarital intercourse at least twice.

intercourse behaves inconsistently. Overall, the model explains a significant but not particularly impressive amount of variance in the use of medical methods.

Source of Pill and IUD

In the 1976 survey, premaritally sexually active young women who had used the pill or the IUD were asked whether they obtained their first pill prescriptions or IUD insertions from a clinic or a private physician. Table 4.11 shows the percentage of women receiving their first pill prescriptions or IUD insertions from clinics by race and, with some inevitable collapsing of categories, by current age, socioeconomic status, family stability, religion, religiosity, and age at first intercourse.

Clinics and private physicians are both important as initial sources for users of modern medical methods—the former somewhat more so in the case of blacks than of whites. The only other variables that appear to be uniformly important among those shown in Table 4.11 are religiosity and age at first intercourse. If intercourse is delayed until age 17 or older, it is much more likely that, if medical methods are used, they will be obtained initially from a private physician. It is worth suggesting, perhaps, that what may be involved here to some degree is privacy and independence. A visit to a physician by a very young, perhaps economically dependent, woman would involve the parents or some adult in paying for services; a trip to a clinic would not. An older, more independent woman with more resources can more often take care of the physician fee herself. Those scoring medium or high on religiosity also are more likely initially to obtain medical contraception from a private physician. Among the other socio-

TABLE 4.11 Percentage of Premaritally Sexually Active Women 15-19 Years of Age in 1976 Who Obtained First Pill Prescription or IUD Insertion from a Clinic

Variable	Total	White	Black
Current Age	(448)	(214)	(234)
15-16	41.2	} 48.2	} 57.0
17	56.8		
18	47.2	41.2	65.1
19	42.2	41.0	46.7
15-19	46.8	43.2	56.6
SES (years)	(429)	(211)	(218)
≤11	49.4	40.2	64.5
≥12	43.8	44.3	41.1
Family Stability	(448)	(214)	(234)
Ideal	45.7	45.1	48.7
Less ideal	45.9	40.0	58.7
Least ideal	50.5	41.7	60.8
Religion	(446)	(213)	(233)
Protestant	47.9	44.7	54.1
Other	45.0	41.6	66.3
Religiosity	(442)	(211)	(231)
Low	51.6	48.8	72.5
Medium/High	41.3	34.4	51.5
Age First Intercourse	(445)	(213)	(232)
≤14	54.6	48.5	61.1
15	49.0	46.3	57.6
16	53.8	51.8	59.6
≥17	36.1	34.7	43.9

NOTE: Estimates are based on weighted sample cases; in addition, see Table 3.1.

logically defined subgroups, whites show little difference in their propensity initially to obtain medical methods of contraception from a clinic, whereas blacks who are of low SES, have an unstable family background, or who are not Protestants are above average in their reliance on clinics as the initial source of medical contraception.

MULTIVARIATE ANALYSIS OF SOURCE

Looking at the effects of these independent variables simultaneously (Table C.19, Appendix C), race and religiosity remain significant predictors—blacks and those with a low religious orientation show some greater preference for clinics even when allowance is made for all the other variables. Current age appears important also but behaves peculiarly—the youngest and the oldest preferring clinics—and is thus hard to interpret. The tendency for those who begin intercourse early, before age 17, to favor clinics as a source for their pill prescriptions or IUD insertions is still evident but fails to achieve statistical significance. Among blacks, those of low SES also opt for clinics, whereas among whites the opposite tendency holds, with those of high SES favoring clinics. In the case of whites, however, SES is not statistically significant.

Reasons for Nonuse

The previous sections of this chapter have shown that young American women often take risks and do not use contraceptives when they engage in premarital intercourse. A significant portion of sexually active women have never used contraceptives, and those that have often have done so sporadically. This section summarizes previously published material (Zelnik and Kantner, 1979) on the reasons premaritally sexually active women give for failing to use contraception.

In the 1976 survey, all premaritally sexually active respondents who had at least one unprotected intercourse were queried about their reasons for not using contraception. We focused on the last unprotected act (for the ever married the reference point was the last unprotected premarital intercourse), recognizing that we thereby ignored differences in the timing of that event as well as in antecedent patterns of use or nonuse.

After identification of those who had no need for contraception, that is, those who were already pregnant or were trying to become pregnant, the remaining cases were asked if they thought there was a good chance they might become pregnant. If the answer was "yes," they were asked why they had not used contraception; if the answer was "no," they were asked why they thought they could not become pregnant.[3]

More than half of the cases, somewhat more so among whites than blacks, thought they could not become pregnant, largely because they "had intercourse at a time of the month when pregnancy could not occur." Other, but less important, reasons for believing pregnancy could not occur were "too young," "had sex too infrequently," and "just couldn't" (become pregnant).

Those who gave "time of month" answers would be called "rhythm users" in everyday parlance. However, they did not associate this de facto use of that method with rhythm, whether involving use of calendar or thermometer, when previously asked about, and shown a list of, specific contraceptives. Apparently, using rhythm means something more deliberate and systematic than taking refuge in ad hoc fashion in the "time of the month."

Some respondents did, of course, explicitly report having used rhythm. This difference in perspective between those who did so and those who did not but had intercourse at a time of the month when pregnancy could not occur, has obvious implications for estimates of contraceptive use. Further complicating the issue is whether either group correctly perceives the period of greatest risk of pregnancy during the menstrual cycle.

Among those who thought there was a good chance of becoming pregnant, the dominant reason for the nonuse of contraception was they "didn't expect to have intercourse." There were a variety of other reasons cited for nonuse, including objections by the partner, fear of using contraception or believing it was wrong to use it, or believing contraception was too difficult to use or that it impinged on the pleasure of sex. Relatively few reported not knowing about contraception or where to get it.

The reasons for nonuse were essentially similar for whites and blacks, allowing for the fact that blacks initiated sexual activity earlier than whites. They are thus somewhat more sexually experienced themselves and live in a milieu in which adolescent sex and pregnancy are more prevalent. Not surprisingly, therefore, they are more apt to see themselves at risk of pregnancy. Otherwise, as among whites, the same tendency to be the victim, and in some cases the beneficiary, of circumstances is apparent.

Summary

Six dimensions of contraceptive use among American teenagers—use at first intercourse, use at last intercourse, patterns of contraceptive use, types of methods used, source of medical methods, and reasons for nonuse—were considered in this chapter. The data indicate that a substantial amount of unprotected intercourse occurs among teenagers. However, the few comparisons that we can make between 1971 and 1976 point toward an increase in contraceptive use among teenagers. Tables 4.12 and 4.13 summarize the results of the multivariate analyses from this chapter.

In the previous chapter, on sexual experience, we documented large differences between the sexual behavior of young white and black women.

TABLE 4.12 Summary of Significance and Consistency of Relationship of Explanatory Variables for Three Aspects of Use of Contraceptive Methods

Variable	Use at First Intercourse 1976 Total	Use at Last Intercourse[a] 1971 & 1976 Total	1976 Reanalysis Total	Pattern of Use: 1976 Always Used Total	Never Used Total
Race	0	0	0	0	0
Current age	x	0	0	x	0
SES	x	x	0	0	x
Family stability	x	0	0	0	x
Religion	0	0	0	0	0
Religiosity	0	0	0	0	0
Age first intercourse	x	x	0	x	x
Marriage plans	—	0	0	—	—
Contraceptive use first intercourse	—	—	x	—	—
Number of partners	—	—	0	—	—
Ever pregnant	—	—	x	—	—

NOTE: x = significant at $p < .10$ and consistent in direction in both surveys or $p < .10$ if only one survey involved; 0 = not significant and/or not consistent; dashes = not applicable.

a. Refers to never-married women.

TABLE 4.13 Summary of Significance and Consistency of Relationship of Explanatory Variables for Four Aspects of Use of Medical Methods of Contraception

	Use Medical Method at First Intercourse 1976			Use Medical Method at Last Intercourse[a] 1971 & 1967			1976 Reanalysis	Ever Use of a Medical Method 1976			Source of Medical Method 1976		
	Total	White	Black	Total	White	Black	Total	Total	White	Black	Total	White	Black
Race	x	—	—	x	—	—	0	x	—	—	x	—	—
Current age	0	0	0	x	x	x	x	x	x	x	x	0	x
SES	0	0	0	0	0	0	0	0	0	0	0	0	x
Family stability	0	0	0	0	0	0	0	x	x	0	0	0	0
Religion	0	0	0	x	0	x	0	0	0	x	0	0	0
Religiosity	0	0	0	0	0	0	0	x	x	0	x	x	x
Age first intercourse	x	x	x	0	0	0	0	0	0	0	0	0	0
Marriage plans	—	—	—	0	0	0	0	—	—	—	—	—	—
Contraceptive use first intercourse	—	—	—	—	—	—	x	—	—	—	—	—	—
Number of partners	—	—	—	—	—	—	0	—	—	—	—	—	—
Ever pregnant	—	—	—	—	—	—	x	—	—	—	—	—	—

NOTE: x = significant at p <.10 and consistent in direction in both surveys or p <.10 if only one survey involved; 0 = not significant and/or not consistent; dashes = not applicable.

a. Refers to never-married women.

In this chapter, we found that when considering cross-tabulations of contraceptive use by race, young black women were less likely to use contraceptives. Thus, total exposure is substantially greater among blacks than among whites—more sexual activity and less contraception. In the multivariate analyses, where age at first intercourse, current age, and several family background variables (socioeconomic status, religion, religiosity, and family stability) were controlled, there was little difference in the extent of use between black and white teenagers. The fact that under controlled conditions we can explain the racial difference in extent of use does not diminish the fact that young black women in our society are highly vulnerable to pregnancy under the uncontrolled conditions of everyday life. Among the remaining independent variables, socioeconomic status was most often related to the extent of contraceptive use—the higher SES teenagers were more likely to use contraceptives at first and last intercourse (but not in the reanalysis of the 1976 data) and fewer of them were never-users; those in the most stable family situations also were more likely to use at first intercourse and less likely to never use. On the other hand, religion and religiosity seem to have little influence on contraceptive use. Variables such as current age, age at first intercourse, previous use, and pregnancy experience are much better predictors of contraceptive use.

The choice of a medical method, on the other hand, had a different set of determinants, the specific determinants varying depending on whether first or last intercourse is considered. Race was more successful in predicting use at first intercourse of a medical method among users than in predicting users among the sexually active; current age, SES, and family stability all play some part in explaining use at first intercourse, but not in explaining use of a medical method. The two variables that explain the current use of a medical method more than any others are the type of method used at first intercourse and experience with pregnancy. Both of these "explanations" beg the question to a degree. On the other hand, race, current age, family stability, and religiosity have some influence on whether medical methods are ever used.

Medical methods (pill and IUD) were obtained in the first instance about equally from clinics and private physicians. Blacks and those who score low on religiosity show some greater preference for the clinic as the place to get their first pill prescriptions and IUD insertions; whites and those inclined toward a religious outlook are slightly partial to the private physician. Many young women, of course, go to neither or do so only after a long delay. If we add together those who never use contraception and those who have never used medical methods, we have around 70 percent of the sexually active who are not being reached through organized services. In addition, there is the large group of young women who ultimately use medical methods, but whose acceptance of these methods comes after an extended period of nonuse, which in many cases involves an unintended pregnancy. In terms of their penetration of the market for teenage contraception, the nation's physicians and clinical services can reasonably be regarded as marginal suppliers. The low cost and anonymity of the clinic would appear from our data to give it certain advantages relative to recruiting the very young and those with limited resources. Thus far they have not capitalized on that advantage.

The reasons given for failing to use contraception reflect the nature of the underlying behavior. Since sex among young people is largely irregular and unplanned, it should not be surprising that little provision is made in advance with regard to contraception. There are, of course, young women who always use contraception. We did not ask them to explain that nor do we know whether their sexual lives are more orderly than those who have not always used contraception. That is a fault of the study design. However, the premaritally sexually active who did not use contraception regularly did give us their reasons. Over half subscribe to the notion that they are not at risk of becoming pregnant—a proposition that we cannot evaluate, but which is almost certainly unfounded in a large number of cases. Some of these young women rely on a de facto version of the rhythm method but not all of them recognize it as such. The remainder of those who thought themselves immune from pregnancy had even less to base their convictions on. Blacks are somewhat less likely to have this largely false sense of security, perhaps because they see more sex and early pregnancy around them. Like the combat soldier who sees a friend go down under fire, the realization that "it could happen to me" is immediate and undeniable.

For those who thought they might become pregnant, the most important reason for not using contraception was that intercourse was unexpected or, not unrelated, that they could not manage to use contraception under the circumstances. Relatively few had objections, moral or otherwise, of their own or of their partners. Events are ascendant over the fear of pregnancy. There are, of course, young women who refuse sex if contraception is unavailable and they think they might become pregnant. But this group, although we do not know its relative size, probably is small compared to those who take a chance.

Since so much has been written by those with a taste for convoluted psychological interpretation about the young woman who seeks a pregnancy because of a variety of psychodynamic subplots, it is worth noting that only about 5 percent of those asked about their last unprotected intercourse were trying to become pregnant. The determined psychodynamicist could claim some of the 15 percent who were actually pregnant at that time (most of whom would probably maintain that they did not want to be in that condition) as well as some of the really involved cases who wanted to become pregnant but used contraception anyhow. Overall, this reason for nonuse, so popular among youth counselors and social workers, does not appear to be manifestly important.

NOTES

1. Following the practice of the previous chapter, we do not show separate results for whites and blacks in those instances where race is not statistically significant in the multivariate analysis of the total population.

2. For a fuller discussion of the differences in these respects between the 1971 and 1976 surveys, see Chapter 5 and the second section of Appendix B.

3. Reasons for nonuse of contraception also were obtained in the 1971 survey. In that survey the question did not refer to a specific event of nonuse and multiple responses were permitted. The data, therefore, are much more difficult to interpret. We should note, however, that having intercourse at a time of the month when (it was believed) pregnancy could not occur was a frequently given reason for the nonuse of contraception (Shah et al., 1975)—a result similar to that of the 1976 survey.

CHAPTER 5

PREMARITAL PREGNANCY

In Chapter 3 we noted an increase in the prevalence of premarital sexual activity between 1971 and 1976. Coincident with this was a drop in the age at first intercourse. At the same time, the use of contraception among never-married young women, as measured by use at last intercourse, became more widespread, with proportionately more of it concentrated among the more effective methods, orals in particular. With the data on hand, we cannot determine whether there was a corresponding change in early use of contraception (for example, at first intercourse) or in the regularity of use prior to pregnancy. Elsewhere we have noted that "there is no evidence that the gap between age at first intercouse and age at first use has narrowed in the last five years" (Zelnik and Kantner, 1977: 67). Thus, it is not apparent before the fact whether overall the prevalence of premarital pregnancy should have gone up, in response to more sexual activity, or down, in response to what appears to be more and presumably better contraception. One would expect, however, that among the sexually active premarital pregnancy should have declined and also that less of it, perhaps, should have been unwanted.

The facts are that between 1971 and 1976 there was, contrary to our expectations, little or no change in the prevalence of premarital pregnancy among sexually active young women. Approximately 30 percent of all premaritally sexually active young women in 1971 had at least one premarital conception, compared to 28 percent in 1976 (Zelnik and Kantner, 1978a). This stability in pregnancy prevalence among sexually active young women appears to have characterized both whites and blacks. For whites, the figures were 24 percent in 1971 and 25 percent in 1976. Blacks registered a small decline—from 47 percent to 40 percent—but, as discussed in Chapter 1 and Appendix B, this apparent decline may well be spurious due to the underreporting of pregnancies by blacks in the 1976 study. Moreover, the proportion of first premarital pregnancies that were unwanted remained essentially the same in the two periods: 68 percent in

1971 and 67 percent in 1976. Thus, on initial examination, more and, theoretically, better contraception does not seem to have diminished the extent of unwanted premarital pregnancy.

With essentially no change in pregnancy among the sexually active but a substantial increase in the overall prevalence of sexual activity, it follows that the proportion of *all* young women experiencing pregnancy must have increased also. It did, and was accounted for entirely by a rise in pregnancy among young white women. The increase was small in absolute terms—for whites, approximately 3 percentage points—but large in relative terms—45 percent, again for whites (Zelnik and Kantner, 1978a).

The central question, therefore, is the unchanging prevalence of pregnancy among young sexually active women in simultaneity with what appear to be somewhat improved contraceptive practices. In this chapter we attempt to penetrate this paradox. We also shall examine factors associated with pregnancy in both periods—patterns of association which, despite an apparent absence of overall change in prevalence, might have changed in consequence of substantial public and private efforts during these years to extend contraceptive services to young women.

That done, we look next at the physical outcome of pregnancy, primarily at abortions and live births and the factors associated therewith. Here again we would expect to encounter change, because of Supreme Court decisions leading to the liberalization of laws regulating abortion followed by the rapid extension of abortion services.

Abortion and marriage represent competing alternatives for many unmarried pregnant women. With the increase in the number of abortions among young women in the United States, there has been a decline in the proportion marrying. While other factors also may be involved in the avoidance of youthful marriage, the availability of abortion certainly is one. Having considered the factors associated with the physical outcome of the pregnancy, we then consider the decision to marry among those young women who carry their pregnancies to term. Finally, we shall look at the factors associated with the rejection of both abortion and marriage— that is, with illegitimacy.

Before considering these issues, it is necessary once more to review the kinds of information available to us, not merely on pregnancy but also on contraception, since we are interested in how one relates to the other. First, contraception.

Since in the second survey we attempted to improve and extend the information on contraceptive use, there inevitably is some lack of comparability between the two surveys. In general, we can say more about contraceptive practice and say it more precisely in 1976 than in 1971.

To describe the differences is complex since in 1976 the data on contraception were collected with respect to different events that might be regarded as checkpoints in a young person's sexual and reproductive career: first intercourse, last intercourse, first use of contraception, last or most recent use of contraception, and first premarital pregnancy. We are interested also in patterns of contraceptive behavior, that is, in determining whether a young woman since first becoming sexually active always, never, or sometimes used contraception. We refer to this classification in terms of consistency of use or nonuse as the respondent's contraceptive status. A classification by contraceptive status is subject to change as always-users fall from grace to become sometimes-users or as never-users begin to contracept and attain the same mixed status. To complicate matters further, the contraceptive status classification, which takes the first intercourse as its benchmark, is defined by reference to some arbitrarily selected terminal event. We have used three such events to close the interval since first intercourse: first pregnancy, marriage, or date of interview. Two of these intervals—first intercourse to first pregnancy and first intercourse to first marriage—are significant segments of one's life course. The interval of first intercourse to interview has the advantage of being available for all sexually active cases, but is somewhat Procrustean as a sociological category.

It may help in understanding the nature of the data we have to work with to list what information is available from each survey (Figure 5.1). Note that we are concerned only with premarital behavior.

The superiority of the 1976 survey with respect to the amount of contraceptive information is immediately evident. Granted that in neither survey do we have a continuous account of contraceptive behavior, the 1976 survey nevertheless provides an abundance of data which are linked, in part to facilitate recall, to significant and/or recent events. The least satisfactory information is that which relates to ever-married women in the earlier survey, for if age at first intercourse, first use, or first pregnancy is the same as the age at marriage, we cannot always be certain that we are dealing with premarital behavior.[1]

A word more needs to be said about the contraceptive status classification in 1976 for the interval up to first pregnancy. The questionnaire does not contain questions which directly ascertain whether contraceptives had always or never been used up to the time of the first premarital conception. Nevertheless, by a process of distillation it is possible to classify all but a handful of cases with respect to their overall contraceptive status up to that event. It works this way: Those who had never or always used contraception up to the time of the survey by definition are classified in

		1971		1976	
		Never Married	Ever Married	Never Married	Ever Married
Before Marriage	**First Intercourse**				
	Date	—	—	x	x
	Age	x	x[a]	x	x
	Used/not used	—	—	x	x
	Method used	—	—	x	x
	Last Intercourse				
	Date	—	—	x	x
	Age	—	—	x	x
	Used/not used	x	—	x	x
	Method used	—	—	x	x
	First Use				
	Date	—	—	x	x
	Age	—	—	x	x
	Method used	x	—	x	x
	Premarital Conception(s)				
	Date(s)	[x]	[x][a]	(x)	(x)
	Age(s)	[x]	[x][a]	(x)	(x)
	Used/not used	x	x	x	x
	Method(s) used	—	—	x	x
To Marriage or Survey	**Contraceptive Status**				
	Method(s) ever used	x	—	x	x
	Never used	x	—	x	x
	Always used	x	$\Big\{$ (x)[b]	x	x
	Sometimes used	(x)		(x)	(x)
To First Pregnancy	Method(s) ever used	—	—	—	—
	Always used	—	—	(x)[c]	(x)[c]
	Never used	—	—	(x)[c]	(x)[c]
	Sometimes used	—	—	(x)[c]	(x)[c]

Figure 5.1 Data on Premarital Contraceptive Use, by Marital Status at Interview

NOTE: [x] = derivable by assuming period of gestation (see section on differences between the two studies, Appendix B); (x) = derivable.

a. Ambiguous in most cases where age at marriage is same as age at the event.
b. Amounts to "ever use" (see section on differences between the two studies, Appendix B).
c. See text.

the same way up to first pregnancy. Included here are those who became premaritally pregnant the only time they were exposed (the one-timers). Their contraceptive status up to first premarital conception is determined by whether or not they used contraception on that occasion. The never and always users as of the survey take care of a large fraction of cases. Other unambiguous cases are those whose first use of contraception occurred after their first pregnancies. They were obviously never-users up to the time of their first pregnancies. Those who, in answer to still another question, said they were using contraception at the time of their first pregnancy but who had not used contraception the first time they had intercourse are classified as sometimes-users. Similarly, those who said they were not using at the time of their first pregnancies, but who had used contraception the first time they had intercourse, are also classified as sometimes-users. Another group of sometimes-users consists of those who did not use at first intercourse but whose first use preceded first pregnancy. At the end of this process the distillate was relatively pure, only a small handful of cases retaining some degree of ambiguity.

In sum, we know a great deal, but not everything, about the contraceptive practice of respondents in the 1976 survey. We know much less, in comparison, about the young women in the 1971 survey, even though for the never married (who make up about 90 percent of the sample) we know at what age they first had intercourse, whether they ever used contraception and, if so, what methods, whether their use was regular or spotty, their age when they first used contraception, whether they used contraception at their last intercourse, what method they had used most recently, and, if ever pregnant, whether contraception was being used when pregnancy occurred. Relative to what was known then about the use of contraception by young women in the United States, this was an abundance of information; relative to the requirements of refined analysis, it was deficient—and as we shall see, capable of leading us and others astray.

Let us return now to the paradox with which we began—the apparent failure of premarital pregnancy rates to respond to increased use of contraception between 1971 and 1976 and to an increase in the use of medical methods in substitution for less effective methods (condoms, withdrawal, douche), all of which experienced decreased usage. Concerning the similar prevalence of premarital pregnancy in the two surveys, there is little serious question. Apart from a few pregnancies to married women that might have been misclassified in 1971, the data on premarital pregnancy would not seem to hold the clue to the puzzle. If anything, since, as we explain elsewhere, there are grounds for suspecting some underreporting in 1976 of black pregnancies that ended in abortion, the pregnancy information understates the issue. So we are left to find its resolution by a close examination of the data on contraceptive use. Given the lack of comparability in this information between the two surveys, we will have to supplement empirical analysis with some deductive argument to make our case.

It is of little help to examine profiles of methods ever used. As is clear from the previous chapter, 1976 looks better in that respect, when by "better" we mean the presumed effectiveness of the methods being used. Ideally, we need to examine the use of contraception up to the first pregnancy, since what is done subsequently in the way of pregnancy avoidance is irrelevant to the question at hand. In other words, we should confine ourselves to an examination of contraceptive practice in the interval from first intercourse to first premarital pregnancy. Unfortunately, we do not have data on methods ever used during that interval for either survey and so we cannot say whether the use of contraception in that interval in 1976 was "better," the same, or "worse."

We can get some idea of what may have happened by looking at comparative data on contraceptive status. In Table 5.1 there is a comparison of the contraceptive status distributions "up to marriage or survey" for 1971 and 1976. Notice that among the never married always use increased from 18 percent to nearly 30 percent (first and fourth columns), but that never use increased also. This is not an equal trade-off; never-users contribute disproportionately to the prevalence of premarital pregnancy (Zelnik and Kantner, 1978b). Part of the answer resides here.

Next, compare the two contraceptive status distributions for 1976—one up to marriage or survey, the other up to first pregnancy, marriage, or survey. These two distributions will differ only to the extent that premaritally pregnant women alter their contraceptive behavior following their first conception. When the terminal point includes first pregnancy, never use stands at 35 percent (last column, fourth row, Table 5.1); when the interval to first pregnancy is ignored, never use falls to 28 percent, indicating that among those who became premaritally pregnant there was a substantial amount of never use. The actual figure for this subgroup, not shown here, was 58 percent. At the same time there is almost no change between the two contraceptive status measures for 1976 in the proportion of always users. Thus it is clear that in 1976 pregnancy induced a shift from never use to use.

Might this not have been the case also in 1971? Undoubtedly, pregnancy did operate then also as an inducement to the adoption of contra-

TABLE 5.1 Percentage Distribution of Premaritally Sexually Active Women 15-19 Years of Age

Race and Contraceptive Status	As of Marriage or Survey							As of Pregnancy, Marriage, or Survey 1976		
	1971			1976					
	Never Married	Ever Married	Total	Never Married	Ever Married	Total	Never Married	Ever Married	Total
TOTAL	(1217)	(212)	(1429)	(788)	(236)	(1024)	(783)	(236)	(1019)
Ever used	83.0	55.5	77.6	76.2	57.8	72.3	67.8	54.9	65.0
Always	18.4	NA	NA	29.8	21.3	28.0	30.7	22.2	28.9
Sometimes	64.6	NA	NA	46.4	36.5	44.3	37.1	32.7	36.1
Never used	17.0	44.5	22.4	23.8	42.2	27.7	32.2	45.1	35.0
Total	100.0	100.0	100.0	100.0	100.0	100.0	100.0	100.0	100.0
WHITE	(548)	(159)	(707)	(379)	(198)	(577)	(377)	(198)	(575)
Ever used	82.6	55.2	76.3	76.7	58.7	72.3	71.1	56.6	67.5
Always	20.0	NA	NA	30.1	22.8	28.3	31.3	23.8	29.4
Sometimes	62.9	NA	NA	46.6	35.9	44.0	39.8	32.8	38.1
Never used	17.4	44.8	23.7	23.3	41.3	27.7	28.9	43.4	32.5
Total	100.0	100.0	100.0	100.0	100.0	100.0	100.0	100.0	100.0
BLACK	(669)	(53)	(722)	(409)	(38)	(447)	(406)	(38)	(444)
Ever used	83.9	58.1	81.8	74.8	50.0	72.3	57.7	39.4	55.8
Always	15.0	NA	NA	28.9	8.0	26.8	29.1	8.0	27.0
Sometimes	68.9	NA	NA	45.9	42.0	45.5	28.6	31.4	28.9
Never used	16.1	41.9	18.2	25.2	50.0	27.7	42.3	60.6	44.2
Total	100.0	100.0	100.0	100.0	100.0	100.0	100.0	100.0	100.0

NOTE: Estimates are based on weighted sample cases. NA = not available.

ception. But it seems unlikely that there could have been as high a proportion then who had never used contraception prior to pregnancy. Were that the case, one would be forced to conclude, since never use to marriage or survey is less in 1971, that the conversion to contraception following pregnancy was greater then than in 1976. This would not seem to be consistent with evidence of greater availability and increased use of contraception by young women generally since 1971.

Resolving the issue of the puzzling resistance of premarital pregnancy to more and better contraception in terms of an increased level of nonuse preceding pregnancy merely raises a new question: Why should there have been an increase in never use? It was not that pregnancy was for some reason more desirable in 1976 than in 1971. In both years two-thirds of the first pregnancies were unintended. One possible explanation is the decline in the age at first intercourse. As we have seen, the older the age at which intercourse begins, the more likely it will be accompanied by the use of contraception. A significant proportion of first pregnancies occur between first intercourse and first use of contraception, thus catching a number of never-users in the interval to first pregnancy. Another "explanation" often heard but seldom supported by evidence is the increased availability of abortion, which, it is alleged, undermines the motivation necessary for the adoption and continued use of contraception. This would appear to have little substance, for, as we have shown elsewhere (Zelnik and Kantner, 1978b) those who have had abortions tend to use contraception *prior to pregnancy* as much as those who have unintended pregnancies that are carried to term.

Prevalence of Premarital Pregnancy

The prevalence of premarital pregnancy varies significantly by race and within racial categories by basic demographic and social variables. In Table 5.2 the percentages of premaritally sexually active women who have ever been pregnant are shown according to current age, age at first intercourse, social status, family stability, religion, and religiosity. As might be expected, premarital pregnancy increases with age, although there is an unexpected dip at age 16 for whites in both surveys and for blacks in 1976.[2] Somewhat unexpected, however, is the change over time at each age; in 1976 premarital pregnancy occurs at ages 15 and 19 with greater relative frequency than in 1971, whereas the reverse is the case for ages 16-18. Thus, underlying the apparent lack of change in the prevalence of premarital pregnancy among sexually active women 15-19 years of age are changes at individual years of age, changes common to both races. Having eliminated a chance explanation, we can think of no reasonable, consistent argument to account for the increased prevalence at some ages and the decreased prevalence at others.

The strong association between current age and prevalence of premarital pregnancy reflects in large part differences by current age in duration of sexual activity. The importance of duration of exposure as related to prevalence of premarital pregnancy can more easily be seen by considering prevalence by age at first premarital intercourse (Table 5.2). At each date each race shows a strong inverse relationship between age at first premarital intercourse and prevalence of premarital pregnancy. The relatively low prevalence rates for whites in 1971 and blacks in 1976 among those who first had intercourse before age 14 are not readily explainable.

The difference between age at first intercourse and current age is equivalent, at least for never-married women, to "years at risk." While in some respects use of years at risk as a variable would be preferable to the joint use of current age and age at first intercourse, we decided to use the latter two in our analysis because of the intrinsic interest in age at first intercourse in discussions of premarital pregnancy. It must be remembered, though, that these data reflect the truncation bias present in cross-sectional surveys (although the inclusion of current age in our multivariate analysis will correct for that bias).

Among the other variables included in our consideration of prevalence of pregnancy, SES and family stability show for each race in each survey a fairly strong association with prevalence. SES is inversely related to prevalence, with differences between the lowest and highest categories of SES somewhat greater in 1971 than in 1976. As for family stability, the "ideal" family setting consistently has the lowest level of prevalence and the "least ideal" case the highest level. On the other hand, there appears to be little or no consistent association between religion and prevalence for either race; religiosity makes no difference among whites, whereas among blacks premarital pregnancy is slightly less prevalent if the respondent ranks high on the religiosity measure.

MULTIVARIATE ANALYSIS OF PREMARITAL PREGNANCY

Analysis of the total population yields somewhat different results for the two surveys. In 1971, race, current age, age at first intercourse, and SES are all significant, whereas in 1976 only current age and age at first

TABLE 5.2 Percent of Premaritally Sexually Active Women 15-19 Years of Age Who Had a Premarital Pregnancy

	1971			1976		
Variable	Total	White	Black	Total	White	Black
Current Age	(1477)	(731)	(746)	(1022)	(576)	(446)
15	16.1	15.1	18.1	22.3	21.8	23.5
16	17.7	9.2	38.8	10.3	7.7	18.2
17	30.5	24.9	46.1	25.4	23.6	31.8
18	35.0	29.2	55.3	29.3	25.5	44.6
19	36.5	29.9	62.9	40.9	35.4	64.1
15-19	29.8	24.3	47.1	28.3	25.2	39.5
SES (years)	(1431)	(726)	(705)	(983)	(567)	(416)
<9	41.9	34.7	53.4	36.1	32.4	43.0
9-11	32.9	26.6	49.8	28.2	26.0	35.8
12	27.1	25.3	37.3	26.7	24.2	37.3
≥13	14.8	13.3	25.8	21.4	20.5	31.2
Family Stability	(1467)	(728)	(739)	(1021)	(575)	(445)
Ideal	24.4	21.2	42.5	23.0	21.6	33.6
Less ideal	32.8	27.8	44.8	31.7	28.8	39.4
Least ideal	43.4	35.0	53.2	39.2	35.0	44.5
Religion	(1476)	(731)	(745)	(1020)	(575)	(445)
Fundamentalist Protestant	33.1	23.1	57.0	27.3	26.4	29.5
Other Protestant	32.1	26.2	45.1	28.4	23.4	41.1
Catholic	26.5	24.4	52.4	27.4	27.2	32.4
None	21.8	15.1	56.0	30.7	26.7	42.8
Religiosity	(1466)	(726)	(740)	(1009)	(568)	(441)
Low	24.6	21.4	53.2	27.2	25.2	43.4
Medium	34.1	29.5	49.5	29.2	24.4	43.8
High	30.6	20.2	43.2	29.1	27.3	31.5
Age First Intercourse	(1443)	(715)	(728)	(1014)	(574)	(440)
≤13	37.1	26.7	58.0	36.9	34.5	40.8
14	42.4	37.0	53.4	37.6	26.1	63.7
15	37.6	31.6	51.7	31.9	30.0	38.4
16	29.8	24.9	44.6	26.8	25.8	30.4
17	24.1	21.4	33.8	23.5	23.0	25.9
≥18	15.6	14.5	27.0	14.3	14.1	16.7

NOTE: Estimates are based on weighted sample cases; in addition, see Table 3.1.

intercourse are significant (Tables C.20 and C.21, Appendix C). This difference in the structure of explanation between the two surveys should not be overinterpreted. The patterns in the prevalence of pregnancy by race, SES, and family stability are similar in both surveys. Some narrowing of differences among the subcategories of these variables in 1976, together with a smaller sample size in 1976, are primarily responsible for the statistical downgrading of these three variables. Generally, they behave in about the same way in both surveys. The main point to emphasize here is that our analysis of the prevalence of premarital pregnancy yields two variables that are consistently significant and that account for almost all of the explained variance: current age and age at first intercourse. The older the current age and the younger the age at first intercourse, the higher the level of prevalence. The lack of a significant effect in 1976 of SES on prevalence of premarital pregnancy is somewhat surprising in light of the findings presented in the previous chapter on contraceptive use. Although SES is not related to always use, it is related to never use, use at first intercourse, and use at last intercourse (but not to use of medical methods).

No other variable is consistently significant across the two surveys. Even race lacks consistent significance, although the pattern for the two surveys is similar; in each survey, blacks show a higher prevalence of pregnancy, significantly so in 1971 but not in 1976. Given that blacks begin sex earlier and given our suspicion about the completeness of reporting of pregnancies by blacks in 1976, some reservation in accepting this latter finding would seem to be justified. The reason for the trend toward convergence by race in the prevalence rates for 1976 is chiefly because of an unexplained drop in the rate for blacks in 1976.

That prevalence of premarital pregnancy is largely a function of the duration of exposure to pregnancy is neither surprising nor of much theoretical importance. What is surprising, however, is the failure of other seemingly basic sociological variables to add significantly to the explanation of variation in prevalence. From a statistical point of view, the analyses may have "explained" a respectable portion of the variance in prevalence of premarital pregnancy; by any other standard we are still in the dark concerning the "causes" of premarital pregnancy other than to say that, if given time, a very high proportion of teenagers will have a pregnancy. The figures are impressive and worth summoning up from the tables: In both surveys about 6 out of 10 sexually active young women 19 years of age had at least one premarital pregnancy.

REANALYSIS OF THE 1976 DATA

As we have noted, the greater detail regarding premarital contraception in the 1976 survey makes it possible to classify the sexually active by their use of contraception prior to pregnancy, marriage, or survey, whichever comes first. At one extreme are the always-users; at the other extreme, the never-users. In between are the sometimes-users, who can be subdivided further into those who used at first intercourse but failed to keep it up and those who did not use at first intercourse but subsequently began to do so.[3] This cannot be done for 1971 since comparable information on contraceptive status prior to pregnancy is not available. Introducing this classificatory scheme in a reanalysis of the findings in Table C.21 (Appendix C) does little to relieve the banality of the previous conclusion that the prevalence of premarital pregnancy is a function of the duration of sexual exposure. This additional analysis, in Table C.22 (Appendix C), shows that the duration of exposure is mediated through the use or nonuse of contraception, and this added information raises R^2 substantially, for the total population from .17 to .27. While the importance of contraceptive status in explaining pregnancy does not come as a surprise, it is not a necessary relationship, since we have not taken account of the regularity or frequency of intercourse, the types of contraception used, the duration of periods of nonuse, or other factors which might negate or weaken the difference between users and nonusers in their true exposure to the risk of pregnancy. Race also is significant, albeit weakly, in the reanalysis of the 1976 data.

The reanalysis includes young women who had intercourse only once, the one-timers, even though they can be classified in terms of contraceptive status only as always-users or never-users. They were retained in the reanalysis so it would be comparable to the earlier analysis of the 1976 data, and they were included there to provide comparability with the 1971 data. Leaving them out of the analysis has no discernible effect on the results.

An oddity that requires some explication is the fact that those who contracepted at first intercourse but not consistently thereafter have a much higher (unadjusted and adjusted) rate of prevalence of premarital pregnancy than those who began to use after some initial period of nonuse. The latter, in fact, have a rate that is closer to that of the always-users than to the other two contraceptive status categories (Table C.22). To a degree these results are an artifact of the method of classifying respondents by contraceptive status. Those who did not use contraception at first intercourse but did so subsequently were never-users up to the time of first use. If they had conceived during that period of nonuse, they would have been classified as never-users. Thus, they "survived," that is, avoided pregnancy, long enough to become users; other, presumably comparable, never-users failed to survive, that is, became pregnant. That these sometimes-users did not conceive prior to first using contraception may have been the result of nothing more than the "luck of the draw." In effect, however, they are young women with a period of zero fecundity during which they did not contracept, followed by a period of contraceptive use. Since all of their pregnancies came after they began to use contraception, it is not surprising that their rate of pregnancy is low and fairly close to the rate among always-users, some of whom also had accidental pregnancies.

However, there is more to the story than mere survival up to the time contraception is first used. As we have pointed out elsewhere, those women who begin to use contraception after some initial period of unprotected intercourse tend to use effective methods (that is, medical methods) of contraception (Zelnik and Kantner, 1977, 1978a). Their distribution of initial methods is more heavily weighted in terms of medical methods than the distribution of methods of those who used at first intercourse or even the distribution of initial methods of those who use consistently, that is, always-users. What accounts for this profile of effective methods among the "late starters" of contraceptive use is not clear. It is not due to their greater age at first use of contraception as compared to those who used at first intercourse since the differences hold at each age. In any event, the relatively low level of prevalence of premarital pregnancy among the sometimes-users who did not initially use contraception but subsequently did is due, in part, to the method of classification, but also to their use of effective methods once they begin to contracept.

Before leaving this point, we should note that the anomalies of classification apply also to those who used contraception at first intercourse but subsequently failed to use it. Prior to first nonuse, these young women were always-users and would have been so classified if they had conceived during that period of use. Thus, they survived long enough to become nonusers of contraception. They thereby combine a period of perfect protection with a period of nonuse, with all of their pregnancies coming at or after the first incidence of nonuse of contraception.

Up to this point in our analysis it has not appeared that contraception among teenagers improved sufficiently after 1971 to make a real dent in

TABLE 5.3 Mean Age at First Premarital Intercourse for All Sexually Active Women 15-19 Years of Age, for Those Who Experienced a Premarital Pregnancy, and Mean Age at First Premarital Conception

Date and Race	Mean Age First Premarital Intercourse		Mean Age First Premarital Conception
	Sexually Active Women	Women Who Had a Premarital Pregnancy	
1971	(1443)	(497)	(511)
Total	16.4	15.9	16.7
White	16.5	16.2	16.8
Black	15.9	15.6	16.4
1976	(1016)	(331)	(336)
Total	16.1	15.7	16.7
White	16.3	16.0	16.9
Black	15.6	15.2	16.2

NOTE: Estimates are based on weighted sample cases; in addition, see Table 3.1.

the first premarital pregnancy rate. It is relevant to observe that the delay in marriage that was evident during this period increased the risk of *premarital* pregnancy. Thus, some improvement in protection against pregnancy can be assumed since otherwise a rise in the rate would have been expected. Nevertheless, much of the improvement in contraceptive practice, it seems, came subsequent to pregnancy. For the period up to first pregnancy, an increase in regular use of contraception (always use) presumably was offset by an increase in never use. There is one qualification to this conclusion which may give some comfort to birth control advocates who had hoped to see a greater yield from their efforts and from federal dollars. If we consider the interval from first intercourse to first premarital pregnancy, the "waiting time" until pregnancy, we find that, although the mean age at first pregnancy remained the same at 16.7 years in both surveys (Table 5.3), the mean age at first intercourse declined. For both races, whether considered separately or together, the difference between mean age at first intercourse and mean age at first pregnancy widened by some 3.6 months for all sexually active women and about 2.5 months for those who became pregnant. This is consistent with the idea that there was in fact some improvement in contraceptive practice, which, though it did not reduce the prevalence of first pregnancies, did stretch out the time until they occurred. We say that this conclusion regarding the effect of contraceptive practice is consistent with the facts, but it is no more than that. A moderation in the frequency of intercourse, for example, could have had the same effect. We do not have the data necessary for a choice among these or other reasonable alternatives. To us, however, it seems most likely that the prolongation of the waiting time to first pregnancy does reflect some upgrading of contraceptive practice between 1971 and 1976.

Mean Age at First Premarital Pregnancy

Analysis of factors associated with variation in age at first premarital pregnancy involves, in addition to race and current age as "control" variables, SES, family stability, religion, religiosity, age at first intercourse, pregnancy intention, that is, whether the pregnancy was wanted and if not, whether contraception was being used at the time of conception. We cannot subdivide those using contraception at time of conception by type of method because the number of sample cases in 1976 is too small to allow such a further break, and in 1971 that information was not obtained.

We have already observed the differences by race in the mean age at first conception (Table 5.3). Blacks become pregnant earlier—by almost 5 months in 1971 and more than 8 months in 1976—although their waiting time to first conception is as long or longer than the waiting time for whites. The cross-tabulation of other variables with mean age at first premarital pregnancy is given in Table 5.4. We do not show current age because the relationship is neither surprising nor of much significance. Further, we do not provide a race break for each variable because, looking ahead to the multivariate analysis, race is not significant at either date in the presence of other factors. The figures in Table 5.4 indicate, not surprisingly, a strong association between age at first intercourse and mean age at first premarital conception—as age at intercourse increases, so does mean age at pregnancy. SES shows a positive, but relatively weak, association with mean age at first premarital pregnancy: The higher the level of SES, the higher the mean age of pregnancy. As found in Chapter 3, however, the higher the level of SES, the higher the mean age at first intercourse (at least for the total population and for whites). Thus, the relationship between SES and mean age at first conception may reflect the temporally prior relationship between SES and initiation of sex. The other variables generally show either weak or inconsistent association with the advent of pregnancy.

TABLE 5.4 Mean Age at First Premarital Conception

Variable	1971	1976
SES (years)	(488)	(314)
<9	16.4	16.5
9-11	16.7	16.4
12	16.9	17.0
≥13	16.9	17.2
Family Stability	(506)	(336)
Ideal	16.9	16.9
Less ideal	16.1	16.6
Least ideal	16.6	16.4
Religion	(511)	(336)
Fundamentalist Protestant	16.0	16.3
Other Protestant	16.8	16.6
Catholic	16.7	16.8
Other	15.9	16.8
Religiosity	(508)	(332)
Low	16.5	16.8
Medium	16.8	16.7
High	16.6	16.3
Age First Intercourse	(496)	(331)
≤13	15.3	15.5
14	15.5	15.5
15	15.9	16.3
16	17.1	17.3
≥17	18.1	18.1
Pregnancy Intention	(487)	(336)
Wanted	16.7	16.7
Not wanted/using contraception	16.8	16.7
Not wanted/not using contraception	16.6	16.7

NOTE: Estimates are based on weighted sample cases; in addition, see Table 3.1.

MULTIVARIATE ANALYSIS OF AGE AT FIRST CONCEPTION

The amount of variance in age at first conception that is explained is relatively high: .63 in 1971 and .57 in 1976 (Table C.23, Appendix C). However, almost half of the explained variance at both dates is accounted for by age at first intercourse; much of the rest is accounted for by current age, a relatively meaningless variable in this situation and suffering badly from truncation bias. Thus, there is little we can say to explain when first pregnancy occurs other than to note that the earlier one embarks on sex, given the prevailing levels of use and effectiveness of contraception among young women, the sooner pregnancy can be anticipated. It is not without interest, however, that social status, family background, and religion have little to do with it.

Religiosity is of some importance, but in an unexpected fashion: Those highest on the religiosity scale become pregnant somewhat earlier than the less devout. The careful reader will recall that this group (high religiosity) was found, in the analysis of age at first intercourse in Chapter 3, to tend toward late initiation of sex. While that does not affect the figures in Table C.23, which are adjusted for differences in age at first intercourse, it does indicate that young women for whom religion is an important aspect of their lives begin to have sex later but become pregnant sooner than others. Is it because the more religious young woman is bound for marriage and more likely to become pregnant intentionally? Not if our measure of pregnancy intention is reasonably valid. Is she less sophisticated and thus apt to run greater risks? The analysis reported in Chapter 4 on contraception does not provide an unequivocal answer. Religious women are not distinguished by greater use of contraception, although, if white, they are more likely in 1976 ever to have used a medical method. The data cannot be focused sharply enough to resolve the question.

As we noted earlier, race is not significant at either date—in effect, the adjusted mean age at first premarital pregnancy is the same for blacks and whites. At first glance, this result is perhaps surprising in view of the earlier age at which blacks tend to initiate sexual activity and, as we noted earlier, the unadjusted data, which show blacks becoming pregnant, on average, at a younger age. However, controlling for that earlier initiation leads with comparable waiting times to comparable ages at first conception. This result is consistent with previously published life table estimates of the risks of premarital pregnancy, which gave similar results for blacks and whites when duration of sexual exposure was controlled (Zabin et al., 1979).[4]

Outcome of First Pregnancy

The outcome of the first premarital pregnancy can be considered along two dimensions: What happens to the pregnancy—how does it end and what happens to the young woman? Does she marry during pregnancy and thus legitimate the birth? These two axes are not independent of one another; for example, an aborted pregnancy cannot subsequently be legitimated, while the woman who marries during the pregnancy is unlikely to end that pregnancy with a voluntary abortion. In this section we consider the outcome of the pregnancy itself, the physical outcome, and in the following section we consider the question of marriage among those whose premarital pregnancies end in live birth. Finally, we consider both dimensions jointly, that is, illegitimacy, since if abortion and marriage are both rejected, the consequence (except in the case of miscarriage) is an illegitimate birth.

To analyze the outcome of first premarital pregnancy, we distinguished between women who had live births or stillbirths and those who had miscarriages or abortions. Excluded from the analysis are those young women who were pregnant for the first time at the time of the survey. There were very few stillbirths reported in either survey and their inclusion with live births has little effect on the results. The decision to combine miscarriages with abortions is more debatable; it reflects our impression that some miscarriages, although reported correctly, may have been brought on by the respondent because of her desire to end the pregnancy. In addition, some pregnancy terminations reported as miscarriages actually may have been abortions, although we are inclined to doubt that such misreporting was of any considerable magnitude. Miscarriages represent 34 percent of all fetal deaths in 1971 and 28 percent in 1976.

For the analysis of the outcome of first premarital pregnancy we consider race, current age, the four familiar social variables, age at first conception, and pregnancy intention. In Table 5.5 we show for 1971 and 1976 the proportion of premaritally pregnant women whose first pregnancies ended in live births by each of the independent variables. The categories shown there for each variable are those used in the subsequent multivariate analyses of the total populations; for the analysis of whites, as in Table C.25 (Appendix C), it is necessary to combine categories for a number of the variables.

We do not include any data for blacks in Table 5.5. There are several reasons for this. First, the overwhelming majority of black women in our surveys ended their first pregnancies with live births, 86.1 percent in 1971 and 86.9 percent in 1976. There was relatively little variation in this regard among the categories of any of the variables. Second, but not unrelated to the first point, we suspect substantial underreporting of abortions to black women, at least in 1976. Third, we did in fact subject the data for blacks to multivariate analysis, with the result that we failed completely in both 1971 and 1976 to account for the dependent variable—the R^2s generally did not differ significantly from zero.

There has been a massive and dramatic shift in the disposition of premarital pregnancies since 1971. Almost 4 out of 5 (79 percent) of first

TABLE 5.5 Percentage of Premaritally Pregnant Women 15-19 Years of Age Whose First Pregnancy Ended in a Live Birth[a]

	1971		1976	
Variable	Total	White	Total	White
Current Age	(426)	(142)	(298)	(140)
15-16	72.5	58.8*	54.0	45.4*
17	78.0	76.3	57.6	43.8
18	82.3	77.6	68.8	58.7
19	79.2	74.9	68.1	59.5
15-19	79.0	74.3	64.8	54.8
SES (years)	(405)	(140)	(277)	(137)
<9	80.9	76.6	81.3	71.3
9-11	83.9	79.0	70.7	66.5
12	72.9	72.2	55.7	44.3
≥13	65.4	58.2*	32.4	24.8
Family Stability	(422)	(142)	(298)	(140)
Ideal	79.3	77.8	60.0	55.4
Less ideal	69.7	58.4	62.0	48.8
Least ideal	87.0	85.5	76.2	62.5
Religion	(426)	(142)	(298)	(140)
Fundamentalist Protestant	79.5	76.6*	68.3	54.7*
Other Protestant	81.0	75.9	67.7	54.0
Catholic	78.6	75.6	60.9	60.9
Other	62.4	56.1*	57.8	42.5*
Religiosity	(423)	(142)	(294)	(138)
Low	73.3	70.0	55.8	52.9
Medium	85.2	83.6	67.9	52.4
High	74.7	54.7	81.3	75.8
Age First Conception	(425)	(142)	(298)	(140)
≤14	79.6	68.2*	80.5	71.0*
15	79.5	74.3	74.8	67.2
16	88.1	86.8	67.9	60.7
≥17	72.5	67.8	51.8	43.5
Pregnancy Intention	(401)	(131)	(298)	(140)
Wanted	89.6	90.0	92.5	91.2
Not wanted	78.6	71.4	51.2	35.6

NOTE: Estimates are based on weighted sample cases; in addition, see Table 3.1.

a. Includes a small number of stillbirths.

*n<20

premarital pregnancies to the 1971 study population ended in live births, as compared to 65 percent among those surveyed just 5 years later. Among whites the percentage ending in live births declined from 74 percent in 1971 to 55 percent in 1976. An equally notable feature of Table 5.5 is that while in 1971 a few of the variables show weak albeit systematic association with a live birth outcome, 1976 presents a much clearer picture. Not only do more of the variables appear to be related to the dependent variable in 1976, but the associations appear to be stronger. Especially striking in the 1976 data is the inverse association between the proportion of women having live births and SES. Those in the highest SES level are only about one-third as likely as those in the lowest SES to carry to term.

Age at first conception, which in 1971 seemed to have little to do with the nature of the pregnancy outcome, shows a definite inverse association with the live birth option in 1976. If a conception occurred at age 17 or over, it was only about 60 percent as likely to end in a live birth as those conceived at age 14 or younger. An informed reader who knows that the ratio of abortions to live births is high, often greater than unity at young ages, may find this latter finding puzzling. An even more sophisticated reader, however, will realize that these high ratios are artifactual in that official data for both abortions and live births refer to the age at which these events occur. This guarantees that in many cases, perhaps as many as half or more, the two outcomes that are being compared arise from groups that differ by age at time of conception. Because it takes longer to produce a birth than an abortion, live births arise from a group that was younger at time of conception than the group responsible for the abortions. If the number of births and abortions did not vary much by age, there would be no problem, but during the adolescent years, when both are increasing rapidly with age, it is not surprising to find for a particular age a large number of abortions relative to the number of births. In Table 5.5, where we are dealing with age at conception rather than age at outcome, this difficulty is avoided and we see clearly that a live birth outcome is more likely among young teenage women than among those who were several years their seniors when they became pregnant (Zelnik et al., 1979). We cannot say for certain why this is so. Very possibly it has something to do with the older girl's greater sophistication in the early recognition of pregnancy and her greater competence and freedom in the search for a solution.

The proportion of pregnancies ending in live births is sharply differentiated also by whether or not the pregnancy was wanted—91 percent of the wanted pregnancies among whites ended in a live birth, in contrast to 36 percent of the pregnancies that were not wanted. Even with allowance for a certain amount of post factum rationalization of behavior this is an impressive difference. The relatively high proportion of women carrying to term among those who score high on religiosity may reflect negative attitudes toward abortion, which one would expect to be more salient in 1976 than in 1971 because of the prominence given to abortion as a political and moral issue subsequent to the action of the Supreme Court. The data fit this interpretation.

MULTIVARIATE ANALYSIS OF PREGNANCY OUTCOME

Table C.24 (Appendix C) provides the results of the MCA for the total populations in 1971 and 1976. In 1971, R^2 is .08, the entire equation is only moderately significant ($F < .10$), and only race, age at first conception, and pregnancy intention are significant variables. In short, these variables singly and together had almost nothing to do with pregnancy outcome. By contrast, in 1976, R^2 is .31, the overall F-ratio is significant at $p < .01$, and race, current age, SES, religiosity, age at first conception, and pregnancy intention are all significant variables, with the last accounting for about 30 percent of the explained variance. A similar difference between 1971 and 1976 is found for whites (Table C.25, Appendix C): In 1971 age at first conception and pregnancy intention are significant, although the complete model is not ($F > .10$); in 1976, R^2 is .38, the F-ratio is highly significant with current age, SES, age at first conception, and pregnancy intention all significant, with the last accounting for just over half of the explained variance.

Earlier (Chapter 3) we indicated our "doubt that the manner in which the underlying forces operate altered in such a short period" (that is, between 1971 and 1976). While we adhere to that conviction with regard to some of the behavior we have analyzed, with respect to outcome of pregnancy it is clear that things did change. Between 1971 and 1976 the legalization of abortion and the extension of abortion services to young women were among the most salient social changes of the period for young people and their parents. Nevertheless, many women were unable to obtain abortion services because of lack of facilities or access to facilities, state restrictions regarding consent procedures (an especially critical factor where very young women are involved), or for financial reasons. Not surprisingly, these limitations are most likely to impede the poor and thus, whereas SES was not significant in 1971, in 1976 those of higher SES were much more likely than those of lower SES to abort their pregnancies. In both periods, if the pregnancy was not wanted and if the first conception was delayed to late adolescence there was a better than average likelihood of abortion. This was more true in 1976, when the abortion option was more available, but nevertheless held also in 1971. What is different in the two periods is the social difference in the outcome of pregnancy that has resulted as the daughters of the better educated have increasingly opted for abortion.

Before leaving this section, we would note for the technically inclined reader who may have noted that the proportion having live births is positively related to current age, but negatively related to age at first conception, that these results are not inconsistent. There is no reason that they need match up. For example, those who conceived at age 15 or under are "currently" anywhere from age 15 to age 19. On the other hand, a young woman currently age 19 who was pregnant at age 15, in the prelegalization period, would have been less likely to obtain an abortion than the young woman currently age 15 who has just conceived.

Marriage During First Premarital Pregnancy

While, strictly speaking, marriage during a premarital pregnancy is not an "outcome" in the same sense as an abortion, miscarriage, or live birth, it is intertwined with these as part of the social resolution of pregnancy. It is extremely rare for an abortion to occur if marriage intervenes between conception and the outcome of the pregnancy. In other words, where marriage follows on the discovery of a premarital pregnancy, the outcome, barring an involuntary fetal loss, tends to be a live birth. Whether the mother or her child ultimately benefit from her recourse to marriage when confronted with a premarital pregnancy is uncertain. We know of no convincing evidence that a marriage undertaken to legitimate an expected birth has any bearing on the subsequent fortunes of a young woman or a young couple. Statements are to be found in the literature indicating "that marriage around the time of the birth of the child indeed contributes slightly to subsequent occupational attainment for the father and even more to subsequent marital stability for the mother" (Card, 1977: 75). The data put forward in support of this conclusion are not themselves conclusive. What matters, it seems, is not whether a birth occurs within or without marriage, but whether the young woman's educational progress is disrupted as a result (Freedman and Thornton, 1979; McCarthy and Menken, 1979). One student of the problem (Furstenberg, 1976), in fact, suggests that in terms of disadvantages resulting from a premarital pregnancy, the most perilous course may be for the woman to try to raise the child alone; the least disadvantageous strategy possibly is for her to remain at home with the baby and, with the help of supportive parents, pick up her life as it was before becoming a single parent. In between is the marriage option—less risky than going it alone, but less advantageous than avoiding early marriage. No one, it appears, is very sure of the pros and cons of the marriage option and this must include the principals in the case and those who seek to advise or pressure them.

In this section we attempt an analysis of the decision to marry during the first pregnancy. The analysis is confined to young premaritally pregnant women who carried their conceptions to term[5] —regardless of whether or not they wanted the pregnancy. Some of them married during pregnancy; others did not. Insofar as our data permit, we want to see if we can achieve some understanding of the factors involved in this crucial decision. In addressing the question, we are more handicapped than usual because of the relatively small numbers of women involved. The analysis must of necessity be somewhat less detailed and confined to the total population, even though, as shown by the multivariate analysis, there are large and significant differences by race with respect to the marriage option. We have eliminated religion from the analysis also, because most cases fall into the category "Other Protestants."

There was no change between 1971 and 1976 in the proportion of women who married during the first pregnancy among those who carried that conception to term (Table 5.6). Finding themselves premaritally pregnant, whites who rejected abortion, or perhaps found it unavailable, were 6 to 7 times as likely to marry as blacks in the same situation. This was true of the respondents in both surveys. While the association with race is the most striking, most of the other variables also appear to have some association with the decision to marry. The exception to this is religiosity, which behaves in an inconsistent fashion. It seems reasonable that those who wanted the pregnancy, were somewhat older, or came from a more stable family situation should be more likely to marry when faced with a premarital pregnancy—remembering always that these are cases who did not resolve the issue through abortion. Less obvious, perhaps, is the tendency for those in the higher SES category to favor marriage, although it is not hard to speculate in this connection. In the next section we see to what extent these associations withstand the rigors of multivariate analysis.

TABLE 5.6 Percentage of Premaritally Pregnant Women 15-19 Years of Age Whose First Pregnancy Ended in a Live Birth and Who Married While Pregnant

Variable	1971	1976
Race	(349)	(223)
White	64.8	61.8
Black	9.0	10.4
Total	40.9	40.4
Current Age	(349)	(223)
≤17	35.0	27.0
18	35.5	46.1
19	49.6	44.3
SES (years)	(332)	(204)
≤11	35.6	34.6
≥12	58.7	60.6
Family Stability	(345)	(223)
Ideal	51.1	57.7
Less ideal	37.9	29.5
Least ideal	24.7	28.3
Religiosity	(347)	(221)
Low	42.8	40.9
Medium	45.0	38.7
High	30.7	43.9
Age First Conception	(349)	(223)
≤14	33.3	14.6
15	42.6	32.7
16	29.9	49.9
≥17	51.6	52.3
Pregnancy Interntion	(341)	(223)
Wanted	60.2	55.1
Not wanted	29.9	27.3

NOTE: Estimates are based on weighted sample cases; in addition, see Table 3.1.

MULTIVARIATE ANALYSIS OF THE DECISION TO MARRY

Given the large racial differences shown in Table 5.6 in the proportion of women electing to carry a pregnancy to term who marry during the pregnancy, it is not surprising that race is highly significant even after controlling for other variables (Table C.26, Appendix C). Race accounts for two-thirds of the explained variance in 1971 ($R^2 = .40$) and about half of the explained variance in 1976 ($R^2 = .49$). Otherwise the variables that are significant in both years are social status and pregnancy intention: If the pregnancy was wanted or if the young woman comes from a background characterized by above-average education, there is a greater than average tendency to marry. Age at first conception was moderately significant in 1971, but only because of the low propensity to marry among those who conceived at age 16. Before spinning out a line of speculation about this, it is well to note that although this item is not significant in 1976, those who conceived at age 16 had the highest proclivity for marriage. We are inclined to dismiss the 1971 results for this variable as a statistical aberration.

Illegitimacy

In the previous two sections we have considered separately the physical outcome of premarital pregnancy and the tendency to marry during the pregnancy. In this section we look at these two alternatives simultaneously and consider the factors involved in the rejection of both abortion and marriage during a pregnancy, that is, the factors involved in illegitimacy.

The unmarried, pregnant young woman faces two alternative ways of resolving the pregnancy so as to prevent an illegitimate birth. She can seek an abortion or, failing that, she can marry during the pregnancy. Only the young woman who rejects both of these options is slated to become the unwed mother, the bearer of an illegitimate birth. Our analysis of the physical outcome of the pregnancy indicated only a few variables that were significant in both 1971 and 1976: race, pregnancy intention, and age at first conception. We also noted that while SES was not significant in 1971 it was so in 1976 and that because of the changes that had occurred between the two dates we were inclined to accept this as a real change in the importance of social status as a factor explaining pregnancy outcome. The decision to marry during the pregnancy also involved few variables significant at both dates: race, SES, and pregnancy intention.

If we focus on 1976, we note, and here we are repeating ourselves, that although there is no (statistically significant) difference among social status categories in the prevalence of premarital pregnancy, women of high SES are more likely to have abortions than women of low SES, and among those premaritally pregnant women who carry to term, women of high

SES are more likely to marry during the pregnancy than women of low SES. Thus, we would expect that a woman of high SES is much less likely than a woman of low SES to deliver an illegitimate live birth. This expectation is borne out by the data presented in Table 5.7. Among the total population those in the lowest SES category were 9 times as likely to deliver illegitimate births as those in the highest category; among whites the differences are even more extreme, in that none of the women in the highest category delivered an illegitimate birth, all of their illegitimate pregnancies having been "resolved" either by abortion or by marriage.

It is somewhat more difficult to advance an argument for the likely effect of SES on illegitimacy in 1971. At that date not only were there differences in prevalence of premarital pregnancy by SES, but SES was not a significant variable in terms of the physical outcome of that pregnancy. The figures presented in Table 5.7 show an association between SES and illegitimacy, but that association is less consistent and less marked than the association in 1976.

The reader may recall that pregnancy intention was significant at both dates with respect to the physical outcome of the pregnancy and the decision to marry during the pregnancy. However, in this instance, that is, illegitimacy, we would expect the effect of pregnancy intention to be somewhat diluted—unlike the case of SES (in 1976) in which the effects were additive. Our argument is that those who want the pregnancy are likely to have a birth, and, among those who do, are likely to marry. Thus, the level of illegitimacy among those who want the pregnancy should be relatively low since the two separate alternatives complement one another. However, those who do not want the pregnancy are likely to have abortions, or, if not, to remain single. In this instance the two alternatives are somewhat offsetting in that those who have abortions thereby are not "eligible" to have illegitimate live births. Further, the greater the recourse to abortion, the lower the proportion of illegitimate live births from premarital pregnancies. We would therefore expect less difference by pregnancy intention in 1976 than in 1971, since there were proportionately more abortions in 1976 than in 1971.

These expectations are borne out by the data in Table 5.7. Differences in the proportion of premaritally pregnant women having an illegitimate live birth by pregnancy intention are smaller in 1976 than in 1971. What may be initially surprising is that the direction differs between the two dates. This is not unexpected, however, and results from the effect of changing levels of abortion. Putting it in its most extreme form, simply for illustrative purposes, if none of the women who did not want the pregnancy had abortions, then (ignoring marriage) all of them would have illegitimate births; on the other hand, if all of the women who did not want the

TABLE 5.7 Percentage of Premaritally Pregnant Women 15-19 Years of Age Whose First Pregnancy Ended in an Illegitimate Live Birth

	1971		1976	
Variable	Total	White	Total	White
Current Age	(426)	(142)	(298)	(140)
15-16	43.4	5.4*	43.2	27.3*
17	52.6	34.7	38.9	19.2
18	53.1	39.3	37.1	16.6
19	39.9	18.0	35.8	20.9
15-19	46.5	26.2	37.6	19.9
SES (years)	(405)	(140)	(277)	(137)
<9	49.4	25.2	59.0	40.8
9-11	55.4	34.4	40.6	24.9
12	29.8	20.5	24.1	7.1
≥13	27.7	12.3*	6.5	0.0
Family Stability	(422)	(142)	(298)	(140)
Ideal	38.6	25.7	25.0	15.7
Less ideal	43.2	16.6	41.5	18.6
Least ideal	64.8	42.5	53.9	33.1
Religion	(426)	(142)	(298)	(140)
Fundamentalist Protestant	54.1	39.3*	40.9	19.2*
Other Protestant	48.4	23.6	39.8	14.0
Catholic	40.2	30.2	28.7	28.3
Other	37.6	19.2*	41.7	20.0*
Religiosity	(423)	(142)	(294)	(138)
Low	41.3	31.6	33.0	26.0
Medium	46.7	27.6	40.0	14.5
High	51.8	7.0	43.5	15.1
Age First Conception	(425)	(142)	(298)	(140)
≤14	51.8	16.2*	67.3	42.1*
15	45.6	19.8	50.4	30.2
16	61.8	51.8	31.2	15.1
≥17	35.0	16.1	24.2	14.1
Pregnancy Intention	(401)	(131)	(298)	(140)
Wanted	35.1	17.2	41.5	25.8
Not wanted	55.1	33.6	35.6	16.8

NOTE: Estimates are based on weighted samples cases; in addition, see Table 3.1.
*<20

pregnancy had abortions, then the percentage having illegitimate live births would be zero.

Among the other variables shown in Table 5.7, only religiosity and family stability show a consistent association in both 1971 and 1976, but in each case only for the total population and not for whites. Thus, young women in the ideal family setting have a lower rate of illegitimacy than young women in the other family types; young women of low religiosity also have low rates of illegitimacy relative to those of medium or high religiosity. The remaining variables show no pattern of association with the dependent variable. As in other instances, multivariate analysis is required to disentangle the interwoven effects of the several variables.[6]

MULTIVARIATE ANALYSIS OF ILLEGITIMACY

The results of the multivariate analyses are shown in Table C.27 for the total population and in Table C.28 for whites (both tables appear in Appendix C). The only variables which are significant for both surveys are race, with blacks showing a rate of illegitimacy about 3 times as great as the rate for whites, and age at first conception. With respect to the latter variable, we pointed out in our discussion of the decision to marry that the 1971 results for age at first conception appeared to be a statistical aberration (as were the results for 1976, although in that case the variable was not significant). Since the pattern of adjusted proportions of women having illegitimate live births is the same as the pattern prevailing in the analysis of the decision to marry—highest adjusted rate at age 16 in 1971 and lowest adjusted rate at age 16 in 1976—we suspect that we are dealing here with the same statistical aberration and thereby dismiss these results as of no meaning.

In 1971 the only other significant variable is current age, and that is weakly significant. Social status in 1971 shows no association with the dependent variable; by contrast SES in 1976 is highly significant, being inversely associated with the proportion of premaritally pregnant women having illegitimate live births. Thus, our earlier supposition about the importance of social status in 1976 relative to the bearing of an illegitimate child has withstood the rigor of the multivariate analysis.

A similar result holds for whites, for whom no variable was significant at both dates. Some collapsing of the social status categories was required, but the figures in Table C.28 indicate that in 1976 the likelihood of an illegitimate birth from a premarital pregnancy was 6 times greater among women of low social status as compared to those of high status. SES is, in fact, the only variable that is significant in 1976 and thereby accounts for almost all of the explained variance ($R^2 = .13$).

Summary

In this chapter we have concentrated on three problems: why premarital pregnancy failed to fall in response to increased availability of and access to contraception; what factors are associated with the prevalence of premarital pregnancy and with the age at which those pregnancies first occur; and what factors determine the outcome of pregnancy. In connection with the discussion of pregnancy outcome, we have looked at the physical outcome of the pregnancy, then at the tendency to marry during the pregnancy, and finally at the effect of both dimensions jointly, that is, illegitimacy.

The apparent resistance of premarital pregnancy to improved contraceptive practice turns out to be explained by a not readily explained increase in the nonuse of contraception prior to the first pregnancy which more than offsets a simultaneous increase in the proportion of young women who are regular users. It is possible that the drop in the age at first intercourse is partially responsible for the increase in never use in the interval prior to first pregnancy.

Premarital pregnancy is explained, insofar as we are able to do so, almost entirely by the duration of exposure—the difference between the age at first intercourse and current age. Social variables such as social status, religion, and family stability are of negligible importance in accounting for variation in the prevalence of premarital pregnancy once the length of exposure is taken into account.

The age at first premarital conception is very closely related to the age at which a young woman becomes sexually active and to her current age. Again, it is the duration of exposure that is most important. There is little variation in the timing of the first pregnancy that is attributable to the social variables employed in the analysis. Nor is race, which is so often associated with differences in other aspects of sexual and reproductive behavior, involved in any simple fashion in explaining the age at which the first conception occurs. Blacks start earlier to have sex but whites have a somewhat shorter "waiting time" to the first pregnancy. The result is no difference in the mean age of first pregnancy for blacks or whites. Is race then a factor? Certainly—but indirectly.

Over the 5-year period covered by these 2 surveys there has been a massive shift in the way premarital pregnancies are dealt with. In 1971, 79 percent of first pregnancies ended as live births; in 1976, 65 percent did so (Table 5.5). For whites, the shift away from a live birth outcome was greater still. The search for an explanation of differences in pregnancy outcome—as between abortion or live birth—was unavailing in 1971. In

1976, when the option to resolve unwanted pregnancies through abortion was more widely available, we are able to explain a fair amount of the difference in outcome, primarily in terms of the "unwantedness" of the pregnancy, but also in terms of race, current age, SES, religiosity, and age at first conception. The wantedness of the pregnancy was of some importance in 1971 also, but the ability to do something about it was, by comparison with the situation in 1976, greatly circumscribed. In 1971, 82 percent of the unintended pregnancies were carried through to live birth outcomes; in 1976, only 64 percent were (Table C.24, Appendix C). There is evidence in 1976 that the less advantaged, operationally those scoring low on our SES measure, were the least likely to abort a pregnancy.

It is uncertain whether marriage during a premarital first pregnancy reduces the disadvantages occurring to mothers and their children from an illegitimate birth—in contrast to the relatively imperceptible consequences resulting from a premarital conception alone. The appropriate group to study in this respect is young women who decide to have their babies, since abortion effectively eliminates the problem. Such young women show no change over the five-year period under observation in the propensity to marry in their situation. There is an enormous difference between the races, whites being more than 6 times as likely to opt for marriage during a premarital pregnancy. Some of these pregnancies are intended and in some instances marriage plans may have been in prospect. The variance in the tendency to marry is explained largely by race. In addition, there is some greater propensity toward marriage on the part of those who intended to become pregnant and young women from more educated backgrounds. These results imply that, although there is no (statistically significant) difference in 1976 among SES categories in the prevalence of premarital pregnancy, a young woman of high SES is much less likely than a woman of low SES to bear an illegitimate child because of her greater recourse to abortion and to marriage during the pregnancy. This implication subsequently was examined by considering simultaneously the physical outcome of the pregnancy and the marriage alternative. Not unexpectedly, whites are much less likely than blacks to have illegitimate births. Among whites, however, there is in 1976 a sharp differentiation in this respect, with a woman of higher social status much less likely to have an illegitimate child than a woman of lower social status. This difference did not prevail in 1971.

To put it all together, we provide in Table 5.8 a summary of the variables used in the analyses of the several aspects of premarital pregnancy considered in this chapter. As before, we distinguish between those

TOTAL 5.8 Summary of Significance and Consistency of Relationship of Explanatory Variables for Four Aspects of Premarital Pregnancy

	Prevalence of Premarital Pregnancy			Mean Age at First Pregnancy	First Pregnancies Carried to Term		Legitimation of Term Pregnancy
	Total	White	Black	Total	Total	White	Total
Race	0[a]	—	—	0	x	—	x
Current age	x	x	x	x	0	0	0
SES	0	0	0	0	0	0	x
Family stability	0	0	0	0	0	0	0
Religion	0	0	0	0	0	0	—
Religiosity	0	0	0	x	0	0	0
Age first intercourse	x	x	x	x	—	—	—
Pregnancy intention	—	—	—	0	x	x	x
Age first conception	—	—	—	—	x	x	0

NOTE: x = significant at p<.10 and consistent in direction in both surveys; 0 = not significant and/or not consistent; dashes = not applicable.

a. Significant in both surveys when contraceptive status is included as a variable in the 1976 analysis.

variables that are significant at both dates and those that are not. It is clear that any single aspect of premarital pregnancy involves few significant variables and that no variable plays a part in all four aspects. Even race, which is highly significant once a premarital pregnancy occurs (that is, in terms of outcome of the pregnancy and whether legitimation occurs), is not significant in terms of when pregnancy occurs and may or may not be (consistently) significant in terms of whether or not it occurs. Overall, variables involving age (current age, age at first intercourse, and age at first conception) and pregnancy intention appear to be the most important variables in the several analyses. With but two exceptions our social variables play no consistent part in the analysis of premarital pregnancy: religiosity in the analysis of mean age at first conception and SES in the analysis of legitimation of term pregnancy. We have not felt it necessary to include in Table 5.8 a summary of the analysis of illegitimacy.

It is possible that our rule of "requiring" a variable to be significant at both survey dates is too stringent. We did in fact relax the rule in our discussion of the analysis of outcome of premarital pregnancy. The relaxation of the rule acknowledged the interim legalization of abortion and the subsequent effect of that change as mediated through our variables. Other events occurred between 1971 and 1976—increased public attention to teenage premarital intercourse and pregnancy, as well as increased access of teenagers to contraceptive supplies and services—that may have led to changes in the manner in which our variables affected various forms of behavior: sexual and contraceptive, as well as pregnancy.

A review of the various analyses presented in the three chapters on premarital sexual behavior, contraceptive use, and premarital pregnancy indicates that the interpretation of all four of the social variables has been affected by our rule. Thus, our summary table in Chapter 3 shows, for example, that SES for whites was not significant at both dates in the analysis of the prevalence of premarital intercourse. It was, however, significant in that analysis for 1976 ($p < .05$). Was this a real change in "the manner in which underlying social forces operate?" In this particular instance it is difficult to reconcile the direction of change, from nonsignificance to significance, with the changes in the broader social milieu. Intuitively we would have argued that in the more restrictive period preceding the 1971 survey SES would have been (negatively) related to prevalence of intercourse and that the social changes that occurred between 1971 and 1976 would have led to a diminution of this relationship and possibly its total disappearance. The empirical results show the opposite—not significant in 1971 but significant in 1976.

Thus, when we hold to our rule with but few exceptions, we may be overlooking a significant variable at a particular point in time in terms of a specific form of behavior. However, we also are less likely to attribute significance to a "chance relationship." In the absence of a body of confirmed relationships and some integrating schema, we prefer to err on the side of caution in identifying "causes."

NOTES

1. A full description of the procedures used in such instances is provided in the second section of Appendix B.
2. For estimates of the cumulative probability of premarital pregnancy at individual years of age, see Zelnik et al. (1979).
3. Prior to the first use or first nonuse, sometimes-users are, of course, never-users or always-users.
4. That paper dealt only with the 1976 survey and was restricted to an analysis of those women who were aged 18 or 19 at the time of the survey. Unpublished material based on the entire sample yields similar results.
5. Women who married shortly after conception but subsequently miscarried are excluded; those who had stillbirths are included.
6. As before, we do not include in Table 5.7 any data for blacks, and the categories shown in that table for each variable are those used in the multivariate analyses of the total populations; for the analysis of whites, categories are combined for some of the variables (see Table C.28, Appendix C). Unlike in our earlier discussion of the (physical) outcome of the pregnancy, we have not combined stillbirths with live births in our analysis of illegitimacy.

CHAPTER 6

SUMMARY AND CONCLUSIONS

Pathways to Pregnancy and Beyond

The birth of an illegitimate child is, speaking analytically, the end point of a complex, convoluted chain of events. Sexual intercourse is a necessary but obviously not sufficient prior event. When the young woman first has intercourse, whether she continues to have it and with what regularity, and within what kind of relationship, all have antecedents or "causes." Each of these, however, is itself a precursor or factor involved in subsequent events.

The sexually active young woman may begin to contracept at the time she first has intercourse and may be consistent in that usage; further, she may use one of the more effective methods and use it effectively. At the opposite extreme is the young woman who never uses contraception. In between are a wide range of alternative patterns or series of events. Some young women may begin to use contraception simultaneously with beginning intercourse, but eventually stop using it; some may begin to use it after an interval of nonuse; some may start with one method and switch to another and sometimes continue to switch; some may adopt one method and stay with it; some may use the methods properly and effectively, others may not. These different contraceptive regimens may be associated with prior sexual events, such as the age at which intercourse first occurs, but usually in ways that make it difficult to determine the direction of cause and effect. Does regularity of intercourse lead to regularity of use of contraception, or does regularity of use lead to regularity of intercourse? Whatever the direction of the association, the different patterns of use are themselves important antecedents of subsequent events.

Why young women do not use contraception, whether that nonuse is regular, sporadic, or an isolated event, is not a simple question and does not have a single, simple answer. Unpublished data from a survey we carried out in 1979 in metropolitan areas of the United States indicate that virtually every sexually active young woman knows of at least one contraceptive method (and may know of several), the best known method being the pill. Among those knowing of the pill, most rate it the most effective in terms of preventing pregnancy. Nevertheless, some of these women, even though evincing a desire to avoid pregnancy, do not use the pill because of fears, correct or otherwise, of side effects. Parenthetically, this is an important reason for attempting to inform young women about side effects and about alternative methods of contraception.

Some young women, regardless of how knowledgeable they are about various methods of contraception, may discount the risk of pregnancy for themselves. Not uncommonly, they believe they cannot become pregnant because of their young age or the infrequency with which they have intercourse. These ideas are not necessarily false and, further, may be quite rational in that they are based either on the young woman's own experience or that of close friends. Many young women, although menstruating, do not begin to ovulate at menarche or do not ovulate in every period. And certainly, even among married couples who want a pregnancy, it generally takes some period of time during which intercourse is frequent and regular for the pregnancy to occur. Trusting in the belief in one's relative infecundity can ultimately be dangerous, since a young woman cannot tell reliably if she is ovulating during a menstrual cycle or has started to do so with some regularity.

Some young women know that pregnancy is not likely to occur during certain phases of the menstrual cycle, but they are often wrong in their assessment of when those are. Other young women have moral objections to the use of contraception or partners who resist its use, some believe its use destroys the pleasure of sex, eliminates the cherished spontaneity of the act, or otherwise diminishes the romantic aura of the relationship. Some young women may have sex somewhat unexpectedly and thus be unable to prepare for it; others, even though having sex with some frequency, presumably are unwilling or unable to accept this about themselves and are therefore equally unprepared. Some young women are unable to overcome various psychological, social, logistical, or financial barriers to obtaining contraceptives. And some young women do not use contraception because they want to become pregnant—whether because marriage is imminent and the couple wants to have a child quickly, or because pregnancy satisfies some psychological need.

Regardless of what contraceptive pattern is followed, regardless of what method is used, and regardless of the reasons for nonuse, some women eventually become pregnant—although the likelihood of that happening differs considerably depending on the consistency of use and the method involved, as well as a number of other factors. The young unmarried pregnant woman has essentially three options available to her, in principle, but not necessarily in fact. Ignoring involuntary fetal death, she can abort, she can marry during the pregnancy, or she can deliver a live birth outside of marriage. She can, of course, combine these options: marry and abort (few do), abort and marry (also rare in the short run), marry and bear the child (quite common), or vice versa.

Many young unmarried women are morally opposed to abortion; some who are not nevertheless would face overwhelming family opposition should they consider it; some may live in communities where abortion is not easily available; and some may not be able to afford it. Marriage also is not necessarily a realistic option, requiring as it does not only the girl's acceptance of that course but also that of a partner, be he the baby's father or someone else. Only in those instances where neither abortion nor marriage occurs is the end result an illegitimate birth.

Many who write and speak on the subject see the progression from intercourse to illegitimacy as a simple process, easily understandable and amenable to simple, sometimes diametrically opposed, solutions. Make contraceptives and/or abortion more readily available, make them less available, make sex education universally required, eliminate it from schools, strengthen the family as the focus for moral instruction, teach morality in the public schools, and on and on. Such proposals generally ignore political, social, and organizational impediments to their implementation. They also fail to recognize the variety of tastes, interests, motivations, experiences, and moral values of the actors involved—the young women and their partners. It is the complexity of this progression, the diversity of pathways, that has required us in the preceding chapters to treat sex, contraception, and pregnancy separately, while at the some time looking for the linkages between them.

The Nub of the Matter—Illegitimacy

It is a sociological truism that every society has a rule of legitimacy and, therefore, of illegitimacy. Depending on the society, the rule for social legitimacy may also be given legal expression, although, as with all laws, the two can differ. Regardless of the function of the rule of social legitimacy, whether to determine the allocation of responsibility for the proper socialization of the child or the child's social placement, illegitimacy is to some extent a threat to the integrity and continuity of a society. According to Goode (1964): "To focus on illegitimacy, then, does not betray a value judgment on the part of the social analyst; but is required by the importance it assumes for the form and meaning of the family structure. The society must be concerned with social placement or jeopardize its continuity."

The rule of legitimacy is violated, in varying degrees (as are all rules and normative standards), in all societies. If placement of the child cannot be ensured outside of a family, or if other functions having to do with its socialization cannot be met adequately, a question arises as to what level of illegitimacy can be tolerated by a society before it does become seriously disruptive. In the United States, the proportion of births that are illegitimate rose from 11 percent in 1970 to 16 percent in 1978 (National Center for Health Statistics 1973; National Center for Health Statistics, 1980). At the latter date, 9 percent of white births and 53 percent of black births were illegitimate.

Illegitimacy ratios for women under the age of 20 are even higher. Some women who have an illegitimate child may marry subsequently while the child is still young, but others will delay longer or not marry at all. There is some reason to believe that the level will continue to rise in the United States. At what point, if any, does this phenomenon become a direct or indirect threat to the continuity of society? How much can it be offset by subsequent marriage? How much delay is tolerable? With such questions before us, we turn to a consideration of what has been learned in the previous chapters that would increase our understanding of the various stages leading to illegitimacy or suggest what is likely to lead to altering the situation.

Methodological Caveats

Before we summarize the findings of the previous three chapters and distill them for their meaning and implications, we should repeat some of the qualifications and caveats scattered throughout those chapters. First is the problem of numbers. Although the total samples of the two studies are fairly large, the number of cases available for analysis diminishes significantly once the focus of interest moves beyond sexual intercourse to a consideration of prevention of pregnancy or the resolution of pregnancy. While all sample surveys might benefit from larger samples, the incremental gain from additional cases is particularly great where teenagers are the focus of attention. It may do in studies of married women, for example, to consider women aged 20-24 or 25-29 as fairly homogeneous with respect to development, social context, and behavior. This is a much less valid assumption for teenagers, since small differences in age are associated with important changes in development, social situations, and

Summary and Conclusions

behavior. Moreover, older women exhibit more of the behavior of interest: more are sexually active, more are or have been pregnant. The analysis, in short, need not be so fine grained as among younger women.

Second, much of the behavior we are concerned with involves *two* extremes, with no gradations in between. Is the young woman sexually active?—"yes" or "no"; was contraception used at first intercourse?—"yes" or "no"; has this person experienced a premarital pregnancy—"yes" or "no." In principle, the explanation of extremes might be thought to be a simpler, easier task than the explanation of finer gradations. However, that task is complicated by two conditions. The first is the cross-sectional nature of our two studies; the second is the relative crudeness of available techniques for analyzing dichotomous situations. The result is that less can be "explained" statistically than would otherwise be the case.

A related problem is the relatively short span of time during which the events under study could have occurred. While some of the young women may have experienced 7 or 8 years of sexual activity, for most the interval is considerably less. This short interval may reduce the likelihood of recall error, but it simultaneously reduces the opportunity for events to occur. The interval, or period of observation, is independent of whether a study is cross-sectional or longitudinal. However, given that we have to work with cross-sectional surveys, we could have increased the period of observation only by enlarging the age range of eligibility, and then only at the upper end. For example, to compare the probability of pregnancy after a year of exposure of a young woman who becomes sexually active at age 15 with one who starts at age 19, we would have to take 20 year olds into the sample. While there is much to be said in favor of having done so from a theoretical perspective, matters of a more mundane nature precluded that possibility.

Another problem, a universal one, relates to measurement. Our variables are, for the most part, fairly crude and do not capture, or they blur over, important elements or components. Socioeconomic status is more than the average level of completed education of parents (or the persons who raised the respondent). Our family stability variable leaves out many elements of the structure and interrelations of families which are undoubtedly important for an understanding of the behavior of young women; further, the residual family stability category lumps together a wide range of family situations, a problem that might have been alleviated partially but not wholly with larger samples.

Aside from the variables we did employ, there are others we believe to be important that were not included, either because we did not know how to obtain the data or how to collapse them into a usable form, or because we avoided data tainted by the problem of circularity. An example of the former is the omission from the analysis of data relating to patterns of leisure activity, peer relations, and so on. In the 1971 survey, a number of questions were devoted to those topics, but we found it virtually impossible to collapse the responses in ways that made them amenable to analysis. As a result, such questions were omitted in 1976.

Educational aspirations and patterns of mobility are two areas that we believe, on theoretical grounds, to be important components in the explanation of adolescent sexual behavior. In both instances the data suggest strong associations with that behavior, but in both instances the problem of circularity is significant. This problem is encountered in many studies and different investigators cope with it in different ways; we have chosen to limit our variables to those unaffected or only minimally affected by circularity.

Finally, there is, of course, the question of the quality of the data. In this respect we have noted one area of deficiency: the reporting of abortions (and presumably, therefore, of pregnancies) to blacks in the 1976 study. While this is an important defect, we have reason to believe that the data from both surveys are at par with other social surveys from which the bulk of information about U. S. fertility is derived. To say that we are up to standard for the "state of the art" is not, however, reason for complacency or for expecting certainty of results.

Results

SEX

In this and following sections, in which we summarize our findings, it should be understood that statements are made in the context of multivariate analysis and are subject to certain self-imposed restrictions. Thus, if we say that variable x is related to variable y, we mean that this was so consistently in both surveys (if both were involved) and in the presence of all other variables specified for the analysis. Relationships which failed any of these tests are ignored. The reader is free, of course, to adopt other rules. There are instances in which relationships among variables appear much the same in the two surveys but are significant in one but not the other, due sometimes to an insufficiency of cases or to the way cases are distributed. Of the various ways of dealing with this situation, such as by pooling the samples, we chose to present the results in a way that seemed most straightforward, that is, to let the reader see the data as they fall in each survey and to assess their statistical significance in terms of the design

Summary and Conclusions

of that survey. In these data it is seldom, if ever, true that the variables we exclude from further discussion by virtue of our rule contribute much to the explanation of variance, even for the survey where they are significant.

For the most part, we have not been very successful in explaining the various aspects of behavior we have subjected to analysis. On the other hand, the failure of a variable widely presumed to be important in accounting for the behavior in question is not an unimportant finding. In areas of behavior such as we are dealing with, there is much speculation and "theorizing" with little empirical testing. Our negative findings, then, may have a salutory effect.

The various analyses fall into two categories—either we explain a trivial amount of the variation in behavior, or explain a sizable proportion, but the explanation is of little significance or importance except, again, in a negative sense. To learn, for example, that prevalence of premarital pregnancy is largely a function of the period of risk to pregnancy is hardly an exciting finding. On the other hand, such a finding is a contribution to the degree that it helps to clear away some of the untested speculation about the prevalence of premarital pregnancy that, through repetition in writings on the subject, has come to be regarded as "confirmed scientific fact." In general, our most consistent and powerful variables are such items as age (current or at time of the event), duration of exposure, and race. The sociological variables, for the most part, are of little importance. It is the infrequent situation where such variables are consistently significant at both dates for each race.

Race is a significant item with respect to sex—whether we consider prevalence, mean age at first intercourse, number of partners, or frequency of intercourse. Blacks have higher prevalence and a lower mean age, whereas whites have more partners and higher frequency. SES, family stability, religiosity, and age at menarche play some small part in explaining prevalence and mean age, but the single most important factor (other than race) is current age. On the other hand, none of these factors play any part in explaining number of partners or frequency of intercourse. Current age is not explicit in these analyses but enters into them implicitly as part of the duration of risk variable (which, in the analysis of frequency of intercourse, is itself replaced by a proxy, number of partners) and is the single factor of any significance to come out of the analysis of number of partners. Frequency, at least among whites, to the degree it is accounted for, is explained primarily by the imminence of marriage and secondarily by the use of a medical method of contraception at last intercourse.

CONTRACEPTION

Contraception presents a very different picture. Race plays no part in determining whether contraception is or is not used at first intercourse or last intercourse or whether contraception is always used or never used. Given the partial overlap which logically occurs between use at first intercourse and always use, it is not surprising that current age and age at first intercourse are significant in both analyses (remembering that, unlike other situations, only one survey, 1976, is being analyzed and therefore our rule requiring consistency and significance in both surveys is not enforceable). It should be noted, however, that the same overlap exists between use (or nonuse) at first intercourse and never use, but here the effect of the two age variables is reduced. Beyond this, SES and family stability play some small part in explaining use at first intercourse but no part with respect to always use. However, both of these social variables do have a significant effect on never use. In other words, there is seemingly a social dimension to the avoidance of contraception, but not to the timing or regularity of use by those who accept contraception. This is puzzling perhaps, although it appeals to common observation that there might well be social factors involved in the total rejection of contraception, whereas the discipline required for regularity of use might be diffused among users of contraception without regard to social coordinates.

Use of contraception at last intercourse appears to be marginally explained by SES and age at first intercourse. However, when the data are reanalyzed by excluding one-timers and those pregnant at last intercourse, the effects of SES and age at first intercourse are eliminated, and use at last intercourse is seen to be a function of whether contraception was used at first intercourse and whether there had been an intervening pregnancy. Thus, those who begin their sexual activity with contraception continue to use it and those who do not contracept initially and experience a pregnancy contracept afterwards. In effect, use begets use and pregnancy provides a powerful inducement to prevent additional pregnancies.

If race makes no difference in whether contraception is used, the same cannot be said for the methods used by those who do contracept. Among contraceptors, blacks are more likely than whites to use medical methods. This is true for the first intercourse, the last intercourse (however, see below), and for methods ever used. Beyond race, only age at first intercourse is significant in terms of use of a medical method at that time and only current age and religion with respect to use of a medical method at last intercourse. It should be noted, however, that the reanalysis of use of a medical method at last intercourse, removing the one-timers and those who were then pregnant and introducing additional variables, eliminates the effect of race and religion and again highlights the importance of use of a contraceptive at first intercourse and the stimulus to effective use of an intervening pregnancy.

Since there is some overlap between use of a medical method at first or last intercourse and ever use of a medical method, it is perhaps not surprising that analysis of characteristics associated with ever using medical contraception again shows the significance of current age. On the other hand, family stability and religiosity, of no significance in the analysis of use of a medical method at first or last intercourse, are of significance in terms of ever use. Clearly, there are few common threads running through the fabric of use of contraception or use of a specific type of method. Onset and timing of use and the use of particular methods are the least influenced by social factors; more generalized responses, such as the rejection of contraception altogether or trying oral contraception, at times appear to be more socially conditioned.

Blacks are more likely than whites to obtain medical methods of contraception from a clinic; whites are more likely to rely on private practitioners. Other than race, only current age and religiosity are significant in terms of initial source of medical contraception.

PREGNANCY

Summarizing the analyses of the various aspects of the first premarital pregnancy is in some ways simpler than was the case with sex or contraception. Although initially race did not appear to be a consistently significant factor with respect to the prevalence of premarital pregnancy, reanalysis of the 1976 data, taking contraceptive status into account, indicated it to be so. Other than race, current age and age at first intercourse are the only two consistently significant variables in the explanation of premarital pregnancy. The racial differences found with respect to prevalence of premarital pregnancy are not evident for mean age at first pregnancy. The two age variables again are significant, as is religiosity.

Major differences by race exist with respect to the outcome of premarital pregnancy. Premaritally pregnant blacks are more likely than whites to carry the pregnancy to term, are less likely in that case to marry during the course of the pregnancy, and, as a result, are more likely than whites to have an illegitimate live birth from a premarital conception. The decision to carry a pregnancy to term (that is, not to have an abortion) is influenced by whether the pregnancy is wanted and by the age at which the conception occurs. Marriage, among those who reject the alternative of abortion, is also a function of whether the pregnancy was wanted (but not a function of age at conception). SES is also a significant factor in the decision to marry, the tendency to marry being greater among those with better educated parents. Surprisingly, perhaps, the bearing of illegitimate live births among all women who conceive premaritally is related consistently and regularly only to race—the likelihood of such an outcome being several times greater among blacks.

In presenting and discussing our results, we have established a "rule" that requires a variable to be statistically significant in both surveys for us to take it seriously as an explanatory factor. Imposition of this rule recognizes the short interval, historically speaking, between the two surveys and our assumption that, though the prevalence of behavior may have changed, we would not expect radical changes in underlying social dynamics. Some exceptions to the rule were noted and in some analyses of contraceptive use, such as use at first intercourse, the rule could not be applied because only one survey was involved. The results, or the meaning of the results, would have been different, and possibly more confusing, without this rule. Certainly our sense of explanatory factors would differ if each survey had been analyzed independently. In this respect we see it as an advantage to have analyzed the two surveys simultaneously. To follow this criterion reduces the number of "findings" in a quantitative sense but gives us greater confidence in those that meet the test. Since we provide the results of all analyses and show the level of significance for each variable at each date, the reader is, of course, free to adopt a quite different rule and reinterpret our results.

We have also made less than some analysts might of variables which do not pass the test of statistical significance, even though in some cases the data are suggestive of sometimes interesting relationships. Some of these deserve further study under circumstances of sample size, measurement technique, and so on, more adequate for their investigation. To have included all relationships where a chance of explanation could not be eliminated would have defeated this attempt at summarization. In the main body of the text we sometimes toy with the possible meaning of some of these relationships, but we have subjected ourselves to a sterner discipline here.

In summary, then, blacks are more likely than whites to have premarital intercourse and to experience it initially at a younger age. They are as likely as whites to use contraception and, among those who do use contraception, they are more likely than whites to use medical methods. Blacks may or may not be more likely than whites to experience a premarital pregnancy, but, among those who do become pregnant, blacks and whites have a comparable mean age at first conception when allowance is made for the earlier age at which blacks begin sexual activity. Racial differences do, however, assert themselves with regard to the outcome of the premarital pregnancy—fewer blacks have abortions, fewer

Summary and Conclusions

marry during their pregnancies, and, consequently, proportionately more premaritally pregnant blacks than whites have illegitimate births.

Age, whether current or at time of an event, for example, first intercourse, is important and pervasive in its influence. It determines whether a young woman is sexually active, uses contraception and if so what type, or experiences a pregnancy. Some of these age effects appear to be due to duration of sexual activity, others do not. Age has little or no effect, it seems, on the outcome of a premarital pregnancy, whether in terms of carrying the pregnancy to term or marrying during the pregnancy. This may be one of the most unexpected findings that we report.

Besides race and age, SES is frequently significant, but often in an inconsistent manner. It has some moderate effect on prevalence of intercourse and mean age at first intercourse. Analysis of the 1976 survey suggests that young women of high SES are more likely to use contraception at some time but are no more likely to be always-users. This greater use does not lead, however, to statistically significant differences (in 1976) in the prevalence of pregnancy, although there is a trend in that direction. There is some indication also, again only for 1976, that premaritally pregnant women of higher SES are more likely than those lower on the SES scale to have abortions or to marry during pregnancy and therefore to have fewer illegitimate births.

The other variables used throughout the analysis, family stability, religion, and religiosity, have isolated and limited effects. Aside from those variables used in all analyses, items used in specific situations, such as pregnancy intention, tend to have powerful effects but are for the most part "obvious."

These results are disappointing from a theoretical perspective and have relatively little significance for the development of policy or the improvement of services. The latter defect is especially important in light of the findings of a survey carried out in 1979—too recently for detailed analysis to be included in this volume. Preliminary results from the 1979 survey indicate an increase in sexual activity among young women, all of it attributable to an increase among whites, and an increase among the sexually active in premarital pregnancy (Zelnik and Kantner, 1980). The rise in premarital pregnancy occurred despite an increase in the use of contraception and in the consistency of that use—more of the sexually active used a contraceptive at first intercourse and more always used—and a decline in never use.

The increase in pregnancy is not due to an increase in the duration of exposure to the risk of pregnancy, as there was no change between 1976 and 1979 in mean age at first intercourse. Rather, an important factor appears to be a shift among contraceptors from more effective methods to less effective methods. Examination of first method used and last method used shows a decline in use of the pill and an increase in withdrawal, the decline more prominent in the case of first method than last method used.

However, the shift from more to less effective methods is only a partial explanation. Each contraceptive status group showed an increase in the likelihood of pregnancy. Since changes in contraceptive practices do not affect the never-users, some other factor or factors must be at work to account for the increase in pregnancy among this group.

The 1979 survey also revealed a continuation of changes that occurred between 1971 and 1976: Proportionately fewer of the premaritally pregnant married during the pregnancy, and, among those who remained unmarried, proportionately fewer wanted the pregnancy and proportionately more ended it by voluntary abortion. As a result of the combined effect of the changes in prevalence of pregnancy, marriage, and abortion, proportionately more of the premaritally pregnant young women in 1979 experienced an illegitimate live birth.

The data from the 1979 survey indicate that young women are increasingly trying to prevent or terminate unwanted pregnancies. That they are somewhat less successful in preventing pregnancies than their earlier counterparts is only partially a result of a shift to less effective methods of contraception—a shift that may or may not be due to recent reporting about the side effects of the pill and the IUD. The complexity of the situation, as revealed by the analyses in the present volume, belies easy answers and defies easy solutions.

Conclusions

The material presented in the previous chapters as well as in other publications relating to the 1971 and 1976 surveys does not lead to a satisfactory explanation for the continued rise in premarital pregnancy; nor does that material lead to suggestions for feasible ways to reduce the prevalence of pregnancy. Many young women have an incorrect notion of the period of greatest risk of pregnancy during the monthly menstrual cycle; others believe themselves immune to pregnancy because of their young age or the infrequency with which they have intercourse. Others, although accepting their vulnerability to pregnancy—and not desirous of experiencing it—have a variety of reasons for not using contraception.

Sex education might be thought an appropriate solution to the problems of ignorance and the "excessive risk taking" engaged in by some young women, particularly those who have sex infrequently. Courses in sex education vary considerably in their content, the ages at which they

Summary and Conclusions

are taught, and the degree to which students are exposed to them. Even assuming well-designed, well-taught courses attended by all students, such instruction may come too late for those who have already experienced intercourse or have picked up misinformation from friends, popular literature, and so on. Further, even strong advocates of sex education cannot expect that all information will be transmitted correctly, that what is transmitted will be understood correctly by all students, or that students will retain everything transmitted to them. Fairly high levels of ignorance and error about the menstrual cycle persist in our society, despite the educational efforts, formal and informal, lay and professional, devoted to the subject. Even beyond the issues of transmission, understanding, and retention of information, there is the question of whether students act on the basis of that information. These problems will be alleviated, but not overcome, if courses are well designed and well taught and if the students who might benefit from such courses are exposed to them. However, at present, many, if not most, courses are poorly designed, poorly taught, and unavailable to many who need them.

We are not suggesting that sex education be removed from the schools and returned to parents—who always had and still have the right to provide such information in a manner and at a time they believe most appropriate for their children; it is their continuing failure to do so that has led to the demand that schools take on the responsibility. Rather, we are suggesting that there are limits to what sex education can accomplish. There are some people who argue that sex education could accomplish a great deal if done "properly"—the right teachers with the right training, a professionally designed curriculum, with all students exposed to it early enough in life for it to be effective. This strikes us as naive, for aside from the almost total absence of evidence supporting this assertion, the argument ignores the very factors in our society which heretofore have prevented the effective development and presentation of sex education programs. There is little likelihood that these factors will diminish in the near future; it is more likely that whatever sex education programs now exist will themselves be diminished in scope and rendered even less effective than they are now.

There are those young women who accept and acknowledge their vulnerability to pregnancy when they engage in unprotected intercourse, yet reject the use of contraception because of moral qualms about its use (qualms which do not seem to extend to intercourse itself) or because of beliefs about its effect on the pleasure or spontaneity of sex. Such notions, whether of a moral or hedonistic nature, are difficult to counter. To the extent that these beliefs are operative, the young women who hold them are not likely to seek contraceptive services.

Other young women, the largest group among the contraceptively unprotected, who see themselves as vulnerable to pregnancy, report having failed to use contraception because they did not expect to have intercourse. When sex is unplanned and sporadic, coitus-dependent methods are appropriate. These methods, however, tend to be the less effective ones, especially in the hands of inexperienced users. The effective methods provide continuous protection, but are most appropriate when sex is regular and contraception routinized. The young sexually active woman therefore faces a dilemma: She is interested in reliable protection against pregnancy, yet the most effective methods are poorly adapted to her sex life; the methods that are adapted to her sex life do not provide the same degree of protection.

This dilemma has been resolved for her, in a way, by the decision of service providers to emphasize effective methods—the pill primarily, despite its recognized drawbacks as a method for unmarried teenage women. So great is the publicity given to the pill in magazines, newspapers, and books that for many young women contraception or "birth control" is synonymous with oral contraception, with use of "the pill." It is possible that greater publicity for the condom and greater stress on this method by service providers when appropriate would lead eventually to increased and more effective use of the method, but we doubt it. Clearly, however, simply making contraceptives available is not sufficient—as our own experience and that of family planning programs around the world show.

A word needs to be said about another proposed "solution" to the problem of teenage pregnancy, namely the development of a new contraceptive better suited to the unplanned sexual lives of young women. Ignoring problems of effectiveness and acceptability, and recognizing that a perfect contraceptive is a scientific will-o'-the-wisp, informed opinion is that any new contraceptive is at least 10, and more likely 20, years away from being commercially available. This "solution," then, has no applicability to today's problem. What the situation may be 10 or 15 years down the road we cannot say. Work on the development of improved contraceptives should go forward, of course. Our point here is that, given that nothing very promising has come out of the laboratory for testing, and given the years of testing that are required before a new drug can be released, we will have to make do with current contraceptive technology for some time to come.

If we appear overly pessimistic about the likelihood of a solution or a dramatic diminution of the problem, we should remind the reader not only that many young women are not sexually active, but that many young women who are sexually active are effective users of contraception

Summary and Conclusions

and do not become pregnant. That some do become pregnant is hardly sufficient to argue for the elimination of contraceptive service programs. While the claims of those favoring sex education, contraceptive services, and even abortion have clearly been overstated, less than complete success should not be deemed complete failure. The problem is that the increase in regular, effective use of contraception is not keeping up with the increase in sexual activity, with an inevitable increase in pregnancy. A continuation of present programs and policies will not, we believe, alter these trends; new approaches that view sexual activity in its broad social context are needed.

If it is difficult to explain the continued rise in premarital pregnancy and to suggest ways to reduce its prevalence, it is less difficult to suggest ways that will not assist in reducing premarital pregnancy among young women. Banning sex education from the schools is unlikely to reduce the level of premarital pregnancy or the level of sexual activity. Similarly, making abortion illegal or difficult to obtain is unlikely to reduce the level of premarital pregnancy or of sexual activity and, other things equal, would substantially increase the level of illegitimacy. The inability of young people to obtain contraceptive services is unlikely to have a negative effect on the prevalence of pregnancy or of intercourse. Lest the reader think we are reaching toward the absurd, each of these propositions has been put forward seriously by persons concerned with the rising level of sexual activity and premarital pregnancy.

At the same time, there is little reason to believe that premarital pregnancy among teenagers can be reduced significantly in a social context that is relatively accepting of it among slightly older women. More broadly, there is little reason to believe that a society can prevent some form of behavior when it neither penalizes those who engage in it nor rewards those who do not. In an effort to improve life for the "innocent" offspring, society's attitude toward the mother has become less punitive, less condemnatory, and more accepting, more supportive, more ameliorative. This is not to suggest that teenage mothers suffer no hardship, but increasingly policies are aimed at reducing or eliminating those hardships, at "equalizing" life chances. Those hardships that persist are more a consequence of factors over which the young mother has no control—essentially, her place in the social system—than of her behavior. In effect, if a society imposes no clear sanctions against certain unwanted behaviors and has no rewards to offer those who abstain, and if, simultaneously, comparable behavior by some members of society is ignored or even accepted for those in the public eye, it can hardly expect not to encounter the behavior it does not want.

There are those who decry what they perceive as the disappearance or deterioration of the American family and who lay the blame for this on the "heavy hand of the government." The argument appears to be that with less intrusion of the government in matters directly affecting the family, there would be less premarital pregnancy and less premarital intercourse. It seems likely that to reduce premarital intercourse in the United States would require far more governmental intrusion than now exists, and at a cost of personal rights that many would be unwilling to accept. Thus, teenage sexuality might recede if we could bring ourselves to accept greater censorship of movies, television, books, and magazines, including the advertising therein, combined with regulations to discourage the participation of more than one parent in the labor force at any one point in time, combined with greater restrictions on the daily movements of teenagers and on their finances, combined with greater surveillance of "trysting" places—whether motels or open fields—combined with a drastic reduction in unchaperoned social activities for teenagers and an increase in "family" activities, combined with restrictions to prevent young people from leaving home for either work or school, combined with social sanctions against open displays of affection by young people, combined with the imposition of punishment in some form for those who stray from clearly marked "paths of righteousness." Traditional societies which characteristically enforce restrictive, punitive codes against youth and women typically have little sex or illicit reproduction among their young women.

It may be that not all of the above items are necessary, and it may be that some that are necessary have been omitted. However, some of those we have listed are, we believe, essential if the prevalence of premarital sex is to be diminished significantly. Each in turn has obvious and far-reaching implications; they would all require greater governmental involvement in our daily lives and would entail the loss or serious attenuation of what we now regard as inalienable rights and privileges. To the degree that a society is a social fabric, the picking and choosing of one item as "the way" to reduce teenage sexuality would have no effect. We suspect that many who argue for a return to the traditional family have given little or no thought to the implications of their rhetoric and would themselves object to what might be needed to return us to those halcyon (but never experienced) days which they celebrate. For ourselves, we prefer to cope with the consequences of early sex as an aspect of an emancipated society, rather than pay the social costs its elimination would exact.

APPENDIX A:
HISTORY AND DESIGN OF THE STUDY

PRELIMINARY EFFORTS

Our initial efforts at raising funds to study the fertility of young women were met with the objection that there were too many uncertainties inherent in the subject to justify the expenditure of a large sum of money. Moreover, there was some question, in the aftermath of the social unrest of the late 1960s, as to whether household surveys could achieve reasonable completion rates. Limited, restricted, and anecdotal evidence seemed to suggest increasing resistance, especially in central-city inner areas, to participating in such surveys. Along with the potential problem of screening a large number of households to identify eligible respondents and determine their willingness to participate in any type of survey was the issue of whether young women would be willing (and allowed, by parents, guardians, relatives, husbands, and so on) to participate in a survey that focused on sexual experience, contraceptive practices, and pregnancy and its resolution. Doubt was expressed whether interviewers could be found who would feel at ease asking questions about such subjects and who would be able to establish rapport with respondents. Further, what type of interviewers would be needed? Non-empirically based claims argued that black respondents would be more likely to give interviews to black interviewers and that young respondents would most readily talk openly to young interviewers. The time was 1969, when agitation over racial and generational differences had the country on edge. Since most trained interviewers available in the market are white and middle-aged, we faced a potential problem if these claims were valid. Also in contention was the question of whether there were regional and perhaps racial differences in the way various sex-related subjects were referred to; in effect, could a questionnaire be designed that would deal satisfactorily with the full gamut of topics pertinent to adolescent fertility and be serviceable for use with a national sample of young women? And finally, since a longitudinal study was being proposed, could young women successfully be located for reinterview at a period in life when many would be leaving their parental homes and, in many cases, also changing their surnames?

A grant was received from the Social and Rehabilitation Service, DHEW, to attempt to resolve these concerns and questions. To learn the language of sexual behavior and related topics, we held 24 group discussions (involving, on the average, 7 participants each) in 4 different locations. These sessions, conducted by trained moderators who unobtrusively led and guided the discussions to ensure inclusion of relevant topics, were video-taped and subsequently subjected to careful, if informal, scrutiny and analysis. What was gleaned from these sessions has been reported on elsewhere (Kantner and Zelnik, 1969; Zelnik and Kantner, 1970). In general, these discussions indicated that, while some terms were subject to several varying interpretations and others had numerous and often localized synonyms, there was a stratum of terms which were clearly understood even though often substituted for by colloquial, nonclinical modes of expression. Thus, construction of an intelligible questionnaire for use with a national sample appeared to be a feasible task.

To determine the feasibility of tracing and locating respondents for reinterview and testing different procedures for so doing, we selected three different test populations:

(1) 98 black women randomly selected from those who had been respondents in the 1965 National Fertility Study
(2) 102 black girls from poverty areas in Philadelphia who were enrolled in the tenth or eleventh grade in a public school in 1967
(3) 74 participants from the group discussions (referred to above) that were held during April 1969

These three populations were used in the tracing effort simply because of their availability. Fortunately, they included cases which were expected to make tracing of more than average difficulty: low-income blacks with varying intervals since last contact and varying amounts and kinds of information available for tracing. For the first group, the available information relevant for tracing purposes consisted of respondent's name, address, phone number, husband's or head of household's name, and the names, addresses, and phone numbers of references given by the respondent at the time of interview. These women had been interviewed on the average of three and one-half years before tracing was attempted.

Tracing techniques used included both telephone directory and post office services, with an aim toward confirmation of address without incurring the expense of direct contact by telephone or actual field investigation. To trace each of the 98 women, 5 separate and independent efforts were made: 2 telephone directory searches involving different amounts of information and slightly different procedures; mailing of letters to all of the references named by a respondent, asking for confirmation of respondent's address; a direct mailing of regular mail to the respondent; and a second direct mailing to the respondent, with address correction requested of the post office. Approximately 84 percent of the women were traced successfully by one or more of these procedures, a reasonably high rate of success given the interval between interview and tracing. For a small number of cases the information received from the different efforts varied, a problem that presumably could be resolved if, as would be the case in the actual situation, the tracing procedures were employed in a complementary rather than an independent manner. However, this was a sample of ever-married women, older on the average than those we wished to study, and therefore only a partial test of our tracing techniques. Thus, there was considerable interest in seeing how well we could do in locating high school students.

The elapsed time interval for tracing the 102 students was approximately 2 years. Information available for tracing was minimal, consisting only of names and addresses of the young women at the time they were in school. Further, the Philadelphia Board of Education stipulated that no direct contacts were to be made with them. This limited tracing methods used to post office mailing list correction services. These efforts resulted in approximately 72 percent being counted as "finds"—that is, with an address confirmed by the post office as being the young woman's present place of residence. Presumably many who were not "found" could have been located had we been able to contact references and to employ other devices available in a well-planned longitudinal investigation. This, then, was an encouraging result.

For the third group, those who had participated in the group discussions, about six months had elapsed when tracing began. The only information available for these women was name, address, and, in most cases, telephone number. The basic tracing device used was a mail questionnaire inquiry about the group discussion experience, which was accompanied by a postage paid return envelope. In addition, the envelopes containing the questionnaires and return envelopes were stamped "address correction requested." Using only these postal services, we succeeded in contacting 92 percent of the women.

These results suggested that high rates of successful tracing could be achieved by keeping the time interval between contacts with the respondents to a reasonably short interval (for example, one year), but supplementing information about the respondent with the name of the head of the household and with information about references who would be most likely to know the current address of the respondent, and by using all available information and procedures (telephone directory services, post office services and direct mailings, and direct telephone contact) for the actual tracing.

When the 1971 teenage study was ultimately funded, the longitudinal design was accepted provisionally and funds provided for the initial interview as well as for tracing efforts to be carried out one year after that contact. The rationale was that if the survey could be carried out in a satisfactory manner, and if the first tracing effort could provide a correct current address for a significantly high proportion of the respondents, then subsequent funding would be provided for additional rounds of interviewing and intervening tracing.

To ensure as much success as possible in tracing, the following information was collected at the time of the initial interview: respondent's name, address, and telephone number; the name of the head of the household; the names, addresses, and telephone numbers of two persons who would always be expected to know where to locate the respondent; the address where the respondent thought she would be living one year after the interview; if the respondent was a student, the name and address of the school she was attending; if the respondent was employed, the name and address of her employer. Utilizing this information (which, of course, varied in amount among respondents), tracing began one year after the interview (in 1972). For an address to be classified as confirmed, we required return mail from a respondent of a simple questionnaire asking current marital status, educational attainment, and address, or, when this was not forthcoming, direct telephone contact with the respondent or a member of her immediate family and provision of her current address. Under these requirements, confirmed addresses were secured for 90 percent of the original panel. In spite of this high rate, and in spite of the success of the 1971 survey itself, it eventually proved impossible for reasons never stated to obtain additional funds to maintain the panel and to reinterview them.

The design and pretesting of the questionnaire to be used in the main survey was conducted in 3 waves (yielding a total of 406 interviews), while simultaneously carrying out 2 experiments designed to determine whether (1) small incentives would induce greater cooperation from potential respondents, and (2) interviewer characteristics (race and age) would have an effect on securing household screenings and completed interviews. The incentives, where applicable, were offered at the household screening stage. By predesignation, the informant at a housing unit received either $1.00 in cash, a postal card which in return entitled the sender to a pair of panty hose, or nothing (representing a control condition). A comparison of completed screenings for each of the 3 conditions showed little variation among them. At the same time, interviewers noted several disadvantages or concerns related to the 2 gift conditions. Because of the lack of difference among the 3 conditions in completed screenings, and because of the problems raised by the offering of the 2 gifts, the decision was made to drop the idea of using any incentive in the proposed study.[1] While an

Appendix A

incentive of greater value might have been more acceptable and might have led to a higher rate of successful screenings, a significant increase in the value of an incentive appeared beyond our means for a sample of around 5000 respondents.

To determine the effect of race and age of interviewers in securing screenings and interviews, interviewers were divided into 2 age groups, under 26 years of age and 26 years of age and over, with black interviewers assigned to black neighborhoods (and therefore presumably to black households) and white interviewers to either black or white neighborhoods. No attempt was made to ensure that black interviewers would interview white respondents, since the majority of professional interviewers are white and same-race interviewing among whites was not regarded as a problem. The most successful group, in terms of obtaining completed listings and completed interviews, were the older white interviewers. This was perhaps not surprising since more experienced interviewers fall within this category than any other. Since the neighborhoods were predominantly black, the results did not support the viewpoint that black interviewers would necessarily gain access more easily to black respondents; nor did the results support the viewpoint that younger respondents would necessarily relate more easily to younger interviewers. The net effect of this test was the conviction that a study of young women could be conducted with the existing professional cadre of experienced interviewers without the need for training a special corps of young and/or black interviewers.

The pretest interview with 406 young women 15-19 years of age was carried out in 3 waves, thereby allowing for minor modifications in the ordering and wording of questions. The results of this (pretest) survey have been reported on elsewhere (Zelnik and Kanter, 1972a). The essential point of this exercise was not the substantive results themselves but the demonstration that young women could be interviewed about their sexual experience, their experience with contraception, and their handling of premarital pregnancy.

THE 1971 AND 1976 SAMPLES

The 1971 Sample

The original study design called for approximately 5000 interviews with females 15-19 years of age living in the continental United States. The respondents were to be selected by two independent national probability samples, the first (and larger) of women living in households and the second of women living in college dormitories. The household sample was to provide equal numbers of interviews with blacks and whites. However, mindful of the difficulties that might be encountered in attempting to interview such a large number of black 15-19-year-old women within a national probability sample, it was decided to carry out the household study in two waves. In the first wave, an attempt would be made to interview 2500 whites, but only 1250 blacks. This first stage was to determine the feasibility for the second stage of black interviews. The first wave was to begin no later than the middle of March (of 1971) and the second wave (if undertaken) was to be completed by no later than the middle of June, so as to minimize the problems of summer vacations.

The 1970 National Fertility Study, the fieldwork for which was carried out by the same organization we used in 1971, was in the field just in front of us. Delays encountered by NFS were passed on to our study, since certain personnel were involved in both surveys. As a result, the fieldwork for the 1971 survey started somewhat later than originally planned. Due to that delay and to various problems that arose during the course of listing households for the first wave, it was not feasible (or even possible) to undertake the second wave. Even with the elimination of the second wave, interviewing continued through the end of June, creating problems we had hoped to bypass. However, the yield from the first wave was greater than anticipated, with a total of 4611 interviews conducted—1479 with blacks and 3132 with whites. The household sample provided 4392 interviews and the college sample 219. The major factor accounting for the difference between the actual and anticipated number of interviews was the high level of coverage of households in the listing stage.

SELECTION OF THE SAMPLE OF HOUSEHOLDS

Selection of the Primary Sampling Unit

For the study, a general-purpose national probability sample was employed which was designed to be representative of all housing units (HUs) in the continental United States and which utilized area sampling methods. In this sample a primary sampling unit (PSU) was defined as an area which included 10,000 HUs in 1960. The PSUs were stratified by census division and by metropolitan-nonmetropolitan character. There were thus 9 strata defined by the 9 census divisions and 6 strata defined by metropolitan-nonmetropolitan character. These 6 strata were:

(1) central cities of standard metropolitan statistical areas (SMSAs) with a population of 1,000,000 or more in 1960
(2) remainders of SMSAs with a population of 1,000,000 or more in 1960
(3) central cities of SMSAs with a population less than 1,000,000 in 1960

Appendix A

(4) remainders of SMSAs with a population less than 1,000,000 in 1960
(5) urban places with a population between 2,500 and 50,000 in 1960 and outside of SMSAs
(6) urban places with a population under 2,500 and rural areas outside of SMSAs

Zones of equal size, namely, 940,000 HUs, were established within each stratum. Each zone comprised 94 equal-sized PSUs of 10,000 HUs. The boundaries of the zones cut across cities, counties, census tracts, blocks, and enumeration districts, but not across strata. None of the last zones of the strata included exactly 940,000 HUs because zones did not cross from one stratum to another. These incomplete zones were filled out with "paper HUs," which were given the same probabilities of selection as real HUs. Within each zone, two selections of PSUs were made so that the probability of selection of a given PSU was $(2 \times 10,000)/940,000 = 1/47$. Overall, 126 PSUs with actually existing HUs were selected. In most zones, two PSUs of 10,000 actual HUs were selected, but there were cases in which one or both of the selected PSUs consisted of less than 10,000 actual HUs in 1960.

Selection of Listing Areas Within Sample PSUs

Each of the 126 sample PSUs was divided into 125 listing areas (LAs) of approximately equal size—that is, 80 HUs based on 1960 census data or paper units in the case of incomplete zones. These LAs all had clearly identifiable boundaries, such as rivers, streets, or railroads, or were combined into a set of LAs which had clear boundaries. Where an area surrounded by clear boundaries included well over 80 HUs in 1960, and could not be subdivided into smaller units with clear boundaries, two or more LAs were combined into a larger cluster.

In each PSU, 16 of the 125 LAs were selected with equal probability of selection and, within each selected LA, all HUs were included in the sample. Where a cluster of LAs was selected, all HUs in the cluster were listed and then subdivided into a set of individual LAs from which one was selected. The overall probability for the selection of HUs was thus $(1/47 \times 16/125) = 1/367.2$. In fact, only blacks in "black" listing areas were selected at this rate (see below). In order to increase the proportion of the sample which was black, whites were subselected at the rate of 1/3.86 (since blacks represented about 11.5 percent of the population but the goal was half the number of interviews with blacks as with whites; thus $[100.0 - 11.5] \times \frac{1}{3.86} = 22.9$, or approximately twice the expected yield of blacks).

Subselection of whites was carried out in three ways: (1) LAs were subselected before HUs were listed; (2) LAs were subselected after HUs were listed; and (3) HUs were subselected within selected LAs after they had been listed. A description of the details of these procedures follows:

Subselection of LAs prior to listing of HUs. An estimate of the racial composition of each selected LA was made using data from two sources, the 1960 census and estimates of the racial composition of nearby LAs selected for a study carried out six months earlier. (Data from the 1970 census were not yet available.) Within each PSU the LAs were divided into two groups—one in which the population was thought to be all white, and another where the population was thought to include at least some blacks or where no reasonable estimate of the racial composition could be made. The LAs that were thought to be all white were then subselected at the rate of 1/3.86. There were 75 PSUs in which all 16 LA were thought to be all white and therefore 4 or 5 of the LAs were subselected in each of these PSUs. There were 15 additional PSUs in which some, but not all, of the LAs were thought to be all white, and this smaller set of "white" LAs were also subselected at the rate of 1/3.86. The other LAs in these 15 PSUs remained in the sample with certainty. All LAs in the remaining 36 PSUs were believed to contain at least some blacks. Therefore, the 16 LAs in each of these 36 PSUs were retained with certainty.

Subselection of LAs after HUs were listed. In all selected LAs (those that were subselected at the rate of 1/3.86 or retained with certainty) interviewers were asked to list all HUs and to estimate the proportion of HUs that were occupied by blacks. In the group of LAs previously retained with certainty, those LAs which the lister thought to be all white were now subselected at the rate of 1/3.86. All LAs still appearing to include at least some blacks were again retained with certainty in the sample.

Subselection of HUs within listed and subselected LAs. There were now 2 sets of LAs remaining in the sample. The first set, referred to as "white" LAs, were those which had been subselected at the rate of 1/3.86 either prior to or subsequent to the listing. These were later found to be about 2.5 percent black. The second set, referred to as "black" LAs, were those in which there had been no subselection. These were found to be about 44 percent black at the time of interviewing.

The first set, "white" LAs, had been selected at the rate of $(1/367.2 \times 1/3.86) = 1/1417.3$ and interviews were attempted with all eligible respondents living in these LAs. The second set of LAs had been selected at the rate of 1/367.2. The whites living in this second set of LAs were then subselected at the rate of 1/3.86 via a simple procedure involving blue and

Appendix A

pink screening forms. Of every 3.86 households in these LAs, one was assigned a pink screening form, while the remaining households were assigned blue forms. Among white females aged 15 to 19, only those found in HUs that had been assigned pink forms were considered to be part of the sample. Black females aged 15 to 19 were considered to be part of the sample whether the screening form was pink or blue.

White households were thus selected at a constant probability of 1/1417.3 whether they were located in LAs including blacks or not. Black households were selected at the rate of 1/367.2 unless they were located in "white" LAs where the probability of selection was 1/1417.3. The introduction of this differential selection is a result of having made subselections of entire LAs. However, subselection of LAs reduced the amount of listing that had to be done by about 50 percent and the number of houses to be contacted by about 60 percent. Had there been no subselection of LAs, the number of black interviews would probably have been increased by about 150 to 200, but, given the time and expense associated with listing households and screening out whites, these would have been extremely costly interviews.

Selection of Respondents Within Households

Within each sample household, all eligible respondents were listed alphabetically by first name, and the person whose first name was earliest in the alphabet was selected as the respondent. Assuming that there is no correlation between the first letter of the first name and any of the study variables, this amounts to a simple random selection of respondents within households.

EVALUATION OF THE SAMPLE OF HOUSEHOLDS

Evaluation of Listing

There were 81,005 listings recorded in the selected LAs, of which 38,154 were in "white" LAs and 42,851 in "black" LAs. For the white LAs, 1.43 percent of the listings were found not to be HUs and for black LAs, 2.83 percent[2] were not HUs, leaving an estimated (38,154 x .987) = 37,610 HUs listed in white LAs and (42,851 x .9717) = 41,638 HUs listed in black LAs. Applying the appropriate sampling fractions, the sample estimate of the number of HUs in the continental United States is (37,610 x 1,417.3) + (41,638 x 367.2) = 68.59 million, which is quite close to the 68.37 million HUs counted in the 1970 census.

Again, based on HUs where at least one contact was made, and subtracting listings for non-HUs, 7.84 percent of the HUs in white LAs and 6.54 percent of the HUs in black LAs were found to be vacant, leaving 34,658 occupied HUs in white LAs and 38,915 occupied HUs in black

LAs. Applying the appropriate sampling fractions, the sample estimate of the number of occupied HUs in the continental United States is (34,658 x 1,417.3) + (38,915 x 367.2) = 63.41 million. This is a close approximation of the 1970 census count of 63.17 million occupied HUs. The sample estimate and census count of the vacancy rate are 7.55 percent and 7.61 percent, respectively.

Assuming a small increase in households between the date of the census count and the study date, the enumeration of households appears to have been quite accurate.

Evaluation of the Listing of Household Residents

The estimates presented in the preceding section indicate that the sample of households was listed adequately. The second and more difficult statement of coverage is the enumeration of all eligible respondents living within the sample households. In a study such as this, where a large proportion of households does not include an eligible respondent, this is often problematic, particularly where screening is on the basis of a variable, such as age, which cannot be observed by the interviewer. The evaluation of this stage is done here separately for blacks and whites.

There were 1,268,697 black females aged 14 through 18 living in the continental United States at the time of the 1970 census. Assuming that mortality and migration among this group is minimal, this is approximately the number of blacks in the study population, that is, aged 15-19, in the spring of 1971 when interviewing was done.

As of the 1970 census, 96 percent of black females 15-19 living in the continental United States were living in households. The estimate, therefore, of the number of study-eligible black females living in households is (1,268,697 x .96) = 1,217,949. In the sample, the average number of eligible blacks found in households in which a black respondent was interviewed was 1.265. Therefore, an estimate of the number of black households including an eligible is (1,217,949 ÷ 1.265) = 962,806. This figure is 15.59 percent of the total number of black households (962,806/6,176,540). From the study sample data, the estimate of black households including an eligible respondent is 11.07 percent,[3] or 71 percent of the estimate from census data (that is, 11.07/15.59).

The estimated undercount of households including eligible whites was smaller. There were 8,331,349 white females aged 14 through 18 in the continental United States at the time of the 1970 census. Since 7 percent of the white females 15-19 years of age were not living in households, the estimate of the number of white females 15-19 years of age living in households at the time of the study is (8,331,349 x .93) = 7,748,154. In the sample the average number of eligible respondents found in white households was 1.160. Therefore, an estimate of the number of households including a white eligible is (7,748,154 ÷ 1.160) = 6,679,444, which

TABLE A.1 Percentage of Distribution of Females 15-19 Years of Age: Household Sample and Census Estimate

Age	White		Black	
	Sample	Census	Sample	Census
15	22.2	22.1	24.3	22.4
16	23.3	21.8	23.6	21.6
17	23.8	21.1	21.2	20.3
18	16.4	17.9	18.0	18.3
19	14.3	17.1	12.8	17.4

is 11.72 percent of all white households (6,679,444/56,991,060). The sample estimate of the proportion of white households including an eligible is 9.94 percent, or 85 percent of the figure estimated from census data (that is, 9.94/11.72).

Eligible respondents within sample households thus appear to have been underenumerated, and more so for blacks than for whites. A comparison of the household sample and census distribution of eligibles[4] is given in Table A.1. By contrast with the census, 18- and 19-year-old survey respondents are deficient. These are ages of increased mobility, when contacts become more difficult. For the census it is sufficient that a report *about* household members be obtained; for the survey an actual contact was required.

Completion Rates

In this section overall completion rates are calculated in the standard manner by determining the proportion of eligible respondents who in fact provided completed interviews. For blacks, the proportion of actual interviews among identified eligibles is 89.34 percent, and for whites, 83.45 percent. This difference between black and white success rates is largely accounted for by refusal rates. The proportion of blacks who refused an interview (including refusal by eligibles or others) was 7.19 percent of the households in which an eligible was identified. For whites, the corresponding figure is 11.02 percent. This is generally consistent with survey experience, in that blacks have been found to be somewhat more cooperative than whites at the interview stage, once screening information has been obtained and eligible respondents have been located. In addition, the eligible not-at-home rate was twice as great for whites (4.25 percent) as for blacks (2.17 percent).

These figures (83.45 percent for whites and 89.34 percent for blacks) are success rates in interviewing enumerated eligibles. However, since there were some potential eligible respondents who were not enumerated, the figures are overestimates of true completion rates. That is, it is necessary to adjust these rates by estimating, and then taking into account, the proportion of those with nondetermined eligibility who would probably have been eligible.

Because no contact was made with an eligible respondent in these cases, or at least no determination was made as to whether there was an eligible respondent, it is necessary to make assumptions in accounting for the potential "yield" from the several close-out categories. On the basis of these assumptions, the proportion of identified eligibles to estimated total eligibles is 95.14 percent for blacks and 88.13 percent for whites. The largest single factor accounting for the difference between the two figures is no-contact households. That is, there were proportionately more white households than black households that interviewers never contacted. There are several reasons for this difference. First, the no-contacts were largely due to the fact that interviewing was halted because of time constraints before interviewers had completed their assignments. Special efforts had been made to complete listing of HUs in black areas first because of anticipated difficulties with those listings. In addition, some white areas had grown considerably since 1960 and required more extensive listing procedures, so that actual interviewing assignments were delayed.

In order to adjust the original completion rates which were calculated on the basis of known eligibles, it is only necessary to multiply those rates by the estimated eligibility proportions given above, that is, (.8934 x .9514) = .8500 for blacks and (.8345 x .8813) = .7354 for whites. The difference between these completion rates and the unadjusted completion rates is due to the effect of non-contacted households, which were more frequent in white than in black areas.

THE COLLEGE DORMITORY SAMPLE

Selection of the Sample

Selection of the college dormitory sample[5] proceeded in four stages, as follows:

Redefining and selecting PSUs. The PSUs, as used in selecting the household sample, were redefined to coincide with county and SMSA boundaries. If a PSU in the household sample was located in one county or SMSA, then that county or SMSA became the PSU for the purposes of selecting the college sample. This was done in order to accurately place colleges and universities in PSUs. The measure of size of a redefined PSU was the number of housing units enumerated in the 1960 census. Just as there were 126 selections of PSUs in the household sample, there were 126 selections of the redefined PSUs in the college sample. Redefined PSUs in which more than one household sample PSU had been selected were correspondingly selected more than once in the college sample.

It was estimated that 200 interviews would be conducted with college women if they were selected at the same rates with which young women in the household sample were selected. If 20 women were interviewed per selected university, then 10 universities were needed in the sample. It was estimated that 10 such universities with women living in dormitories or sorority houses could be easily found in a subselected group of 18 PSUs. Therefore, the set of 126 selections was subselected at the rate of 1 in 7.

Selection of colleges within PSUs. The colleges in each of the selected PSUs were then listed and selected with equal probability, except that if the college was predominantly black it was selected at twice the rate. The overall probability of selection of a given college, if the college was not predominantly black, was 1/164.5. If the college was predominantly black, the probability of selection was 2/164.5. Only one predominantly black university was selected.

Selection of dormitories and sorority houses. Interviewers were sent to the selected colleges and universities to obtain lists of all dormitories and sorority houses and estimates of the numbers of rooms in which 15-19-year-old females might be found. The dormitories and sorority houses were then assigned a measure of size, which was the estimated number of rooms in which a 15-19 year old was living. The dormitories and sorority houses were listed and selected systematically, with an expected 20 rooms to be subsequently selected per dormitory or sorority house.[6]

Selection of rooms and respondents within dormitories. For each selection of a particular dormitory or sorority house, a cluster of an expected size of 20 rooms was selected. The probability of selection of a given room in a selected university was 1/8.62 and the overall probability of selection of a given room was (1/164.5 x 1/8.62) = 1/1418.0 ~ 1/1417.3. For predominantly black universities, the probability of selection of a given room from a selected university was 1/4.47 and the overall probability of selection was (2/164.5 x 1/4.47) = 1/367.7 ~ 1/367.2. In this manner, 15 dormitories and sorority houses were selected from 8 colleges and universities.

Within the dormitories, 1 eligible was selected per room. There were 357 eligibles, an average of 1.63 per room in the 219 rooms where an eligible respondent was interviewed.

EVALUATION OF THE COLLEGE DORMITORY SAMPLE

Almost all eligible respondents who were contacted were interviewed in the college sample. A total of 219 interviews were obtained in 224 attempts, giving a success rate of 97.8 percent. There were 3 refusals, 1 case where the eligible was never home, and one noninterview for "other" reasons. There were also 6 vacancies and 157 rooms where there was no eligible. The high response rate is consistent with general survey experience in interviewing students, who are usually quite willing to be interviewed once they are contacted.

Inflating the sample counts by the inverses of the appropriate sampling fractions and by the average number of eligibles per room, we get a sample estimate of 15-19-year-old white and 15-19-year-old black females in college dormitories and sororities. Based on the data of the 1970 census, we estimate that the number of women 15-19 years of age living in college dormitories and sororities in 1971 was slightly larger than the inflated sample estimate in the case of whites and slightly smaller in the case of blacks.

WEIGHTING OF THE SAMPLE CASES

Since blacks were overrepresented in the sample, any attempt to provide estimates of the relevant aspects of behavior for the total population aged 15-19 would require some form of weighting of the sample cases. Since a reasonably close approximation to the census count was important for making the kinds of comparisons we present in the fifth section of Appendix B, we decided to calculate the sample weights from the 1970 census counts of young women aged 14-18, that is, those who were aged 15-19 at the time of the 1971 survey. The census data were compiled, by single years of age and race, for each of the strata underlying the sample— the 9 census divisions and within each division by the metropolitan-nonmetropolitan classification given above. In the latter instance we did not attempt to distinguish between urban places and rural areas outside of SMSAs, but rather combined them. Thus, we compiled census counts for 45 strata, rather than for 54.

In compiling the data, Alaska and Hawaii were excluded and SMSAs were defined by 1960 standards. Further, no attempt was made to distinguish between household population and college dormitory population or between the latter and the remainder of the group quarters plus the institutional population. In effect, we used the total population. The task of separating out the household population and the college dormitory and sorority house population was not possible at that time nor was it thought to be essential. Almost all young women live in households, with the bulk

Appendix A

of those not in households living in college dormitories and sorority houses.

With the census data compiled by single years of age and race for each of the 45 strata and the sample cases similarly identified, dividing the former by the latter would give the (average) weight for each cell in the matrix. However, some cells had very few cases. Instead of computing weights based on very small numbers of sample cases, certain cells were combined. Among blacks all census divisions, with the exception of South Atlantic, were combined. Within the non-South Atlantic grouping a further combination eliminated the difference based on size of SMSA for the population living outside of central cities, that is, in remainder of SMSAs. And lastly, 18- and 19-year-old blacks in remainder of SMSAs outside of South Atlantic were combined. Among whites, New England and Middle Atlantic were combined into one unit, as were South Atlantic, East South Central, and West South Central. No further combinations were necessary for whites.

The 1976 Sample

The study design called for approximately 2500 interviews with females 15-19 years of age living in households (HUs) in the continental United States. The sample was to yield 800 interviews with black females and 1700 interviews with white females. Respondents were to be selected by a general-purpose national probability sample designed to be representative of all HUs (in the continental United States) and which utilized area sampling methods. As in 1971, only one eligible was to be selected (randomly) per HU and the only criterion of eligibility was age. Interviewing was to begin in March and to be completed by the first week of June; however, the fieldwork progressed somewhat more slowly than anticipated and interviewing continued through most of June. The final yield of 2193 completed interviews—702 with blacks and 1491 with whites—was 88 percent of the desired number. Even if all funds available for fieldwork had not been exhausted by then, stretching the interviewing into July was undesirable.

SELECTION OF THE SAMPLE OF HOUSEHOLDS

The Primary Sample

The sampling frame used to identify sampling areas for the 1976 survey consisted of 1675 primary sampling units (PSUs) based on data from the 1970 census. These PSUs were defined as: (1) entire SMSAs which were either self-representing (SR) or non-self-representing (NSR) SMSAs lying within a single census division; (2) that portion of an SMSA located within the boundaries of a single census division; and (3) counties or groups of continguous counties outside of SMSAs. All SMSAs remained intact as a single PSU unless the SMSA crossed census division boundaries, in which case the SMSA pieces in different divisions were defined as separate SMSA PSUs.[7] The non-SMSA PSUs were composed of single nonmetropolitan counties that had a 1970 population of at least 20,000. Those counties which did not meet this minimum size requirement were combined with one or more contiguous nonmetropolitan counties until the minimum size requirement was met.

The primary sample consisted of 100 distinct PSUs selected from the 1675 PSUs in the sampling frame. The 16 largest SMSAs, defined as SR PSUs, were selected with certainty. The other 84 PSUs were selected from the remaining SMSAs and nonmetropolitan counties after first grouping them into 42 primary strata based on census regions and divisions, metropolitan-nonmetropolitan character, and size of community characteristics.

The NSR PSUs were first stratified by the 4 census regions. Within each region, PSUs were further stratified as either metropolitan (SMSA) or nonmetropolitan (non-SMSA). The 2-way stratification of PSUs by the 4 census regions and metropolitan-nonmetropolitan categories defined 8 basic NSR strata. The PSUs within these basic strata were then ordered in specific manners.[8] The 2-way stratification and controlled ordering of the NSR PSUs were used to ensure geographic dispersion of the sample and to maximize the homogeneity of PSUs within primary strata.

The final step in the primary stratification process involved dividing each of the 8 basic strata into from 2 to 8 final strata, to form a total of 42 final primary strata of approximately equal size (that is, 1970 population of approximately 3 1/3 million). Two sample PSUs were then selected from each of the 42 final NSR primary strata. The sample PSUs were selected with probabilities proportional to 1970 population and without replacement.

The Secondary Sample

The next step was to form a secondary sampling frame of smaller areas, called secondary sampling units (SSUs), for the area covered by each of the 100 PSUs. Census enumeration districts (EDs) and block groups (BGs) were used to define SSUs. Each ED/BG was given a unique residence code, depending on where the majority of its household population was residing. The codes were defined as follows:

for metropolitan PSUs

1 = inner city of the central city of an SMSA[9]
2 = remainder of the central city of an SMSA
3 = urban area outside the central city of an SMSA
4 = rural area of an SMSA

for nonmetropolitan PSUs

3 = urban area
4 = rural area

After the residence codes were assigned, the elements in the frame were arranged in a specified order before making the final stratification. This ordering was completed independently within each of the PSUs. Once the ordering in a PSU had been completed, secondary strata were defined. A total of 960 SSUs was to be selected for the national sample, with two SSUs to be selected in each secondary stratum. Thus, 480 secondary strata were to be defined. Within each of the 84 NSR PSUs, 4 secondary strata of approximately equal numbers of household population were defined, accounting for 336 of the 480 secondary strata. This left 144 secondary strata to be defined in the 16 SR PSUs. These 144 secondary strata were allocated to the 16 SR PSUs in proportion to their household population. From each of the 480 secondary strata, 2 SSUs were selected with probabilities proportional to their household populations and with replacement.

The Third-Stage Sample

The third-stage sample involved the selection of HUs from the SSUs so as to yield a projected total of 2500 interviews with young women 15-19 years of age, with blacks to be oversampled in order to yield 800 interviews. The subcontracting organization responsible for the fieldwork was also under contract (with another investigator) to conduct a household survey of 1500 ever-married white women born from 1900 to 1910. It was decided to combine the screening effort for the 2 samples, each of which was in search of a relatively rare population. Procedures were developed to minimize the number of household screenings needed to meet the sample size requirements of both surveys while simultaneously maintaining acceptable levels of precision.

A total of 4 superstrata of SSUs were formed which combined SSUs with especially high concentrations of the respective target populations. The first stratum contained those SSUs that were relatively rich in older white females per occupied HU. This stratum contained 114 SSUs. The second superstratum contained 170 SSUs rich in young white women per occupied HU. The third superstratum contained 63 SSUs with a relatively high concentration of young black females per occupied HU. The fourth superstratum contained 613 SSUs, the remainder of the 960 SSUs.

An iterative procedure was developed to allocate among the four superstrata the number of households (that is, screenings) required to obtain the desired sample sizes for the three populations of interest while simultaneously controlling the precision (that is, variance) for the three populations. The procedure involved an assumed response rate of 0.75 and assumptions about the average number of eligibles per household having at least one eligible,[10] since only one eligible per household was to be selected.

The number of households allocated to each superstratum by the iterative procedure was divided by the average number of households per SSU to determine the actual number of SSUs in each superstratum needed for the survey. This assumed the (random) selection of 1 area segment, having an average size of 33 households, per SSU. The number of SSUs in the third stratum (high concentration of young black females) was not adequate to accommodate the sample allocation on the assumption of 1 area segment per SSU. Therefore, additional area segments were assigned from a predetermined random ordering of similar area segments defined within the 63 SSUs of stratum 3. At the same time, the number of SSUs available in strata 2 and 4 were sufficiently larger than the required number to permit subsampling of the SSUs in those strata. These various procedures led to defining 982 unique area segments in 813 SSUs.

COMPLETION RATES

A total of 26,036 units were listed during the course of the survey. Of these, 2,783 (10.7 percent) were found to be vacant or structures not meeting the definition of "housing unit." Of the remaining 23,253 occupied HUs, 22,290 (95.9 percent) were screened and 2,732 were found to contain an eligible; 1,875 were white households and 857 were black. Overall, 2,193 eligibles were interviewed, for a success rate of 80.3 percent, with little difference between blacks and whites—702 interviews with blacks (81.9 percent) and 1,491 with whites (79.5 percent). the bulk of the noninterviews (76.0 percent) resulted from refusals by the eligible or, in about equal number, by the parent. Presumably, the need for signed parental consent for eligibles less than 18 years old had an adverse effect on the response rate. However, it is possible that in some households where the parent refused to give permission the eligible would also have refused. It is also possible that some eligibles refused in anticipation of parental refusal.

The rates given above refer to identified eligibles. However, some eligibles were not identified in those HUs that were not screened (there were 963 occupied HUs that were not screened). If we assume that households containing an eligible in the unscreened HUs were in the same proportion by race as the screened HUs with eligibles, then the completion rate for whites is 76.2 percent, and for blacks, 78.5 percent. The figure for whites in 1976 is slightly higher than was achieved in 1971 (73.5 percent), whereas for blacks the 1976 rate is lower than the 1971 figure (85.0 percent).

WEIGHTING OF THE SAMPLE CASES

Weighting of the 1976 sample cases involved the same consideration underlying the procedures used with the 1971 study—namely, to produce inflated sample estimates that closely approximated, by race, the best available estimate of the population that was sampled, that is, females aged 15-19 living in households in the continental United States. In this instance, the best available estimate of the sampled population was provided by the March 1976 Current Population Survey (U. S. Department of Commerce, 1977a).

The single-year age distribution provided by the July 1976 CPS (U. S. Department of Commerce, 1977b) made it possible to estimate the number of women aged 15-17 among the age group 14-17 as of March. Adjustments were then made to the age groups 15-17 and 18-19 for the populations of Alaska and Hawaii and for women living in group quarters. Those adjustments were based on percentage distributions from the 1970 census. The final estimates of women 15-17 and 18-19 years of age, by race and marital status, living in households in the continental United States were used to inflate the sample counts.

NOTES

1. Experience 9 years later with a national survey of young males (and females) suggests that an incentive, in this case $5.00, may be crucial to securing a high completion rate. Thus, the experience of 1970 merely means that for young women,

at that time and for that value received, there was no percentage to be gained through incentives.

2. The 1.43 and 2.83 percents are based on total listings where at least one contact was made.

3. This percentage is based on those households in which definite information was obtained with respect to eligibility.

4. This distribution is based on census counts of females 14-18 years of age in 1970 and the proportions at each age 15-19 in 1970 living in households.

5. College students living in households were eligible for selection in the household sample.

6. A large dormitory had a chance of being selected more than once, in which case another cluster of rooms was selected in that dormitory.

7. In New England, SMSAs, defined by the Bureau of the Census in terms of minor civil divisions, were redefined in terms of counties.

8. The PSUs of each metropolitan-region stratum were ordered, within each division of the region, by 1970 total population; the PSUs of each nonmetropolitan region stratum were ordered, within each division, by the 1970 proportion of the population residing in rural areas.

9. Inner-city areas were defined as low-income or poverty areas in the 65 largest SMSAs—those with a 1970 population of 500,000 or more.

10. These values, for blacks and for whites, were taken from the 1971 survey.

APPENDIX B:
METHODOLOGY AND VALIDITY ISSUES

CONSENT PROCEDURES

Federal regulations pertaining to the protection of the rights of human volunteers participating in research projects were slightly less demanding in 1971 than in 1976. At the former date we were required to get "informed consent" from the eligible respondent (and her parent or guardian where the eligible was less than 18 years of age) before the interview could proceed. Informed consent consisted of verbal approval to the interview after the interviewer informed the eligible (and, where required, the parent) of the nature and purpose of the study, the types of questions that would be asked, that a participant could refuse to answer any question and could terminate the interview at any point, and that all answers would be held in confidence and used only in statistical summaries. The interviewer conveyed this information by reading a form letter that we had prepared; where requested, the respondent (and/or parent) was given the letter to read to herself.

By 1976, the requirements specified that informed *signed* consent be obtained from the eligible (and her parent or guardian where the eligible was less than 18 years of age) before the interview could proceed. In each instance a letter was given to the eligible specifying essentially the same information listed above; the letter, printed on carbonized paper, had to be signed by the eligible, the original retained by her and the copy returned to the interviewer. To assure good faith on the part of the interviewer, she also signed the letter, following a printed pledge to keep all answers confidential. A similar procedure was followed in obtaining signed consent from the parents. Given the nature of the study, general interviewing procedures required that the interview be conducted in private; this requirement was implicit in the 1971 consent letter but explicit in the 1976 consent letter. The form letter used in the 1971 survey and the consent forms used in the 1976 survey are available from the authors.

DIFFERENCES BETWEEN THE TWO STUDIES

Age Eligibility

The only criterion used to determine whether a female was eligible to be included in either survey (aside from sampling procedures to assure the desired oversampling of blacks) was age.[1] However, the definition of age differed slightly between the two surveys. In the 1976 survey, age eligibility was based on having been born between March 1956 and February 1961, with those born between March 1956 and February 1957 classified in the study as "currently" age 19, those born between March 1957 and February 1958 as "currently" age 18, and so on. As a result, respondents selected for the survey represented exactly 60 months of births. Since interviewing occurred over a 4-month span, starting in March, events occurring shortly before the interview could have occurred at an age greater than the respondent's "current" age. For example, a respondent born in March 1956 is classified in the study as "current age 19." If such a respondent were interviewed any time after March 1976, by which time she would have turned age 20, any event occurring after March 1976 would have occurred at age 20, although to a person classified as age 19. Such inconsistencies can occur only for those respondents whose birth dates fall in the earlier months of the years as here bounded.

In 1971, those eligible for inclusion in the study were young women who were 15 through 19 years of age (at last birthday) at the time of screening. In most instances interviewing occurred immediately after screening. However, screening occurred over a 3- to 4-month interval, beginning in March. As a result, respondents included in the 1971 study represented more than 60 months of births. Survey or "current" age was determined as age last birthday as of May 1971, the approximate midpoint of screening activities. To the degree that interviewing followed screening with no delay, no event could occur to a respondent at an age greater than the current age. Such an occurrence was possible only in those exceptional situations where interviewing was delayed.

Obviously, either way of determining age eligibility has problems attached to it, given the impossibility of conducting all screening and interviewing in some very short span of time. For the most part the problems are minimal and, while the two studies are not strictly comparable in respect to age, we regard the difference as of little consequence. In effect, the two studies represent ten consecutive cohorts, that is, those born between March 1951 and February 1961.

Appendix B

Data on Household and Head of Household

Information about the respondent's household and about the head of that household was collected in both surveys for inclusion in an index of socioeconomic status. In 1971 such information was collected from the respondent in the course of the interview. The relevant questions included the (usual) occupation of the head of the household, total family income, and monthly rental or selling price of the house. In the case of family income, monthly rental, and selling price of house,[2] sizable proportions of the sample reported they did not know the amounts, but probings and requests to "take a guess" or to give "your best estimate" resulted in many providing an answer. Although we had no definitive way to check on the quality of the data, subsequent consideration of them suggested that both the outright responses and the "guesstimates" were of relatively poor quality. That most young women do not know total family income or selling price of a house does not strike us as surprising.

To try to improve the quality of data about the household and the head of the household for the 1976 survey, it was decided that the relevant questions would be asked not of the respondent but of the head of the household, and a short questionnaire was designed for this purpose. The interviewers were instructed to conduct the interview whenever possible with the person designated as the head of the household; failing that, second choice was to be some other adult member of the household (anticipated to be, in most instances, the spouse of the head). Only in those instances where it was not possible to obtain the information from the head or other adult member of the household was the interviewer to obtain the information from the (teenage) respondent.[3]

About 27 percent of the household questionnaires were completed by the head of the household, 38 percent by the spouse, 33 percent by the (teenage) respondent, and 2 percent by some other member of the household. Comparison of such items as household income, monthly rental, and selling price of house revealed differences in the distributions by type of informant. While such differences may in fact be real we have no a priori reasons for believing that households where the head is the informant actually differ from households where the spouse is the informant. In addition, the unexpectedly large proportion of household questionnaires completed by the teenage respondents in 1976 leads one to suspect that the part of the field protocol calling for contact with an adult member of the household was not diligently pursued. Here again, however, empirically based judgments about the quality of these data are hard to make.

As a result of these various concerns and our desire for a measure of SES that would include the same components for the two surveys, family income and value (or rent) of the house have not been included in our index of SES. Rather, we have relied on education of the person or persons who raised the respondent. Experimentation with a prestige score for the household head's occupation proved disappointing as a useful measure of general social status. The noncomparability between the occupation of older household heads and younger heads,[4] who were often in transitional phases of their occupational careers, was a major factor in leading us to abandon the use of occupational prestige scores in the construction of a general index of SES.[5]

The Determination of Premarital Events Among the Ever Married

We have, in other sections of this book, dealt with the quality of the responses to the various questions asked in the two surveys. Important in this respect are the results of the (1971) reliability reinterview, the use (in 1976) of the randomized response technique (RRT) as a way of testing the validity of responses to the direct question on sexual intercourse, and the comparisons (at both dates) of various estimates derived from survey data with independent, external sets of data. Our purpose here is to describe the differences in the procedures used in the two surveys to determine whether an ever-married respondent had had premarital intercourse and, for those with a pregnancy, whether it had occurred before or after marriage. We will also describe differences in our ability to determine whether there was premarital use of contraception among the ever married in the two surveys who were premaritally sexually active and in our ability to determine their premarital patterns of contraceptive use.

The differences alluded to stem largely from the use in 1971 of a self-administered questionnaire (SAQ) containing a fairly simple set of questions relating to sex and contraception, as contrasted to the use in 1976 of an interviewer-administered questionnaire with a fairly detailed series of questions on these subjects. The SAQ was completed by the respondent after an interviewer-administered questionnaire had been completed. Thus, in the interviewer-administered part of the 1971 survey, before any questions were asked about intercourse, all respondents were asked if they had ever been pregnant. It should also be noted that only one version of the SAQ was used and the questions themselves made no distinction between pre- and postmarital events. In 1976, separate questionnaires were used for the never married and the ever married. Only those never-married respondents who reported that they had had sexual intercourse were subsequently asked if they had ever been pregnant. For the ever married, the questions on pregnancy preceded questions on sex and contraception, all of which referred to events before (first) marriage.

The greater number and detail of the questions asked in 1976 also means, of course, that we have more information on the sexual and contraceptive histories of the never-married respondents in that survey than we do for the never-married respondents in the 1971 survey. The pregnancy history used in 1976 was also somewhat more detailed than the one used in 1971.

PREMARITAL SEX AND PREMARITAL PREGNANCY

In 1976, the various questions provided, in a fairly straightforward manner, information on premarital intercourse and premarital conceptions among the ever married.[6] In 1971, however, important items, such as whether intercourse had occurred prior to marriage, date of first intercourse, and number of months duration of (first) pregnancy, were missing. In the case of premarital intercourse, one group of the ever married presented no problem of determination, namely, those who reported having had intercourse at an age prior to age at first marriage. A second group, the ever married whose age at first intercourse was the same as their age at first marriage, did present a problem, in that it was not possible from this information alone to determine if first intercourse had preceded or followed marriage. Information contained in or derived from the pregnancy histories indicated that at least some of the ever married whose age at first intercourse was the same as their age at first marriage had, in fact, had intercourse before marriage. This information, then, under some rather arbitrary rules (summarized in Figure B.1), was used in determining which of these respondents should be classified as having had intercourse before marriage.

There are several weak spots in the procedures used to determine whether or not premarital intercourse had occurred among those ever-married women with an age at first intercourse equal to age at marriage. Some of the women who had never been pregnant doubtless had intercourse prior to marriage. However, all such women are assumed to have had intercourse only after marriage. Some pregnancies of 8 or more months duration from time of marriage could have been conceived prior to marriage, or nonimpregnating intercourse could have occurred before marriage. Some births occurring less than 8 months after marriage could have been conceived after marriage (although, again, intercourse could still have preceded marriage). Similar arguments could be advanced for the other pregnancy outcomes. It is likely that the net bias introduced by these rules runs in the direction of underestimating the extent of premarital intercourse among ever-married women. However, the net bias in the estimate of the prevalence of premarital intercourse in the total population, although in the same direction, is likely to be fairly small, since the women to whom these rules apply represent only a small fraction of the total population.

Premarital Intercourse	Not Premarital Intercourse
1. Age first intercourse < age first marriage	1. n. a.
2. Age first intercourse = age first marriage and:	2. Age first intercourse = Age first marriage and:
a. n. a.	a. Never pregnant
b. Ever pregnant and:	b. Ever pregnant and:
Live birth ≤7 months after marriage	Live birth >8 months after marriage
Stillbirth <7 months after marriage	Stillbirth >8 months after marriage
Miscarriage ≤2 months after marriage	Miscarriage ≥3 months after marriage
Currently pregnant (first) due ≤8 months after marriage	Currently pregnant (first) due ≥9 months after marriage

Figure B.1 Determination of Premarital Intercourse Among the Ever Married, 1971

For ever-married women whose age at first intercourse was the same as age at first marriage, the procedure followed to determine premarital intercourse status simultaneously provided the women who had had premarital intercourse and those with premarital pregnancies. To determine premarital pregnancies that occurred to ever-married women whose age at first intercourse preceded age at first marriage, the same rules regarding the timing of conception vis-à-vis the date of marriage were applied where necessary. Obviously, no set of rules regarding premarital conception was needed for the ever married whose first pregnancies terminated prior to first marriage.

It is difficult to assess the direction of net error in the estimation of the prevalence of premarital pregnancy. Some pregnancies judged to have occurred before marriage could in fact have occurred after marriage, and some judged to have occurred after marriage could have occurred before. Whatever the direction of error, it is likely that the amount of error is smaller than the error in the estimate of premarital intercourse.

PREMARITAL USE OF CONTRACEPTION

The questions in 1976 refer only to contraceptive use before marriage, ask for specific dates of use or nonuse, and, in part, relate use or nonuse to certain specified acts of intercourse. The flow of questions makes it possible to categorize ever-married respondents by whether they always, sometimes, or never used contraception before marriage, and, for those who experienced a pregnancy, we can determine whether contraception had always, sometimes, or never been used prior to the pregnancy. We know how many used contraception at first intercourse and how many used at last (premarital) intercourse and we can relate last nonuse to first and last use—that is, whether last nonuse preceded first use, came between first and last use, or came after last use.

Unlike the questions asked in 1976, those asked in 1971 are few in number, do not distinguish between pre- or postmarital events or use, are not related to specified acts of intercourse, and allow for a general rather than specific answer on first use, that is, age rather than date. As a result, the best we can accomplish for the ever married in 1971 is a simple classification of ever or never used contraception (prior to marriage). Even that classification scheme required some judgmental decisions for those cases in which age of first use of contraception was equal to age at first marriage. Each of these cases was carefully reviewed and a decision made, on the basis of the totality of information about reproductive behavior, whether first use preceded or followed marriage. Involved in the decision was the month (and year) of the respondent's birth, the month (and year) of her marriage, the date of outcome of pregnancies (and the inferred date of conception), whether contraception was being used when pregnancy occurred, the number and type of contraceptives ever used, and so on. Although all decisions are judgmental, and may be in error, for the most part the evidence "clearly suggested" how the respondent should be classified. It should be noted also that such decisions were required for a relatively small number of the ever married.

RESPONSE CONSISTENCY

While much concern has been expressed about the quality of data collected in social surveys, especially large-scale national surveys, relatively little has been done to determine what the problematic areas are or to ascertain levels of reliability. One major effort to measure reliability was carried out in conjunction with the 1965 National Fertility Survey (Ryder and Westoff, 1971).[7] A probability subsample of the women interviewed in the course of that study were subsequently reinterviewed on about 60 percent of the questions asked in the original interview. The results of that investigation revealed relatively little inconsistency at the aggregate level (that is, inconsistency as measured by a comparison of the distributions of responses to the same question in the interview and reinterview among those respondents in both interviews) but considerable inconsistency at the individual level of response (that is, inconsistency as measured by a comparison of the responses of each respondent to the same question in the interview and in the reinterview). As might have been expected, behavioral items in general showed lower levels of inconsistency than attitudinal items, but even behavioral items showed fairly high degrees of inconsistency at the individual level of response.

The design of the 1971 study of young women also called for a reliability reinterview among a probability subsample of the original respondents. Reinterviews were attempted with 331 black respondents and 348 white respondents; however, only 267 black reinterviews and 258 white reinterviews were successfully completed.[8] Reinterviews occurred anywhere from one to four and a half months after the original interview. Most reinterviews were conducted by a different interviewer than the one who conducted the original interview. The reinterview questionnaire was a much shortened version of the original interview schedule and included only 29 items, some of which, however, had more than one part.

Our concern here is not with the consistency or inconsistency of actual responses, but rather with the consistency of "blips" on magnetic tape. Differences can and do arise not only because of differing responses, but also from various processing errors, such as recording errors, editing errors, punching errors, and so on. Some differences in response may reflect an actual behavioral or attitudinal change between the two interviews.

Finally, there are the unreliable responses, where the difference is due neither to a processing error nor to a real change in behavior or attitude.

Attempts at measuring reliability or consistency require that the wording of each question in the reinterview schedule be identical to the wording of the (comparable) question used in the original interview (although presumably the number of questions and the flow pattern or ordering of questions, which might differ between the interview and the reinterview, could also have some effect on consistency). Unfortunately, in the present instance the questions included in the reinterview schedule were inadvertently taken from a preliminary version of the interview schedule. As a result, some of the questions asked in the reinterview were slightly different in wording and/or response categories from the comparable questions actually asked in the original interview. For example, in the original interview the question on religious affiliation was, "What is your religion, if any?" whereas the counterpart question in the reinterview was, "Are you Protestant, Catholic, Jewish or what?" Interestingly, however, questions with slightly different forms of wording and/or response categories do not exhibit uniformly higher—or lower—levels of inconsistency than other questions that are identical in wording and response categories.

The methods used here for examining consistency at the aggregate and individual levels differ from those of Ryder and Westoff. As they note:

> It is no simple matter to devise a satisfactory measure of individual inconsistency. Obviously, the proportion giving a different response is not satisfactory, since this proportion is reduced by any tendency for random correspondence [Ryder and Westoff, 1971: 360].

In effect, the observed or apparent level of consistency, represented by the proportion of cases on the main diagonal of a cross-tabulation of responses to the comparable question in the interview and in the reinterview, overstates the "true" level of consistency to the degree that some responses are consistent by chance.[9] To correct for chance or random agreement between responses, Ryder and Westoff use as their measure of individual consistency $M = (1-O)/(1-E)$, where O is the observed proportion giving the same response and E is the expected proportion giving the same response under random conditions.

This measure presumably gives the total proportion responding randomly, whether consistently or otherwise. The measure M assumes a symmetric matrix of responses and is inapplicable or undefined if the matrix is asymmetric; however, an asymmetric matrix of responses implies a "significant" amount of individual inconsistency.[10] Thus, before examining individual inconsistency it is first necessary to determine which of the response matrices are symmetric. For this reason we have reversed the order of Ryder and Westoff's analysis and look first at aggregate inconsistency.

Ryder and Westoff, in effect, equate aggregate consistency of response with "marginal homogeneity" of the response distributions on the first and second interviews. With the model P and data X given by

$$P = \frac{p_{ij} \mid p_{i.}}{p_{.j} \mid 1} \quad \text{and} \quad X = \frac{x_{ij} \mid x_{i.}}{x_{.j} \mid N = \Sigma\Sigma x_{ij}} \quad ; i = 1, \ldots, n; j = 1, \ldots, n$$

the question is whether or not X is consistent with the hypothesis that $p_{i.} = p_{.i}$ for $i = 1, \ldots, n$. Ryder and Westoff suggest as a measure of aggregate inconsistency

$$m = \frac{\sum_{i=1}^{n} /x_{1.} - x_{.1}/}{2N}$$

Although $\Sigma/p_{i.} - p_{.i}/$ is an obvious and well-accepted measure of the difference between two probability distributions, the fact that the marginals are correlated (since the diagonal elements p_{ii} appear in both $p_{i.}$ and $p_{.i}$) makes its use here questionable. In addition, sampling properties of the data matrix X relative to the measure m do not appear to have been worked out.

Although there is available a test of the hypothesis of marginal homogeneity, the procedure requires the iterative maximum likelihood estimation of the cell probabilities $\hat{p}_{ij}$ from the data. Because this is fairly involved, an alternative is to test for symmetry of the model, that is, $H_o: p_{ij} = p_{ji}$ for all pairs i,j. Symmetry implies marginal homogeneity, but is more restrictive except for n = z, where the two are equivalent.

A simple test for symmetry, due to Bowker, is to refer the statistic

$$X^2 = \sum_{i<j} \frac{(x_{ij} - x_{ji})^2}{x_{ij} + x_{ji}}$$

to the χ^2 distribution with n (n−1)/2 degress of freedom. Given acceptance of marginal homogeneity, it is then permissible to look at individual inconsistency as Ryder and Westoff do, but their procedures for the latter, which assume marginal homogeneity, do not make sense for asymmetric matrices.

Thus, we proceed by first looking at aggregate inconsistency. For those items where we reject the hypothesis of symmetry or marginal homogeneity of response distributions we shall not proceed to look at individual inconsistency, since we can assume it to be high (and "significantly" so). However, for those items where we cannot reject the hypothesis of marginal homogeneity, we then proceed to a consideration of individual inconsistency. In so doing we do not make use of the Ryder-Westoff measure $(1-O)/(1-E)$ since we regard it as a less than satisfactory measure of the total proportion responding randomly. This measure is seriously affected by skewed distributions[11] and gives a solution (in the dichotomous response situation) if and only if the conditional probability of a random responder saying yes is equal to the conditional probability of a consistent responder saying yes. Instead we prefer to use a simpler measure, $(O - \frac{1}{n})/(1 - \frac{1}{n})$, where O is the observed proportion giving the same response and n is the size of the matrix. We assume independence between responses in the first and second interviews, and therefore, under random conditions, every cell has an expected frequency of $1/n^2$. The measure therefore tells us the degree to which responses are more consistent than would be expected by chance. Results can vary from -1 to $+1$. A minus result indicates even less consistency than would occur by chance.[12]

Table B.1 gives the statistic

$$\sum_{i<j} \frac{(x_{ij} - x_{ji})^2}{x_{ij} + x_{ji}}$$

for each of the items in the reinterview, by race. A number of items, slightly more for whites than for blacks, have distributions which appear to be nonsymmetric. For blacks, some of the items are "factual" and some attitudinal, whereas for whites the bulk are attitudinal. Among blacks, the single most difficult area of questioning has to do with persons the respondent lived with between her fifth and tenth birthdays, while for whites the discrepant area of questioning relates to factors surrounding marriage.

Table B.2 shows $(O - \frac{1}{n})/(1 - \frac{1}{n})$, our measure of individual consistency, for each item where we did not reject the hypothesis of marginal homogeneity. For the most part, factual items show high levels of consistency (in the 90s), whereas attitudinal items show much lower levels of consistency.

In a recent article published subsequent to the preparation of this appendix, Ryder (1979) assesses the consistency of individual responses (on fertility planning status) by comparing answers from the same respondents in the 1970 and 1975 National Fertility Surveys. The assessment involves a new measure of individual consistency which is less sensitive to

TABLE B.1 Index of Aggregate Consistency for Selected Items Included in the Reinterview of the 1971 Survey

$$\left[\sum_{i<j} (x_{ij} - x_{ji})^2 / (x_{ij} + x_{ji})\right]$$

Survey Question	Item	D.F.	White	Black
1	Age	15	2.80	3.33
8	Catholic school education	1	5.00 <.05	3.00
37	Marital status*	10	1.00	0.00
102	Mother in household**	1	2.00	1.33
102	Father in household**	1	0.11	6.43 <.05
102	Sibs in household**	1	8.33 <.01	36.00 <.01
102	Stepmother in household**	1	1.00	0.33
102	Stepfather in household**	1	3.00	9.00 <.01
102	Others in household**	1	3.24	7.04 <.01
122	Ideal age of marriage	36	19.38	34.43
123	Parents' approval of marriage*	3	7.67	2.67
123	Same race in marriage*	3	3.22	10.56 <.05
123	Same nationality*	3	19.33 <.01	0.37
123	Same religion*	3	6.15	1.07
123	Similar economic background*	3	22.05 <.01	4.91
123a	Sex before marriage—couple	3	9.30 <.01	13.72 <.01
123a	Sex before marriage—male	3	18.08 <.05	3.61
123a	Sex before marriage—female	3	14.71 <.01	4.94
124	Religion*	6***	6.13	8.78
130	Importance of religion	3	4.96	8.60 <.05
166	Desired number of children	15	7.81	19.54
166a	Why this number	21	38.35 <.05	25.11
169	Men chase women	10	17.86	12.79
171	Society condemns unmarried mother	10	24.53 <.01	20.03 <.05
172	Neighborhood condemns unmarried mother	10	13.94	11.37
175	People look down on illegitimate child*	3	10.16 <.05	9.45 <.05
177	Number of unmarried mothers known	15	9.00	8.38
181	Would you adopt	3	1.00	1.02
183	Ideal age to have first baby	36	26.75	25.58
185	Mother of preschool child work	1	0.27	0.10
187	When able to get pregnant*	3	3.53	4.09
189	Ever had a child	1	1.00	1.00

TABLE B.1 Continued

Survey Question	Item	D.F.	White	Black
190	Intend to have children	6	6.33	3.00
191	Intended number of children	21	9.40	17.43
SAQ 7	Responsibility for contraception	3	8.00 <.05	2.42

*Wording in reinterview different from that in interview.
**Refers to period respondent aged 5-10.
***For whites D.F. = 10.

the dimension of the item that the measure $(1-O)/(1-E)$ or other similar indexes. Ryder's (1979: 127) new measure has the "further advantage of producing a superior estimate of consistency of response in situations that are highly skewed." The effect of skewness on the earlier measure $(1-O)/(1-E)$ was discussed above and by Coombs (1977).

VALIDITY OF RESPONSES ON PREMARITAL INTERCOURSE

Perhaps the most frequently asked question about the results of the 1971 survey concerned the validity of the data, especially in regard to premarital sexual intercourse. The 1971 survey included a 10 percent reliability reinterview, the results of which are given in the preceding section of this appendix. Comparisons between estimates based on the sample data and alternative independent sets of data were also made (see the following section). These tests, as well as the internal consistency of the sample data, suggested that, while not wholly free of error, the data were of reasonable and certainly usable quality, especially the data on behavior (as contrasted to the data on attitudes).

Although we had confidence in the quality of the 1971 data, it seemed prudent to attempt to undertake a more specific test of the validity of the data that was to be collected in the 1976 survey. Thus, we included in that survey an application of the randomized response technique (RRT) to test the validity of the responses to the direct question on sexual intercourse.[13] Due to limitations of time and money, as well as procedural problems, no other direct responses were tested by the RRT.

TABLE B.2 Index of Individual Consistency for Selected Items Included in the Reinterview of the 1971 Survey

$$[(0 - 1/n) / (1 - 1/n)]$$

Survey Question	Item	White	Black
1	Age	95.2	94.6
8	Catholic school education	N.A.	97.7
37	Marital status*	99.5	100.0
102	Mother in household**	98.4	91.0
102	Father in household**	93.0	N.A.
102	Stepmother in household**	99.2	97.7
102	Stepfather in household**	97.7	N.A.
102	Others in household**	80.5	N.A.
122	Ideal age of marriage	43.1	33.2
123	Parents' approval of marriage*	56.2	53.4
123	Same race in marriage*	55.1	N.A.
123	Same nationality*	N.A.	40.4
123	Same religion*	57.4	41.4
123	Similar economic background*	N.A.	38.2
123a	Sex before marriage—male	N.A.	46.0
123a	Sex before marriage—female	N.A.	50.2
124	Religion*	94.2	92.5
130	Importance of religion	62.8	N.A.
166	Desired number of children	61.3	67.5
166a	Why this number	N.A.	36.6
169	Men chase women	47.2	39.1
172	Neighborhood condemns unmarried mother	40.9	24.6
177	Number of unmarried mothers known	46.1	31.3
181	Would you adopt	88.2	70.8
183	Ideal age to have first baby	40.9	28.8
185	Mother of preschool child work	74.3	34.6
187	When able to get pregnant	55.5	46.4
189	Ever had a child	99.2	97.0
190	Intend to have children	95.3	91.0
191	Intended number of children	64.2	63.8
SAQ 7	Responsibility for contraception	N.A.	66.0

*Wording in reinterview different from that in interview.
**Refers to period respondent aged 5-10.
N.A. = not applicable.

The application of the RRT took place at the conclusion of the interview and was limited to never-married respondents. Each such respondent was provided with a small box containing beads of three colors; a shaking of the box caused a bead to fall into a small, windowed slot. Each color represented a different question. The respondent was instructed to shake the box and to answer the question associated with the color of the bead she had thereby generated. The questions were printed on the box next to a dot of the appropriate color. The interviewer was not to be told the color of the bead generated or the question being answered, and the answer was to be a "yes" or a "no." The three questions were: "I have had sexual intercourse," "I am a female," and "I am a male." The first question was represented by 70 percent of the beads, the second by 22 percent, and the third by 8 percent.

Given the (known) probability of the selection of the question relating to sexual intercourse and the proportion of the sample that responded affirmatively, it is possible to estimate the proportion who are responding in the affirmative to the question on sexual intercourse. If the shaking of the box did generate beads randomly, if the respondents answered the appropriate question, and if they answered truthfully, then the RRT estimate can be presumed to be valid. Shown in Table B.3 is a comparison of the RRT estimates, for each race and the total population, with the estimates from the direct question on sexual intercourse. These estimates are based on unweighted sample cases. In each instance the estimate from the direct question is slightly below the estimate provided by the RRT, but it falls comfortably within the 95 percent confidence interval of the RRT estimate. Thus it appears that the direct question on sexual intercourse elicited truthful responses from the 1976 study population.

This test of the data, as well as our other tests, increases our confidence in the overall results of the two surveys, although we recognize that we have not definitively demonstrated (nor can we) that "the data are valid." In fact, we know that the 1976 data are defective in at least one respect, the reporting of abortion by blacks (see the following section). In spite of this defect, we regard the foundation underlying what we have presented in this monograph (and elsewhere) to be at least as firm as that of other national surveys on fertility and contraceptive use. We recognize, however, that our confidence in the data may not be shared by all readers.

COMPARISONS OF ESTIMATES BASED ON SAMPLE DATA WITH EXTERNAL DATA

Some of the data collected in the 1971 and 1976 surveys can be used to generate estimates of fertility-related behavior that can be compared with external, independently obtained data. To the degree that the comparisons "validate" the data from a survey, confidence in other but uncompared data from that survey is established, if not increased. Unfavorable comparisons would of course cast doubt on the quality of the survey data, the uncompared as well as the compared. However, the comparisons are affected not only by the quality of the survey data and the fact that these are data from a sample, but also by the quality of the external data and by the degree to which the survey data approach or approximate the universe

TABLE B.3 Comparison of RRT and Direct Question on Intercourse, 1976

	RRT	(SE)	Direct Question
Total	44.1	±1.6	41.8
White	33.6	±2.0	30.8
Black	64.1	±2.6	62.7

represented by the external data. It may be difficult, therefore, to judge whether a comparison is favorable or not. Discrepancies, while possibly troublesome, do not in and of themselves necessarily indicate bias nor invalidate distributions derived from the survey data.

The 1976 survey allows for a comparison of live births and of abortions to women aged 15-18 in 1975 and of children ever born to women aged 15-19 as of 1976. Comparisons involving the 1971 survey are of live births to women aged 15-18 in 1970 and of children ever born to women aged 15-19 as of 1971.[14] These are the only possibilities for comparison of which we are aware.[15]

Comparisons of 1976 Survey Data

LIVE BIRTHS AND ABORTIONS TO WOMEN AGED 15-18 IN 1975

Some common problems arise in estimating live births and abortions in 1975 from the survey data and in attempting to compare these estimates with the external data on births and abortions. The 1976 survey involved interviews with a sample of women aged 15-19 who were living in households in the continental United States as of March 1976. The external data on births and abortions against which we compare the survey estimates derive from data collection systems that attempt to report on each event[16] for all 50 states and, more importantly, for women living in group quarters and in institutions as well as in households. Although we can, and do, make adjustments to nationally reported births and abortions for events occurring in Alaska and Hawaii, we have no way of estimating how many births and abortions occurred to women who were living in group quarters or institutions in 1975. As a result, when we compare numbers of births and abortions, the survey estimates should fall below the external data, but by how much cannot be determined; comparisons of rates, where these are possible, reduce but do not eliminate this major difference in coverage. The effect of the difference in coverage is probably more important at age 18 than at ages 15-17; we also think the difference is more important for abortions than for live births and more important for whites than for blacks.

A survey respondent could have been resident in 1975 in group quarters or an institution. If such a person had a live birth or an abortion while so resident the survey estimate includes that event. On the other hand, a live birth or an abortion to a person then living in a household but in group quarters or an institution in (March) 1976 is excluded from the survey estimate. Also excluded are those events that occurred to women who were living in group quarters or institutions in both 1975 and 1976.

In estimating births and abortions from the survey data, the only ages for which the survey provides 12 months of experience through 1975, during which time one of these events could occur, are ages 15-17. For age 18, the survey population experiences slightly less than a full year's experience. As of January 1, 1975, the maximum age of the survey respondents is 18 years and 10 months, since the oldest respondents were born in March 1956. No one in the survey experienced the last two months of age 18 in January 1975 and no one experienced the last month of age 18 in February 1975, and births (or abortions) that occurred to women at those ages are not represented in the sample. In effect, the number of births and abortions reported by survey respondents at age 18 in 1975 presumably represents 97.9 percent $(141/144)$[17] of what would have occurred in a full year of experience. Although of limited significance, we have adjusted the survey estimates of births and abortions to women age 18 (in 1975) to reflect a full year of events.

A comparable procedure could have been followed to estimate births and abortions to women age 14 in 1975 (the "shortage" of experience in this instance would have been at the end, rather than the beginning, of 1975). However, we have not done so for two reasons. First, external data on births and abortions are not available by single years of age below age 15. While most events occurring to those under age 15 presumably are to women age 14, any attempt to allocate those events to single years of age would result in estimates of very questionable quality.

Second, births and abortions to women under age 15 are relatively rare events (in 1975 there were approximately 13,000 live births and approximately 14,000-16,000 abortions to women under age 15) and are therefore relatively rare events to women age 14. Given the size of our sample and the relatively small number of events, we would not expect the survey to provide an accurate estimate of events at age 14.

The estimates from the survey data represent the number of live births and of abortions occurring in 1975 to respondents who at the time of the event were 15-18 years of age, inflated by sample weights. These weights reflect a respondent's characteristics—age, marital status, and race—as of 1976. While race would not change between 1975 and 1976, age and marital status might. We know of no way by which sample events could have been inflated by weights reflecting the actual characteristics of a respondent when a live birth or abortion occurred in 1975. At the same time, we believe the procedure we have followed is not a source of significant error in the survey estimates.

An alternative weighting scheme was in fact tried. The married 18 year old (in 1976) who gave birth in 1975 at age 17 and was then unmarried, for example, was given the (1976) weight for an unmarried 17 year old. The estimates generated in this manner differed little from the estimates generated in the manner described above. Further, the logic of this alternative procedure seemed to be more questionable than the logic of the one that was used.

An additional, if minor, problem in comparing sample estimates to national data is the difference in racial categories by which events are reported. Where possible, we have reclassified the external data to be consistent with the racial categories of the survey, that is, whites and others, and blacks. This reclassification was possible for numbers of live births, but not for abortions.

Before proceeding to the actual comparisons, one further step, involving the external data, must be described, namely, the allocation of national data on abortions by age and race. Reports of the total number of abortions legally performed each year in the United States are available from two sources, the Center for Disease Control (CDC) and the Alan Guttmacher Institute (AGI). Each organization receives reports from health agencies in those states that have established centralized direct-reporting systems, or surveys hospitals and abortion facilities in those states that do not collect statewide abortion data. AGI claims that its reporting network is more comprehensive than CDC's and therefore that its reports are more complete.[18] According to AGI, there were 1,034,200 legal abortions performed in the United States in 1975 (AGI, personal communication) whereas CDC reports a total of 854,853 (Center for Disease Control, 1977). In comparing our data on abortions to the external data, we use the AGI figure because it presumably is more complete and represents a more stringent "test" of our data.

Unfortunately, information on the characteristics of women receiving abortions is not available from AGI. On the other hand, CDC does provide percentage distributions of the women who received abortions, but only for one characteristic at a time. In addition, detailed information available from CDC on the ages of women under age 20 who received abortions is based on reports from a small number of states and involves only a small proportion of all reported abortions to women under the age of 20.[19]

Since we have accepted as the more complete figure the total number of abortions reported by AGI for 1975, it is necessary to allocate this

Appendix B

figure to arrive at estimates of the number of abortions to women in a race-age group comparable to that which can be provided from our 1976 survey.[20] To do so we use the percentage distributions available from CDC and apply them to the AGI total. Clearly, the only effect of using the AGI total is to arrive at estimates which are larger, by a common factor, than if we used the total available from CDC. Since the CDC distributions are given separately by age and by race, we have assumed that abortions to women under age 20 (accounting for 33.1 percent of all abortions) occurred to blacks (and others) and whites in the same proportions as abortions to blacks (and others) and whites of all ages, that is, 32.2 percent to blacks and others and 67.8 percent to whites. This assumption may be erroneous, but we have no better evidence by which to allocate abortions to women under age 20 by race. The estimated number of abortions to women of each race under age 20 is then subdivided by age group using the distribution provided by CDC of abortions in 8 states to women under the age of 20. The same distribution is used for each race. It is unlikely that the distributions for whites and for blacks and others are identical or that the distribution based on eight states accurately reflects the distribution for all states. Here again, however, these are the only and thus the "best" data available. The number at ages 18-19 is simply divided in half to give an estimate of the number of abortions at age 18.[21]

The final step, preparatory to the comparisons, was to "adjust" the national estimates on births and abortions for those events occurring in Alaska and Hawaii, to provide national, external estimates for the 48-states area, comparable to the (48-state) coverage of the 1976 survey data. We will not detail how the available data for the two states were handled since the numbers involved are small.[22]

The final estimates are shown in Table B.4. The upper panel compares births, the middle panel abortions, and the lower panel the sum of births and abortions.[23] The comparisons involving whites are in the appropriate direction, that is, the estimates from the survey are smaller than the figures from the external, independent data sets. Further, since a higher proportion of pregnancies to women (in this age group) living in group quarters and institutions are likely to be terminated by abortion than would be the case of pregnancies to women living in households, we should expect the survey estimate of abortions to be "less complete" than the survey estimate of births. Although the comparisons lack some degree of precision, the general levels of the survey estimates as well as the differential levels of the two suggest that the reporting of live births and of abortions in 1975 by white respondents in the 1976 survey are of reasonable and satisfactory quality.

A different situation exists for blacks, however. Respondents in the survey appear to have overreported live births and to have underreported

TABLE B.4 Estimates of Live Births and Abortions to Women 15-18 Years of Age in 1975, from 1976 Survey and External Sources

Event and Source	White	Black	All Races
Live Births			
(1) 1976 Survey	235,757[a]	122,398	358,155
(2) NCHS	270,378[a]	117,022	387,400
(3) = (1)/(2)	.87	1.05	.92
Abortions			
(1) 1976 Survey	117,572[a]	16,524	134,096
(2) AGI and CDC	161,869	76,507[b]	238,376
(3) = (1)/(2)	.73	.22	.56
Births and Abortions			
(1) 1976 Survey	353,329	138,922	492,251
(2) External Sources	432,247	193,529	625,776
(3) = (1)/(2)	.82	.72	.79

SOURCES: National Center for Health Statistics (1977); Center for Disease Control (1977); AGI (personal communication).

a. Refers to whites and others.
b. Refers to blacks and others.

abortions, and in fact to have underreported pregnancies. Thus, the combined total of estimated births and abortions from the survey (139.000) is only 72 percent of the combined total of births and abortions from NCHS and AGI/CDC, in comparison to the white ratio of 82 percent. We suspect the black figure is too low.[24] If we assume for the moment that the estimate of black births from the survey should equal 87 percent of the NCHS figure on black births (that is, the same as the white ratio) and that the "excess" of reported births were actually pregnancies that ended in abortion, the survey figure on abortions plus this excess (16,524 plus 15,213) would still represent only 42 percent of the AGI/CDC figure on abortions. In effect, the excess of reported births appears to be smaller than the deficit in the reporting of abortions.

However, it is our contention that the excess of births is not in fact due to the misreporting of the outcome of pregnancy. Of all births occurring to black respondents aged 15-18 in 1975, 95 percent were reported as living in the mother's household (that is, the respondent's household) at the time of the survey. In all such instances a check of the household roster did in fact reveal a named infant along with the sex and date of birth of that infant. It strikes us as highly unlikely that a woman whose pregnancy actually ended in abortion would not only report a live birth but would also report the "created" child as a member of the household and provide it with a name, sex, and date of birth. The roster of household members was not always provided by the respondent, but that only shifts the "burden" for creating the fictitious child to whoever did provide the listing. Since the roster of household members was obtained prior to interviewing, it would also mean that a fictitious child was "created" (that is, listed) in anticipation of the respondent being interviewed and eventually asked about the outcome of pregnancy.

Of course, some small number of live births reported in the survey by blacks may actually represent pregnancies that ended in abortion, but, as suggested, this phenomenon is unlikely to be of significant magnitude and unlikely to account simultaneously for the excess of live births and the deficit in abortions. Although these results refer to events occurring to black women 15-18 years of age in 1975, they probably hold for the reporting of events in other years covered by the survey—too many live births,[25] too few abortions, and a net deficit in pregnancies. While the underreporting of abortions by blacks may not be wholly unexpected, the overreporting of births is, and is something we cannot account for or explain. Whatever the errors in the survey, there are undoubtedly reporting errors on age and race in the external data on both births and abortions. We are inclined to doubt that such errors are an important consideration in the present context.

It also is possible that some pregnancies that actually ended in abortion were reported as ending in miscarriage. External data that would permit us to check the accuracy of the survey reports on miscarriage do not exist. However, since the number of reported abortions is considerably larger than the number of reported miscarriages, the number of pregnancies possibly misreported in this manner must be relatively small and insufficient to explain the deficit in abortions.

CHILDREN EVER BORN TO WOMEN 15-19 YEARS OF AGE AS OF 1976

In June of 1976 the Current Population Survey (CPS) collected information on children ever born to women 14 to 59 years of age who were reported as ever married and to women 18 to 59 years of age who were reported as never married. Shown in Table B.5 are the number of children ever born per 1000 never-married women 18-19 years of age and per 1000 ever-married women 15-19 years of age as estimated from the 1976 survey and as given by the CPS. The CPS data refer to the civilian noninstitutional population (that is, the civilian population in households and group quarters) of the United States, whereas the 1976 survey data refer to the household population in the continental United States.[26] For the ever married, both black and white, and for never-married whites the

TABLE B.5 Estimates of Children Ever Born per 1000 Ever-Married Women 15-19 Years of Age and per 1000 Never-Married Women 18-19 Years of Age, from 1976 Survey and 1976 CPS

Marital Status, Age, and Race	Survey	CPS	Survey/CPS
Ever Married Aged 15-19			
White	524	505	1.04
Black	1023	1021	1.00
All races	569	548	1.04
Never Married Aged 18-19			
White[a]	29	29	1.00
Black	434	296	1.47
All races	89	69	1.29

SOURCE: U.S. Department of Commerce (1977a: 32, Table 18).

a. Refers to whites and other nonwhites.

two sets of data are in close agreement (especially when it is remembered that both sets are generated by samples). Only for never-married blacks 18-19 years of age is there a substantial difference.

Since live births in 1975 are included in children ever born as of 1976, and since the survey appeared to provide an excess of live births to blacks in 1975, the relatively greater number of children ever born to black survey respondents as compared to blacks in the CPS is not unexpected. As indicated, in connection with the reporting of births in 1975, we have no explanation for this phenomenon. Table B.6 provides a comparison of the percentage of women reported as childless in the 1976 survey and the 1976 CPS data. These data are consistent with the figures shown in Table B.5.

In summary, the 1976 survey appears to provide data of reasonable quality on births and abortions to whites.[27] For blacks, abortions appear to be underreported by a substantial amount and births appear to be overreported. However, it does not seem to be the case that any substantial number of pregnancies that actually ended in abortion were reported as ending in live births. The net effect of these two "independent" sources of error probably is an underreporting of pregnancies to blacks in the 1976 survey.

TABLE B.6 Percentage of Women Reported as Childless in the 1976 Survey and the 1976 CPS

Marital Status Age, and Race	Survey	CPS
Ever Married		
Aged 15-19		
White	53.6[a]	57.8
Black	26.3	26.6
All races	51.1	55.1
Never Married		
Aged 18-19		
White	97.6[a]	97.4
Black	67.1	77.2
All races	92.2	94.2

SOURCE: U.S. Department of Commerce (1977a: 34-35, Tables 19 and 20).

a. Refers to whites and other nonwhites.

Comparisons of 1971 Survey Data

LIVE BIRTHS TO WOMEN AGED 15-18 IN 1970

Estimation of live births to women aged 15-18 in 1970 from the 1971 survey essentially involved the same problems and the same procedures as the estimation of births in 1975 from the 1976 survey. However, there are two differences between the two surveys that are relevant in the present context. Whereas the 1976 survey involved interviews with a probability sample of young women living in households, the 1971 survey involved interviews with a probability sample of young women living in households plus interviews with a separate probability sample of young women living in college dormitories. Although the latter sample has been excluded from consideration in various sections of this book, it has been included here. Thus, the 1971 survey, although still differing in coverage from the universe of the birth registration system of the United States, more closely approximates that universe than does the 1976 survey. Births from the 1971 survey should therefore more closely approximate the number of births reported by NCHS for 1970.

The second difference between the two surveys concerns the issue of age eligibility (see "Differences Between the Two Studies," in this appen-

TABLE B.7 Estimates of Live Births to Women 15-18 Years of Age in 1970, from 1971 Survey and NCHS

Source	White[a]	Black	All Races
(1) 1971 Survey	226,448	118,930	345,378
(2) NCHS	282,586	121,734	404,320
(3) = (1)/(2)	.80	.98	.85

SOURCE: National Center for Health Statistics (1973).

a. Refers to whites and other nonwhites.

dix) and its effect on estimated births to women aged 18 in 1970 and in 1975. Taking May 1971 (the midpoint of screening) as the reference date for age, the survey population was aged 13 years 9 months to 18 years 8 months in January 1970 and experienced 134/144 of a full year's experience at age 18 in 1970. Thus, the adjustment to age 18 in 1970 is slightly larger than the comparable adjustment needed for 1975.

Table B.7 shows the number of births to women aged 15-18 in 1970 as estimated from the 1971 survey and as reported by NCHS.[28] Given that the 1971 survey data refer to women in households and college dormitories, the estimated number of white births appears too low, certainly by comparison with the comparable estimate for 1975. On the other hand, although the ratio of estimated black births to registered black births is appropriately below 1.00, it is probably higher than it should be, although we are unable to indicate the level of error.[29] The 1971 survey, then, appears to be slightly deficient in terms of births reported by white respondents (and by implication, therefore, deficient in terms of pregnancies to whites) and, as was the case with the 1976 survey, to provide an excess of live births to black respondents (but less of an excess in 1971 than was the case in 1976).

CHILDREN EVER BORN
TO WOMEN AGED 15-19 AS OF 1970/71

The 1970 census, like previous censuses, collected information on the number of children ever born to women who, at the time of the census, had ever been married. However, unlike the earlier censuses, the 1970 census also collected information on children ever born to never-married women (U.S. Department of Commerce, 1973b). The availability of the 1970 census data on children ever born to women of all marital statuses permits a comparison of these data with comparable information collected in the course of our 1971 study.

Both sets of data are based on samples and are therefore subject to sampling error.[30] The census provides data as of April 1, 1970; the survey data were collected between March and July of 1971. The census refers to all 50 states, whereas the survey refers to the 48 contiguous states. The census covered all women regardless of type of residence they were in, whereas the survey covers women living in households or in college dormitories—that is, it did not cover women living in group quarters other than college dormitories.[31] The census data cited below are for blacks and whites; the survey data are blacks and "whites," that is, whites and other nonwhites.

Keeping in mind the various differences in obtaining the information, we show in Table B.8 the number of children ever born per 1000 women by race, age, and marital status, in the census and in the survey. For single women, whites show a higher rate in the census than in the survey, with the reverse situation for blacks. Among the ever married, the census and survey show substantially the same rate for whites, whereas for black ever-married women, census data provide a higher rate overall than the survey data. The largest relative difference between the census and the survey data is for single white women, the group for whom the bearing of a live child is, in either case, a relatively rare event. For the other three groups, the differences are relatively small.

Part of the differences shown in Table B.8 may be attributable to differences in the universes covered by the census and the survey. If, for example, single white women living in institutions and group quarters other than dormitories (at the time of the 1970 Census) had borne more children per woman than single white women living in households and college dormitories, then the census figure should be higher than the survey figure. However, we suspect that the various differences in coverage or universe are relatively inconsequential. Of great importance, we believe, is the quality of the data collected. As suggested earlier, we have no reason to place greater credibility on one or the other source.

In this respect, it should be noted that the relatively greater number of children born per 1000 women in the census is in large part the result of women enumerated at and allocated to high parities and *not* the result of the survey reporting a disproportionately large number of childless or zero-parity women. Thus, census data show ever-married women at ages 15-19 with 4, 5, and 6 live births and some single women in that age group with at least 4 live births.[32] The survey included no respondent with more than 3 live children ever born to her. However, the proportion at zero parity is higher in the survey only for never-married whites, the category with the largest relative difference in children ever born (Table B.9). If we assume that .4 percent[33] of the single women in the survey were not actually childless, but had had a live birth that was not reported, children ever born to these women still would not equal the census figure of 17 per thousand.

TABLE B.8 Children Ever Born per 1,000 Women: 1970 Census and 1971 Survey

Marital Status and Age	White			Black			Both Races		
	Census	Survey[a]	$\frac{Survey}{Census}$	Census	Survey	$\frac{Survey}{Census}$	Census	Survey[b]	$\frac{Survey}{Census}$
Single	17	8	.47	169	192	1.14	37	34	.92
15-17	10	4	.40	105	104	.99	22	18	.82
18-19	32	16	.50	302	356	1.18	66	63	.95
Ever Married	574	568	.99	1029	888	.86	631	596	.94
15-17	529	489	.92	871	759	.87	578	512	.88
18-19	588	590	1.00	1088	924	.85	648	619	.96
All Women	84	67	.80	268	236	.88	108	89	.82
15-17	34	22	.65	143	118	.82	48	35	.73
18-19	163	136	.83	477	432	.90	202	174	.86

SOURCE: U.S. Department of Commerce (1973b: 14, 17, 376, Tables 4, 5, and A4).

a. Refers to whites and other nonwhites.

b. Refers to all races.

TABLE B.9 Percentage of Women Reported as Childless in the 1970 Census and the 1971 Survey

Marital Status and Age	White		Black	
	Census	Survey[a]	Census	Survey
Single	98.8	99.2	86.2	83.7
15-17	99.3	99.6	90.7	89.9
18-19	97.7	98.3	76.9	72.0
Ever Married	53.6	52.6	31.0	30.4
15-17	56.7	56.4	37.5	31.1
18-19	52.7	51.6	28.6	30.1

SOURCE: U.S. Department of Commerce (1973b: 14, 17, 376, Table 4, 5, and A4).

a. Refers to whites and other nonwhites.

That the high parities reported in the census are a source of difference between the census and the survey is best illustrated, perhaps, by ever-married blacks. Although the ratio of the survey estimate of children ever born to the census figure is .86 (Table B.8), the census and the survey show essentially the same proportion of women as childless.

NOTES

1. In both surveys only one eligible female could be selected (randomly) from any one household.

2. A number of other items that initially were considered relevant but supplementary were also asked. Although these other items appear to have provided data of reasonable quality, they were not subsequently included in the 1976 survey since we did not anticipate need of them in constructing our index of SES.

3. If the head of the household was available and refused to answer the questions, then no further attempt was to be made to get the information from any other person. Thus, we are speaking here of instances where the head of the household was not available for interview but where the head (or spouse) had consented to the interview; see the preceding section for a discussion of the consent procedures followed in the two surveys.

4. Including cases where the respondent herself was the household head or where the respondent was married and her husband was the household head.

5. Additional problems in using occupational prestige scores were posed by those cases where the household head was a housewife (with no usual occupation) and those cases where occupation was not reported.

6. Comparable questions that took into account the difference in marital status provided the same information for the never married. Questions on pregnancy were asked only of those never-married respondents who reported having had intercourse.

7. More correctly, the focus of that effort was in terms of measuring consistency (or inconsistency) as affected by all sources of error rather than just response reliability. Our concern here is also with the broader issue of consistency. In this respect also see Knodel and Piampiti (1977).

8. In two instances, the respondents selected for reinterview claimed they had not been interviewed earlier; other reasons for failing to obtain reinterviews were: respondents had married, were away on vacation, refused, parents refused, or unable to locate.

9. It should be noted that although the focus is on measuring inconsistency regardless of its source, the "true" concern is with response reliability.

10. It can also be shown that if the matrix is symmetric then M equals the total proportion responding randomly when: (1) all responders are consistent; (2) all responders are random; (3) the conditional probability of random responders saying (on a dichotomous yes/no item) yes (no) is equal to the conditional probability of consistent responders saying yes (no); and (4) the conditional probability of random responders saying yes is equal to the proportion of all responders saying no.

11. For example, in the following two matrices:

I

	A	B	
A	.85	.05	.90
B	.05	.05	.10
	.90	.10	1.00

II

	A	B	
A	.45	.05	.50
B	.05	.45	.50
	.50	.50	1.00

although 90 percent of the responses are consistent in each one $(1-0)/(1-E)$ leads to an estimate of 55 percent of the respondents responding randomly in the first matrix and 20 percent in the second. It is not immediately obvious to us that the first matrix involves more random responses.

12. In a sense, minus results indicate a kind of consistency or nonrandomness; that is, that those who replied yes (no) the first time are consistently responding no (yes) the second time.

13. There is a considerable body of literature on the application of the RRT and on alternative ways of applying it. A recent article by Chow et al. (1979) contains a fairly complete list of references.

14. Since abortion had not been legalized by the time the 1971 survey was conducted, there are no reliable external data against which to compare reporting of abortions in that survey. The external data sets involved in the various comparisons are not only independent of the survey data but also of one another.

15. In principle, live births (and abortions in the case of the 1976 survey) could be estimated from the surveys for successively earlier calendar years for successively younger age groups, for example, live births in 1974 to women aged 14-17. There are a number of reasons, some of which will be mentioned below, for not attempting to do so.

16. The most recent test of birth registration completeness in the United States found that 99.4 percent of white births and 98.0 percent of black and other births

Appendix B

occurring over the period 1964 to 1968 were registered (U.S. Department of Commerce, 1973d). No information is available in that study on completeness of birth registration by age of mother.

While the birth registration system attempts to register each birth, some of the published data on registered births is "based on 100 percent of births in selected States and on a 50 percent sample of births in all other States" (National Center for Health Statistics, 1978b).

The reporting of legal abortions is undoubtedly less complete than the reporting of live births, but the extent of underreporting is unknown.

17. The 144 assumes persons at each month of age 18 in each calendar month of the year.

18. CDC acknowledges the underreporting of its system. How complete the AGI system is is unknown.

19. CDC shows a single-year age distribution (except for less than age 15) of abortions to women under age 20 who had those abortions in 6 states. This distribution is based on 15,656 abortions or 7.5 percent of all CDC reported abortions to women reported to be under age 20. Another distribution, for ages less than 15, 15-17 years, and 18-19 years, is based on reports from those 6 states plus 2 others and involves 23,991 abortions or 11.5 percent of all abortions reported to women under age 20.

20. As indicated earlier, comparability on race is not actually achieved for abortions.

21. The distribution given by CDC based on 6 states shows that 51.2 percent of the abortions at ages 18 and 19 were to women aged 18. However, the figures on abortions for these two ages involve only a small proportion of all abortions presumably occurring to 18- and 19-year-old women. In addition, the 6-state distribution differs from the 8-state distribution by being slightly skewed toward the older ages. We have, therefore, resorted to a 50-50 split at ages 18 and 19.

22. External figures on births 15-18 were reduced by 63 black births and 2088 white and other births; the external figures on abortion were reduced by 596 white abortions and 652 black and other abortions. Note the difference in the racial categorization of births and abortions.

23. Rates are available, externally, only for births, but not for the age group 15-18. For the age group 15-17, NCHS gives a rate of 28.3 for whites and 86.6 for blacks. The 1976 survey gives a rate of 28.0 for whites and others and 97.3 for blacks. For all races the NCHS figure is 36.6, compared to 37.6 from the survey data (National Center for Health Statistics, 1977).

24. As previously noted, the AGI/CDC figure on abortions is for blacks and others; even if we assumed that 10 percent of these abortions were to nonblacks, the survey estimate would still be too low (of course, adding 10 percent of 76,507 to the white figure of 161,869 would reduce the completeness of white abortions from the survey, but still not to an unreasonable level).

25. In this respect see the discussion below on children ever born.

26. The weighting problem referred to earlier in the context of estimating births and abortions in 1975 from the 1976 survey does not arise in this situation. Although the CPS gives figures for ever-married women 15-17 and 18-19 years of age, we have refrained from comparisons for these two age groups because of the small number of ever married respondents in our sample, especially for blacks.

In this instance our comparisons involve not the absolute number of children ever born (although that is possible), but rather the ratio of children to women. Use of the ratio minimizes, but probably does not eliminate, differences due solely to the differences in coverage between the CPS and the 1976 survey.

27. It should be noted that the external figures on abortion refer to legal abortions, whereas survey respondents could have reported legal as well as illegal abortions. We do not regard this as very likely or of any real significance.

28. The NCHS figures have been reclassified by race to be consistent with the 1971 survey categories and have been adjusted by the exclusion of births in Alaska and Hawaii.

29. For the age group 15-17, NCHS gives a birthrate of 29.2 for whites and 101.4 for blacks. The 1971 survey gives a rate of 22.8 for whites and others and 88.9 for blacks. For all races the NCHS figure is 38.8, compared to 31.7 from the survey data (National Center for Health Statistics, 1977).

30. The 1970 census data on children ever born that we cite below are based on a 5 percent sample of households and of persons living in group quarters.

31. In 1970 the institutional population was defined by the Census Bureau as a subcategory of the group quarters population.

32. For single women the census parity distribution terminates at "3 or more" live births. However, since the total number of live births to these women is also given, it is a simple matter to determine that some of the 3 or more parity women are of parity 4 or higher.

33. This is the difference between the proportion of white single women reported childless in the census and the proportion reported childless in the survey.

APPENDIX C:
DATA FROM THE STUDY

TABLE C.1 Adjusted Proportion of Women 15-19 Years of Age in 1971 Who Had Premarital Intercourse

Variable	n	Total Adjusted Proportion	n	White Adjusted Proportion	n	Black Adjusted Proportion
Race		***		—		—
White	2848	.26		—		—
Black	1302	.51		—		—
Current Age		***		***		***
15	948	.18	632	.12	316	.32
16	968	.28	660	.18	308	.48
17	960	.35	683	.25	277	.57
18	701	.45	462	.37	239	.63
19	573	.53	411	.44	162	.76
SES (years)		**		N.S.		***
<9	804	.36	413	.24	391	.59
9-11	1455	.36	906	.28	549	.53
12	953	.32	741	.24	212	.49
13-15	732	.30	613	.23	119	.41
≥16	206	.31	175	.24	31	.39
Family Stability		***		***		***
Ideal	2690	.30	2137	.23	553	.46
Less ideal	801	.39	449	.30	352	.58
Least ideal	659	.41	262	.36	397	.56
Religion		**		**		N.S.
Fundamentalist Protestant	305	.32	186	.27	119	.44
Other Protestant	2651	.34	1621	.25	1030	.54
Catholic	933	.31	843	.23	90	.48
Non-Christian	68	.27	68	.17	{63	.50
None	193	.40	130	.36		
Religiosity		***		***		***
Low	951	.43	792	.35	159	.59
Medium	1506	.37	1071	.27	435	.60
High	1693	.25	985	.16	708	.46
Age at Menarche		***		***		**
≤11	848	.36	581	.29	267	.53
12-13	2572	.35	1790	.26	782	.55
14-15	686	.26	458	.18	228	.43
≥16	44	.28	19	.06	25	.56
Grand Mean	4150	.34	2848	.25	1302	.52
R^2		.19		.13		.14
F-ratio		47.55***		22.97***		11.30***

NOTE: Estimates are based on unweighted sample cases. Dashes = not applicable. N.S. = not significant; *p<.10; **p<.05; ***p<.01.

TABLE C.2 Adjusted Proportion of Women 15-19 Years of Age in 1976 Who Had Premarital Intercourse

Variable	Total n	Total Adjusted Proportion	White n	White Adjusted Proportion	Black n	Black Adjusted Proportion
Race		***		—		—
White	1436	.40		—		—
Black	632	.62		—		—
Current Age		***		***		***
15	398	.23	274	.16	124	.40
16	424	.34	301	.24	123	.56
17	431	.50	299	.41	132	.70
18	433	.60	293	.53	140	.75
19	382	.67	269	.59	113	.84
SES (years)		**		**		**
<9	374	.48	206	.36	168	.71
9-11	679	.50	441	.44	238	.64
12	557	.47	406	.38	151	.66
13-15	355	.42	299	.35	56	.53
≥16	103	.36	84	.32	19	.47
Family Stability		***		***		***
Ideal	1249	.41	1007	.35	242	.53
Less ideal	472	.56	288	.47	184	.75
Least ideal	347	.53	141	.45	206	.69
Religion		N.S.		*		N.S.
Fundamentalist Protestant	193	.50	118	.44	75	.63
Other Protestant	1162	.48	713	.40	449	.64
Catholic	517	.42	480	.35	37	.59
Non-Christian	24	.37	22	.24	{71	.74
None	172	.50	103	.39		
Religiosity		***		***		***
Low	618	.57	495	.51	123	.70
Medium	779	.50	533	.41	246	.70
High	671	.33	408	.21	263	.57
Age at Menarche		***		***		N.S.
≤10	152	.58	98	.57	54	.63
11	311	.50	205	.44	106	.63
12	577	.47	408	.40	169	.65
13	609	.46	450	.37	159	.67
14	299	.39	211	.28	88	.63
≥15	120	.43	64	.31	56	.65
Grand Mean	2068	.47	1436	.39	632	.65
R^2		.25		.23		.19
F-ratio		30.90***		20.05***		7.22***

NOTE: Estimates are based on unweighted sample cases. Dashes = not applicable. N.S. = not significant; *p < .10; **p < .05; ***p < .01.

TABLE C.3 Adjusted Mean Age at First Premarital Intercourse for Women 15-19 Years of Age in 1971

Variable	Total n	Total Adjusted Mean	White n	White Adjusted Mean	Black n	Black Adjusted Mean
Race		***		—		—
White	700	16.3	—		—	
Black	669	15.9	—		—	
Current Age		***		***		***
15	167	14.5	70	14.7	97	14.3
16	255	15.5	114	15.5	141	15.3
17	323	16.1	163	16.3	160	15.9
18	322	16.5	172	16.7	150	16.3
19	302	17.0	181	17.4	121	16.5
SES (years)		***		**		N.S.
<9	332	15.9	107	16.2	225	15.6
9-11	536	16.0	251	16.3	285	15.8
12	272	16.2	174	16.5	98	15.9
≥13	229	16.4	168	16.6	61	16.0
Family Stability		***		***		N.S.
Ideal	712	16.2	456	16.5	256	15.9
Less ideal	340	15.9	146	16.2	194	15.7
Least ideal	317	16.0	98	16.2	219	15.7
Religion		**		N.S.		*
Fundamentalist Protestant	95	15.8	47	16.2	48	15.3
Other Protestant	938	16.1	396	16.4	542	15.8
Catholic	230	16.2	186	16.5	44	15.6
Other	106	15.9	71	16.2	35	15.5
Religiosity		**		**		N.S.
Low	381	15.9	290	16.2	91	15.8
Medium	551	16.1	286	16.5	265	15.7
High	437	16.2	124	16.6	313	15.8
Age at Menarche		***		***		***
≤11	311	15.8	175	16.1	136	15.5
12-13	852	16.1	437	16.4	415	15.8
≥14	206	16.4	88	16.7	118	16.1
Grand Mean	1369	16.1	700	16.4	669	15.8
R^2		.33		.35		.27
F-ratio		39.18***		22.89***		15.31***

NOTE: Estimates are based on unweighted sample cases. Dashes = not applicable.
N.S. = not significant; *$p<.10$; **$p<.05$; ***$p<.01$.

TABLE C.4 Adjusted Mean Age at First Premarital Intercourse for Women 15-19 Years of Age in 1976

Variable	n	Total Adjusted Mean	n	White Adjusted Mean	n	Black Adjusted Mean
Race		***		—		—
White	552	16.1		—		—
Black	405	15.8		—		—
Current Age		***		***		***
15	91	14.4	42	14.6	49	14.2
16	142	15.4	73	15.4	69	15.3
17	212	15.7	122	15.9	90	15.4
18	261	16.4	156	16.6	105	16.1
19	251	16.6	159	16.9	92	16.1
SES (years)		*		*		N.S.
<9	201	15.8	84	16.0	117	15.5
9-11	346	15.9	194	16.2	152	15.6
12	254	16.0	153	16.3	101	15.6
≥13	156	16.1	121	16.4	35	15.7
Family Stability		***		***		**
Ideal	460	16.2	335	16.4	125	15.8
Less ideal	280	15.9	144	16.0	136	15.7
Least ideal	217	15.6	73	15.8	144	15.3
Religion		**		N.S.		N.S.
Fundamentalist Protestant	95	15.8	48	16.1	47	15.4
Other Protestant	567	16.0	285	16.2	282	15.6
Catholic	179	16.2	158	16.4	21	15.9
Other	116	15.7	61	16.0	55	15.3
Religiosity		*		N.S.		*
Low	344	15.8	259	16.2	85	15.2
Medium	391	16.0	216	16.3	175	15.6
High	222	16.1	77	16.3	145	15.7
Age at Menarche		***		***		***
≤10	90	15.5	56	15.8	34	15.0
11	159	15.6	93	15.9	66	15.2
12	272	15.9	162	16.3	110	15.4
13	255	16.2	154	16.5	101	15.7
14	117	16.3	63	16.3	54	16.2
≥15	64	16.3	24	16.4	40	16.1
Grand Mean	957	16.0	552	16.2	405	15.6
R^2		.31		.29		.29
F-ratio		20.63***		11.57***		8.16***

NOTE: Estimates are based on unweighted sample cases. Dashes = not applicable. N.S. = not significant; *p<.10; **p<.05; ***p<.01.

TABLE C.5 Adjusted Proportion of Women 15-19 Years of Age in 1971 Who Had Two or More Premarital Sexual Partners

Variable	Total n	Total Adjusted Proportion	White n	White Adjusted Proportion	Black n	Black Adjusted Proportion
Race		*		—		—
White	691	.41		—		—
Black	652	.36		—		—
SES (years)		N.S.		N.S.		N.S.
<9	326	.37	104	.38	222	.37
9-11	526	.38	248	.36	278	.41
12	267	.40	172	.38	95	.42
≥13	224	.41	167	.44	57	.30
Family Stability		***		***		N.S.
Ideal	698	.35	450	.34	248	.36
Less ideal	332	.46	144	.50	188	.42
Least ideal	313	.40	97	.42	216	.38
Religion		N.S.		N.S.		N.S.
Fundamentalist Protestant	93	.41	47	.36	46	.46
Other Protestant	918	.38	390	.38	528	.37
Catholic	228	.40	183	.40	45	.43
Other	104	.44	71	.43	33	.42
Religiosity		**		***		N.S.
Low	377	.44	287	.45	90	.37
Medium	540	.38	280	.36	260	.40
High	426	.35	124	.30	302	.38
Years at Risk		***		***		***
0	342	.13	214	.14	128	.15
1	473	.36	269	.39	204	.32
2	276	.51	112	.56	164	.46
3	134	.64	52	.72	82	.57
≥4	118	.68	44	.73	74	.61
Grand Mean	1343	.39	691	.39	652	.39
R^2		.16		.23		.12
F-ratio		16.88***		14.06***		5.98***

NOTE: Estimates are based on unweighted sample cases. Dashes = not applicable. N.S. = not significant; *p<.10; **p<.05; ***p<.01.

TABLE C.6 Adjusted Proportion of Women 15-19 Years of Age in 1976 Who Had Two or More Premarital Sexual Partners

Variable	n	Adjusted Proportion
Race		N.S.
White	550	.47
Black	398	.50
SES (years)		N.S.
<9	195	.49
9-11	344	.46
12	254	.48
≥13	155	.50
Family Stability		***
Ideal	459	.43
Less ideal	277	.51
Least ideal	212	.55
Religion		N.S.
Fundamentalist Protestant	94	.56
Other Protestant	562	.46
Catholic	180	.48
Other	112	.52
Religiosity		N.S.
Low	344	.50
Medium	386	.47
High	218	.47
Years at Risk		***
0	199	.14
1	324	.37
2	195	.67
3	112	.73
≥4	118	.80
Grand Mean	948	.48
R^2		.27
F-ratio		22.75***

NOTE: Estimates are based on unweighted sample cases N.S. = not significant; *p<.10; **p<.05; ***p<.01.

TABLE C.7 Adjusted Mean Number of Premarital Sexual Partners for Women 15-19 Years of Age in 1976

Variable	Total n	Total Adjusted Mean	White n	White Adjusted Mean	Black n	Black Adjusted Mean
Race		***		–		
White	550	2.8		–		
Black	396	2.2		–		–
SES (years)		N.S.		N.S.		N.S.
<9	195	2.4	83	2.5	112	2.5
9-11	343	2.4	193	2.5	150	2.3
12	253	2.5	154	2.4	99	2.6
≥13	155	3.2	120	3.3	35	2.4
Family Stability		N.S.		N.S.		N.S.
Ideal	458	2.5	335	2.6	123	2.4
Less ideal	277	2.7	143	2.5	134	2.6
Least ideal	211	2.5	72	3.0	139	2.3
Religion		**		*		N.S.
Fundamentalist Prostastant	93	2.7	48	3.0	45	2.5
Other Protestant	561	2.3	284	2.2	277	2.4
Catholic	180	2.8	159	2.9	21	1.9
Other	112	3.3	59	3.4	53	3.0
Religiosity		N.S.		N.S.		N.S.
Low	344	2.8	259	2.7	85	2.9
Medium	385	2.4	213	2.6	172	2.2
High	217	2.4	78	2.4	139	2.4
Years Sexually Active		***		***		***
0	279	1.2	189	1.4	90	1.3
1	290	1.8	191	1.8	99	1.9
2	178	3.0	96	3.0	82	2.9
3	97	4.3	41	5.2	56	3.4
≥4	102	6.0	33	10.3	69	3.6
Grand Mean	946	2.6	550	2.6	396	2.4
R^2		.20		.30		.17
F-ratio		15.41***		16.74***		5.47***

NOTE: Estimates are based on unweighted sample cases. Dashes = not applicable; N.S. = not significant; *$p<.10$; *$p<.05$; *$p<.01$.

TABLE C.8   Adjusted Mean Frequency of Intercourse for Never-Married Women 15-19 Years of Age in 1971

Variable	Total n	Total Adjusted Mean	White n	White Adjusted Mean	Black n	Black Adjusted Mean
Race		**		—		—
White	493	3.0		—		—
Black	543	2.2		—		—
SES (years)		N.S.		*		N.S.
<9	251	2.7	67	3.7	184	2.0
9-11	404	2.5	174	2.7	230	2.3
12	199	2.2	120	2.5	79	2.1
≥13	182	3.1	132	3.8	50	1.9
Family Stability		N.S.		N.S.		N.S.
Ideal	532	2.6	324	2.9	208	2.4
Less ideal	261	2.4	101	3.5	160	1.6
Least ideal	243	2.7	68	3.3	175	2.2
Religion		**		N.S.		N.S.
Fundamentalist Protestant	64	2.0	29	2.8	35	1.4
Other Protestant	708	2.5	270	2.9	438	2.1
Catholic	177	2.4	138	3.0	39	2.0
Other	87	4.1	56	4.5	31	2.9
Religiosity		N.S.		*		N.S.
Low	284	2.9	210	3.6	74	1.8
Medium	410	2.3	194	2.5	216	2.1
High	342	2.6	89	3.1	253	2.2
Marriage Plans		***		***		N.S.
Yes	387	3.5	195	4.6	192	2.4
No	649	2.0	298	2.1	351	2.0
Contraceptive Use Last Intercourse		***		***		**
Medical method	166	4.5	74	6.6	92	2.7
Nonmedical method	296	1.8	153	2.2	143	1.5
None	574	2.4	266	2.7	308	2.2
Number of Partners		**		*		*
1	637	2.3	306	2.7	331	2.0
2-3	274	2.8	112	3.7	162	2.0
≥4	125	3.5	75	3.8	50	3.2
Grand Mean	1036	2.6	493	3.1	543	2.1
R^2		.11		.20		.05
F-ratio		7.60***		7.71***		1.76**

NOTE: Estimates are based on unweighted sample cases. Dashes = not applicable.
  N.S. = not significant; *p<.10; **p<.05; ***p<.01.

TABLE C.9 Adjusted Mean Frequency of Intercourse for Never-Married Women 15-19 Years of Age in 1976

Variable	n	Total Adjusted Mean	n	White Adjusted Mean	n	Black Adjusted Mean
Race		**		—		—
White	360	2.6		—		—
Black	366	1.8		—		—
SES (years)		N.S.		N.S.		N.S.
<9	146	2.2	43	1.9	103	1.7
9-11	263	2.4	123	3.0	140	1.9
12	191	2.2	99	3.1	92	1.3
≥13	126	1.9	95	2.6	31	1.2
Family Stability		N.S.		N.S.		*
Ideal	341	2.2	228	2.6	113	2.1
Less ideal	216	2.5	88	3.4	128	1.7
Least ideal	169	1.9	44	2.6	125	1.2
Religion		N.S.		*		N.S.
Fundamentalist Protestant	69	2.1	27	3.6	42	1.3
Other Protestant	428	2.0	170	2.2	258	1.6
Catholic	142	2.5	123	2.9	19	2.8
Other	87	3.1	40	4.3	47	1.6
Religiosity		N.S.		N.S.		*
Low	273	2.6	190	2.9	83	2.4
Medium	275	2.2	126	3.0	149	1.5
High	178	1.8	44	1.8	134	1.4
Marriage Plans		***		***		N.S.
Yes	237	3.5	138	4.8	99	2.0
No	489	1.6	222	1.6	267	1.5
Contraceptive Use Last Intercourse		***		***		N.S.
Medical method	260	2.9	121	3.8	139	1.8
Nonmedical method	185	1.7	111	2.3	74	1.1
None	281	2.0	128	2.3	153	1.8
Number of Partners		***		***		***
1	334	1.4	189	1.7	145	1.0
2-3	258	2.1	103	2.8	155	1.7
≥4	134	4.5	68	5.9	66	2.9
Grand Mean	726	2.6	360	2.8	366	1.6
R^2		.17		.24		.10
F-ratio		8.85***		7.37***		2.59***

NOTE: Estimates are based on unweighted sample cases. Dashes = not applicable.
N.S. = not significant; *$p<.10$; **$p<.05$; ***$p<.01$.

TABLE C.10 Adjusted Proportion of Premaritally Sexually Active Women 15-19 Years of Age in 1976 Who Used a Contraceptive Method at First Intercourse

Variable	n	Adjusted Proportion
Race		N.S.
White	556	.36
Black	406	.39
Current Age		*
15	91	.47
16	141	.44
17	216	.35
18	261	.39
19	253	.32
SES (years)		*
<9	210	.30
9-11	347	.39
12	257	.38
≥13	157	.43
Family Stability		*
Ideal	467	.40
Less ideal	279	.39
Least ideal	216	.31
Religion		N.S.
Fundamentalist Protestant	96	.44
Other Protestant	570	.38
Catholic	180	.38
Other	116	.32
Religiosity		N.S.
Low	347	.35
Medium	392	.38
High	223	.41
Age First Intercourse		***
≤13	102	.17
14	145	.29
15	229	.35
16	229	.39
17	160	.48
≥18	97	.58
Grand Mean	962	.38
R^2		.07
F-ratio		3.67***

NOTE: Estimates are based on unweighted sample cases. N.S. = not significant; *p<.10; **p<.05; ***p<.01.

TABLE C.11 Adjusted Proportion of Premaritally Sexually Active Women 15-19 Years of Age in 1976 Using a Contraceptive Method at First Intercourse Who Used a Medical Method

Variable	n	Total Adjusted Proportion	n	White Adjusted Proportion	n	Black Adjusted Proportion
Race		***		—		—
White	217	.19		—		—
Black	145	.42		—		—
Current Age		N.S.		N.S.		N.S.
15-16	83	.30	} 82	} .18	} 76	} .44
17	73	.29				
18	110	.26	} 135	} .20	} 69	} .39
19	94	.28				
SES (years)		N.S.		N.S.		N.S.
<9	58	.26	} 100	} .18	} 92	} .41
9-11	134	.29				
12	101	.29	} 117	} .20	} 53	} .44
≥13	69	.29				
Family Stability		N.S.		N.S.		N.S.
Ideal	197	.27	148	.17	49	.43
Less ideal	106	.27				
Least ideal	59	.37	} 69	} .24	} 96	} .41
Religion		N.S.		N.S.		
Fundamentalist Protestant	39	.17				
Other Protestant	220	.30	} 136	} .22		
Catholic	71	.26				
Other	32	.34	} 81	} .14		
Religiosity		N.S.		N.S.		N.S.
Low	115	.29	90	.21	25	.42
Medium	153	.30	92	.17	61	.47
High	94	.25	35	.22	59	.37
Age First Intercourse		**		*		N.S.
≤14	62	.23				
15	82	.20	} 79	} .13	} 65	} .35
16	88	.28	44	.15	44	.47
17	75	.28				
≥18	55	.48	} 94	} .27	} 36	} .48
Grand Mean	362	.28	217	.19	145	.42
R^2		.11		.05		.03
F-ratio		2.49***		1.45*		.61 N.S.

NOTE: Estimates are bases on unweighted sample cases. Religion was not included in the equation for blacks because almost all of them were Protestant. Dashes = not applicable. N.S. = not significant; *$p<.10$; **$p<.05$; ***$p<.01$.

TABLE C.12 Adjusted Proportion of Never-Married Sexually Active Women 15-19 Years of Age Who Used a Contraceptive Method at Last Intercourse

Variable	1971 n	1971 Adjusted Proportion	1976 n	1976 Adjusted Proportion
Race		N.S.		N.S.
White	520	.46	364	.61
Black	585	.43	375	.61
Current Age		N.S.		N.S.
15	155	.40	82	.49
16	227	.40	134	.61
17	284	.46	187	.60
18	245	.47	188	.67
19	194	.50	148	.62
SES (years)		*		**
<9	269	.43	151	.53
9-11	432	.41	267	.62
12	211	.46	194	.58
≥13	193	.53	127	.73
Family Stability		N.S.		N.S.
Ideal	570	.45	347	.61
Less ideal	273	.46	218	.64
Least ideal	262	.43	174	.57
Religion		**		N.S.
Fundamentalist Protestant	70	.36	71	.68
Other Protestant	762	.43	435	.61
Catholic	182	.51	142	.62
Other	91	.53	91	.56
Religiosity		N.S.		N.S.
Low	296	.44	274	.61
Medium	435	.44	283	.62
High	374	.46	182	.61
Age First Intercourse		**		*
≤13	112	.39	87	.46
14	130	.32	116	.61
15	230	.44	175	.60
16	318	.47	172	.63
17	187	.53	118	.68
≥18	128	.47	71	.68
Marriage Plans		N.S.		N.S.
Yes	400	.46	239	.59
No	705	.44	500	.62
Grand Mean	1105	.45	739	.61
R^2		.05		.06
F-ratio		2.60***		2.34***

NOTE: Estimates are based on unweighted sample cases. N.S. = not significant; *p<.10; **p<.05; ***p<.01.

TABLE C.13 Adjusted Proportion of Never-Married Women 15-19 Years of Age in 1976 Who Used a Contraceptive Method at Last Intercourse

Variable	n	Adjusted Proportion
Race		N.S.
White	295	.68
Black	287	.65
Current Age		N.S.
15	52	.62
16	102	.67
17	152	.67
18	155	.68
19	121	.67
SES (years)		N.S.
<9	111	.65
9-11	206	.67
12	156	.64
≥13	109	.71
Family Stability		N.S.
Ideal	275	.68
Less ideal	173	.65
Least ideal	134	.65
Religion		N.S.
Fundamentalist Protestant	54	.71
Other Protestant	336	.67
Catholic	115	.66
Other	77	.62
Religiosity		N.S.
Low	230	.68
Medium	215	.67
High	137	.64
Age First Intercourse		N.S.
≤13	69	.52
14	87	.68
15	140	.68
16	138	.65
17	96	.74
≥18	52	.70
Marriage Plans		N.S.
Yes	192	.65
No	390	.67

TABLE C.13 Continued

Variable	n	Adjusted Proportion
Contraceptive Use First Intercourse		***
Medical method	74	1.00
Nonmedical method	148	.92
None	360	.49
Number of Partners		N.S.
1	219	.63
2-3	244	.67
≥4	119	.73
Ever Pregnant		***
Yes	128	.80
No	454	.63
Grand Mean	582	.67
R^2		.26
F-ratio		9.57***

NOTE: Estimates are based on unweighted sample cases. This table contains data for young women who had intercourse at least twice and were not pregnant at last intercourse. N.S. = not significant; *p $<$ .10; **p $<$ .05; ***p $<$ .01.

TABLE C.14 Adjusted Proportion of Never-Married Women 15-19 Years of Age in 1971 Using a Contraceptive Method at Last Intercourse Who Used a Medical Method

Variable	Total n	Total Adjusted Proportion	White n	White Adjusted Proportion	Black n	Black Adjusted Proportion
Race		*		—		—
White	242	.31		—		—
Black	253	.39		—		—
Current Age		***		***		***
15-16	137	.09	62	.00	75	.20
17	133	.31	61	.26	72	.35
18	121	.48	58	.46	63	.51
19	104	.60	61	.61	43	.56
SES (years)		N.S.		N.S.		N.S.
<9	114	.31			89	.36
9-11	176	.39	}100	}.31	101	.45
12	100	.35	61	.35		
≥13	105	.33	81	.31	}63	}.30
Family Stability		**		N.S.		N.S.
Ideal	267	.30	172	.29	95	.30
Less ideal	120	.43	41	.39	79	.45
Least ideal	108	.40	29	.42	79	.40
Religion		**		***		**
Fundamentalist Protestant	22	.21				
Other Protestant	330	.32	}133	}.27	}219	}.36
Catholic	96	.38	76	.29		
Other	47	.54	33	.59	}34	}.48
Religiosity		N.S.		N.S.		N.S.
Low	135	.35	108	.31	27	.32
Medium	172	.40	98	.37	94	.45
High	168	.30	36	.24	132	.34
Age First Intercourse		N.S.		N.S.		N.S.
≤14	75	.45	27	.29	51	.51
15	95	.41	38	.42	57	.43
16	149	.35	71	.37	78	.35
17	105	.27				
≥18	68	.28	}106	}.26	}67	}.26
Marriage Plans		**		N.S.		N.S.
Yes	185	.40	104	.34	81	.48
No	310	.32	138	.30	172	.33
Grand Mean	495	.35	242	.32	253	.38
R^2		.18		.27		.17
F-ratio		5.36***		4.04***		6.08***

NOTE: Estimates are based on unweighted sample cases. Dashes = not applicable. N.S. = not significant; *$p<.10$; **$p<.05$; ***$p<.01$.

TABLE C.15 Adjusted Proportion of Never-Married Women 15-19 Years of Age in 1976 Using a Contraceptive Method at Last Intercourse Who Used a Medical Method

Variable	n	Total Adjusted Proportion	n	White Adjusted Proportion	n	Black Adjusted Proportion
Race		***		—		—
White	235	.51		—		—
Black	215	.67		—		—
Current Age		***		***		***
15-16	113	.38	52	.26	61	.48
17	114	.63	64	.56	50	.69
18	130	.65	67	.60	63	.72
19	93	.68	52	.61	41	.76
SES (years)		N.S.		N.S.		*
<9	78	.58	}102	}.47	57	.64
9-11	164	.53			83	.63
12	116	.64	59	.56	}75	}.70
≥13	92	.60	74	.55		
Family Stability		N.S.		N.S.		N.S.
Ideal	220	.57	154	.50	66	.68
Less ideal	139	.56	55	.52	84	.61
Least ideal	91	.65	26	.64	65	.69
Religion		*		*		N.S.
Fundamentalist Protestant	45	.55	}129	}.54	}182	}.62
Other Protestant	266	.58				
Catholic	90	.53	78	.43	}33	}.83
Other	49	.75	28	.67		
Religiosity		N.S.		**		N.S.
Low	166	.63	124	.58	42	.59
Medium	177	.58	84	.49	93	.69
High	107	.52	27	.32	80	.65
Age First Intercourse		N.S.		N.S.		***
≤14	103	.65	36	.55	67	.74
15	103	.60	55	.60	48	.60
16	110	.54	61	.47	49	.60
17	83	.54	}83	}.48	}51	}.64
≥18	51	.57				
Marriage Plans		N.S.		N.S.		**
Yes	146	.60	92	.52	54	.70
No	304	.57	143	.52	161	.64
Grand Mean	450	.58	235	.52	215	.65
R^2		.11		.15		.09
F-ratio		2.95***		2.60***		1.48**

NOTE: Estimates are based on unweighted sample cases. Dashes = not applicable. N.S. = not significant; *p<.10; **p<.05; ***p<.01.

TABLE C.16 Adjusted Proportion of Never-Married Women 15-19 Years of Age in 1976 Using a Contraceptive Method at Last Intercourse Who Used a Medical Method (Reanalysis)

Variable	n	Adjusted Proportion
Race		N.S.
White	205	.59
Black	181	.69
Current Age		*
15-16	92	.52
17	99	.67
18	112	.70
19	83	.64
SES (years)		N.S.
<9	65	.65
9-11	141	.58
12	100	.69
≥13	80	.66
Family Stability		N.S.
Ideal	194	.64
Less ideal	113	.63
Least ideal	79	.64
Religion		N.S.
Fundamentalist Protestant	37	.67
Other Protestant	225	.62
Catholic	80	.58
Other	44	.77
Religiosity		N.S.
Low	151	.67
Medium	148	.63
High	87	.60
Age First Intercourse		N.S.
≤14	90	.61
15	90	.66
16	92	.58
17	73	.67
≥18	41	.72
Marriage Plans		N.S.
Yes	129	.63
No	257	.64
Contraceptive Use First Intercourse		***
Medical method	72	.91
Nonmedical method	136	.40
None	178	.71

TABLE C.16 (Continued)

Variable	Always Used		Always Used	
	n	Adjusted Proportion	n	Adjusted Proportion
Number of Partners			N.S.	
1			150	.62
2-3			160	.62
≥4			76	.71
Ever Pregnant			***	
Yes			88	.81
No			298	.58
Grand Mean			386	.64
R^2				.30
F-ratio				6.58***

NOTE: Estimates are based on unweighted sample cases. This table contains data for young women who had intercourse at least twice and were not pregnant at last intercourse. N.S. = not significant; *p $<$ .10; **p $<$ .05; ***p $<$ .01.

TABLE C.17 Adjusted Proportion of Premaritally Sexually Active Women 15-19 Years of Age in 1976 Who Always Used Contraceptives and Who Never Used Contraceptives

Variable	Always Used n	Always Used Adjusted Proportion	Never Used n	Never Used Adjusted Proportion
Race		N.S.		N.S.
White	476	.24	476	.36
Black	351	.28	351	.34
Current Age		***		N.S.
15	63	.35	63	.24
16	113	.36	113	.28
17	188	.26	188	.33
18	232	.24	232	.37
19	231	.18	231	.40
SES (years)		N.S.		***
<9	174	.20	174	.43
9-11	294	.29	294	.40
12	222	.24	222	.31
≥13	137	.27	137	.20
Family Stability		N.S.		***
Ideal	397	.29	397	.29
Less ideal	241	.24	241	.35
Least ideal	189	.20	189	.45
Religion		N.S.		N.S.
Fundamentalist Protestant	84	.34	84	.30
Other Protestant	488	.25	488	.35
Catholic	156	.28	156	.37
Other	99	.19	99	.34
Religiosity		N.S.		N.S.
Low	308	.26	308	.35
Medium	332	.24	332	.35
High	187	.28	187	.33
Age First Intercourse		***		**
≤13	89	.07	89	.50
14	128	.18	128	.39
15	199	.22	199	.33
16	196	.28	196	.35
17	138	.35	138	.27
≥18	77	.43	77	.24
Grand Mean	827	.25	827	.35
R^2		.07		.08
F-ratio		3.06***		3.50***

NOTE Estimates are based on unweighted sample cases. This table contains data for young women who had premarital intercourse at least twice. N.S. = not significant; *p<.10; **p<.05; ***p<.01.

TABLE C.18 Adjusted Proportion of Premaritally Sexually Active Ever-Contracepting Women 15-19 Years of Age in 1976 Who Ever Used a Medical Method

Variable	n	Total Adjusted Proportion	n	White Adjusted Proportion	n	Black Adjusted Proportion
Race		***		—		—
White	356	.59		—		—
Black	271	.79		—		—
Current Age		***		***		***
15	43	.36	}62	}.33	}66	}.57
16	85	.47				
17	141	.69	85	.59	56	.81
18	175	.77	94	.71	81	.85
19	183	.74	115	.64	68	.88
SES (years)		N.S.		N.S.		N.S.
<9	126	.64	47	.60	79	.73
9-11	215	.67	115	.54	100	.82
12	171	.67	104	.57	67	.80
≥13	115	.73	90	.68	25	.70
Family Stability		**		*		N.S.
Ideal	311	.62	226	.55	85	.75
Less ideal	182	.70	88	.64	94	.78
Least ideal	134	.75	42	.73	92	.82
Religion		N.S.		N.S.		**
Fundamentalist Protestant	63	.66	32	.65	31	.68
Other Protestant	371	.67	181	.58	190	.77
Catholic	116	.64	103	.55	}50	}.89
Other	77	.76	40	.71		
Religiosity		**		***		N.S.
Low	232	.71	172	.66	60	.79
Medium	249	.67	134	.57	115	.79
High	146	.62	50	.43	96	.76
Age First Intercourse		**		***		N.S.
≤13	56	.79	}59	}.53	}100	}.84
14	103	.66				
15	155	.69	89	.66	66	.75
16	142	.62	88	.55	54	.74
17	112	.65	}120	}.60	}51	}.76
≥18	59	.71				
Grand Mean	627	.67	356	.59	271	.78
R^2		.15		.15		.11
F-ratio		5.42***		3.74***		2.21***

NOTE: Estimates are based on unweighted sample cases. This table contains data for young women who had premarital intercourse at least twice. Dashes = not applicable; N.S. = not significant; *$p<.10$; **$p<.05$; ***$p<.01$.

TABLE C.19 Adjusted Proportion of Premaritally Sexually Active Women 15-19 Years of Age in 1976 Who Obtained First Pill Prescription or IUD Insertion from a Clinic

Variable	Total n	Total Adjusted Proportion	White n	White Adjusted Proportion	Black n	Black Adjusted Proportion
Race		**		—		—
White	207	.42		—		—
Black	213	.57		—		—
Current Age		**		N.S.		**
15-16	62	.39	}65	}.48	}89	}.55
17	92	.58				
18	134	.54		.38	66	.67
19	132	.44		.42	58	.45
SES (years)		N.S.		N.S.		**
≤11	222	.53	81	.38	141	.62
≥12	198	.45	126	.45	72	.44
Family Stability		N.S.		N.S		N.S.
Ideal	181	.48	118	.46	63	.50
Less ideal	130	.48	57	.38	73	.58
Least ideal	109	.53	32	.39	77	.60
Religion		N.S.		N.S.		N.S.
Protestant	289	.50	120	.47	169	.56
Other	131	.47	87	.36	44	.58
Religiosity		***		**		*
Low	159	.60	113	.51	46	.69
Medium/high	261	.43	94	.32	167	.53
Age First Intercourse		N.S.		N.S.		N.S.
≤14	107	.53	28	.47	79	.58
15	102	.52	54	.46	48	.58
16	88	.54	45	.49	43	.62
≥17	123	.41	80	.35	43	.47
Grand Mean	420	.50	207	.42	213	.56
R^2		.08		.06		.11
F-ratio		3.05***		1.26 N.S.		2.57***

NOTE: Estimates are based on unweighted sample cases. Dashes = not applicable.
N.S. = not significant; *p<.10; **p<.05; ***p<.01.

TABLE C.20 Adjusted Proportion of Premaritally Sexually Active Women 15-19 Years of Age in 1971 Who Had a Premarital Pregnancy

Variable	n	Total Adjusted Proportion	n	White Adjusted Proportion	n	Black Adjusted Proportion
Race		***		—		—
White	702	.28		—		—
Black	678	.40		—		—
Current Age		***		***		***
15	168	.00	70	.00	98	.00
16	260	.14	116	.02	144	.28
17	327	.32	163	.21	164	.44
18	322	.49	172	.36	150	.64
19	303	.57	181	.42	122	.72
SES (years)		***		***		**
<9	335	.40	107	.32	228	.48
9-11	542	.36	252	.26	290	.45
12	274	.34	175	.27	99	.39
≥13	229	.22	168	.15	61	.28
Family Stability		**		N.S.		*
Ideal	717	.32	457	.22	260	.40
Less ideal	342	.33	147	.27	195	.42
Least ideal	321	.40	98	.30	223	.49
Religion		N.S.		N.S.		N.S.
Fundamentalist Protestant	96	.33	47	.21	49	.45
Other Protestant	946	.34	397	.26	549	.42
Catholic	231	.36	186	.24	45	.54
None	107	.32	72	.20	35	.51
Religiosity		N.S.		N.S.		N.S.
Low	382	.32	290	.21	92	.46
Medium	555	.37	287	.28	268	.46
High	443	.32	125	.25	318	.42
Age First Intercourse		***		***		***
≤13	142	.50	57	.34	85	.63
14	167	.59	65	.48	102	.67
15	297	.50	131	.40	166	.59
16	386	.29	201	.25	185	.34
17	234	.16	131	.14	103	.17
≥18	154	.00	117	.00	37	.00
Grand Mean	1380	.34	702	.24	678	.44
R^2		.22		.16		.24
F-ratio		19.40***		6.67***		11.17***

NOTE: Estimates are based on unweighted sample cases. Dashes = not applicable. N.S. = not significant; *p<.10; **p<.05; ***p<.01.

TABLE C.21 Adjusted Proportion of Premaritally Sexually Active Women 15-19 Years of Age in 1976 Who Had a Premarital Pregnancy

Variable	n	Total Adjusted Proportion
Race		N.S.
White	556	.30
Black	407	.35
Current Age		***
15	90	.08
16	142	.03
17	217	.25
18	262	.39
19	252	.55
SES (years)		N.S.
<9	202	.38
9-11	347	.32
12	257	.30
≥13	157	.28
Family Stability		N.S.
Ideal	466	.29
Less ideal	280	.33
Least ideal	217	.36
Religion		N.S.
Fundamentalist Protestant	95	.24
Other Protestant	570	.31
Catholic	181	.36
None	117	.36
Religiosity		N.S.
Low	348	.30
Medium	393	.34
High	222	.31
Age First Intercourse		***
≤13	102	.45
14	144	.51
15	231	.40
16	228	.29
17	161	.19
≥18	97	.01
Grand Mean	963	.32
R^2		.17
F-ratio		9.82***

NOTE: Estimates are based on unweighted sample cases. N.S. not significant; *p<.01; **p<.05; ***p<.01.

TABLE C.22 Adjusted Proportion of Premaritally Sexually Active Women 15-19 Years of Age in 1976 Who Had a Premarital Pregnancy (Reanalysis)

Variable	n	Total Adjusted Proportion	n	White Adjusted Proportion	n	Black Adjusted Proportion
Race		*		—		—
White	555	.30		—		—
Black	405	.35		—		—
Current Age		***		***		***
15	90	.07	42	.15	48	.03
16	141	.06	73	.01	68	.19
17	216	.26	124	.23	92	.28
18	261	.38	157	.31	104	.48
19	252	.53	159	.45	93	.64
SES (years)		N.S.		N.S.		N.S.
<9	201	.35	84	.35	117	.40
9-11	346	.31	194	.27	152	.34
12	256	.31	155	.26	101	.38
≥13	157	.32	122	.27	35	.41
Family Stability		N.S.		N.S.		N.S.
Ideal	466	.30	338	.26	128	.33
Less ideal	278	.33	144	.31	134	.39
Least ideal	216	.34	73	.30	143	.39
Religion		N.S.		N.S.		N.S.
Fundamentalist Protestant	95	.26	49	.25	46	.27
Other Protestant	569	.31	285	.26	284	.38
Catholic	180	.36	159	.32	21	.40
Other	116	.35	62	.30	54	.44
Religiosity		N.S.		N.S.		N.S.
Low	346	.30	261	.26	84	.32
Medium	392	.34	216	.27	176	.43
High	222	.32	78	.35	144	.34
Age First Intercourse		***		***		***
≤13	102	.40	38	.35	64	.45
14	144	.49	67	.32	77	.62
15	229	.39	134	.37	95	.41
16	228	.29	137	.30	91	.29
17	160	.21	106	.24	54	.15
≥18	97	.05	73	.05	24	.06

(Continued)

TABLE C.22 (Continued)

Variable	n	Total Adjusted Proportion	n	White Adjusted Proportion	n	Black Adjusted Proportion
Contraceptive Status		***		***		***
Always used	267	.16	157	.15	110	.16
Used First—not always	95	.37	60	.30	35	.48
Not First—used later	236	.20	147	.20	89	.19
Never used	362	.50	191	.44	171	.58
Grand Mean	960	.32	555	.28	405	.37
R^2		.27		.19		.43
F-ratio		15.43***		5.56***		13.24***

NOTE: Estimates are based on unweighted sample cases. Dashes = not applicable. N.S. = not significant; *p<.10; **p<.05; ***p<.01.

TABLE C.23 Adjusted Mean Age at First Premarital Conception for Women Aged 15-19 Years of Age

	1971		1976	
Variable	n	Adjusted Mean	n	Adjusted Mean
Race		N.S.		N.S.
White	162	16.4	155	16.5
Black	286	16.4	152	16.5
Current Age		***		***
15-16	87	15.8	38	15.9
17	106	16.3	60	16.3
18	129	16.7	89	16.7
19	126	16.7	120	16.8
SES (years)		**		N.S.
<9	144	16.4	80	16.5
9-11	196	16.3	110	16.4
12	79	16.7	78	16.6
≥13	29	16.6	39	16.7
Family Stability		**		N.S.
Ideal	197	16.5	124	16.5
Less ideal	113	16.2	93	16.6
Least ideal	138	16.5	90	16.5
Religion		N.S.		N.S.
Fundamentalist Protestant	33	16.4	25	16.5
Other Protestant	321	16.5	186	16.6
Catholic	65	16.3	54	16.5
Other	29	16.3	42	16.4
Religiosity		**		***
Low	100	16.5	106	16.8
Medium	203	16.5	132	16.5
High	145	16.3	69	16.2
Age First Intercourse		***		***
≤13	54	15.2	39	15.6
14	72	15.7	64	15.7
15	122	16.0	81	16.3
16	115	16.9	65	17.1
≥17	85	17.7	58	17.8
Pregnancy Intention		N.S.		N.S.
Wanted	133	16.5	107	16.5
Not wanted/using contraception	40	16.5	31	16.8
Not wanted/not using contraception	275	16.4	169	16.5
Grand Mean	448	16.4	307	16.5
R^2		.63		.57
F-ratio		36.04***		18.68***

NOTE: Estimates are based on unweighted sample cases. N.S. = not significant; *p < .10; **p < .05; ***p < .01.
a. Includes a small number of stillbirths.

TABLE C.24 Adjusted Proportion of Premaritally Pregnant Women 15-19 Years of Age Whose First Pregnancy Ended in a Live Birth[a]

Variable	1971 n	1971 Adjusted Proportion	1976 n	1976 Adjusted Proportion
Race		**		***
White	130	.78	135	.65
Black	248	.89	138	.83
Current Age		N.S.		***
15-16	70	.80	29	.51
17	82	.79	53	.69
18	107	.89	80	.79
19	119	.88	111	.79
SES (years)		N.S.		**
<9	129	.83	72	.83
9-11	165	.86	100	.77
12	63	.81	68	.68
≥13	21	.98	33	.59
Family Stability		N.S.		N.S.
Ideal	166	.87	108	.71
Less ideal	100	.82	85	.74
Least ideal	112	.86	80	.78
Religion		N.S.		N.S.
Fundamentalist Protestant	32	.80	24	.73
Other Protestant	270	.86	165	.74
Catholic	51	.83	46	.77
Other	25	.85	38	.72
Religiosity		N.S.		**
Low	83	.82	93	.65
Medium	173	.88	118	.79
High	122	.84	62	.79
Age First Conception		**		**
≤14	59	.89	40	.86
15	106	.89	68	.78
16	95	.90	70	.77
≥17	118	.76	95	.64
Pregnancy Intention		***		***
Wanted	108.9	.93	95	.93
Not wanted	270	.82	178	.64
Grand Mean	378	.85	273	.74
R^2		.08		.31
F-ratio		1.63*		6.30***

NOTE: Estimates are based on unweighted sample cases. N.S. = not significant; *p<.10; **p<.05; ***p<.01.

TABLE C.25 Adjusted Proportion of Premaritally Pregnant White Women 15-19 Years of Age Whose First Pregnancy Ended in a Live Birth[a]

Variable	n	1971 Adjusted Proportion	n	1976 Adjusted Proportion
Current Age		N.S.		**
≤17	40	.70	38	.45
18	42	.86	39	.66
19	48	.79	58	.69
SES (years)		N.S.		***
≤11	83	.78	77	.71
≥12	47	.78	58	.48
Family Stability		N.S.		N.S.
Ideal	77	.82	69	.62
Not ideal	53	.73	66	.61
Religion		N.S.		N.S.
Protestant	90	.81	77	.60
Catholic	29	.74	42	.66
Other	11	.68	16	.54
Religiosity		N.S.		N.S.
Low	48	.71	64	.59
Medium/high	82	.83	71	.64
Age First Conception		**		**
≤16	81	.86	73	.69
≥17	49	.67	62	.52
Pregnancy Intention		**		***
Wanted	46	.89	55	.88
Not wanted	84	.72	80	.43
Grand Mean	130	.78	135	.61
R^2		.11		.38
F-ratio		1.59 N.S.		8.68***

NOTE: Estimates are based on unweighted sample cases. N.S. = not significant; $*p<.10$; $**p<.05$; $***p<.01$.

a. Includes a small number of stillbirths.

TABLE C.26 Adjusted Proportion of Premaritally Pregnant Women 15-19 Years of Age Whose First Pregnancy Ended in a Live Birth and Who Married While Pregnant

Variable	n	1971 Adjusted Proportion	n	1976 Adjusted Proportion
Race		***		***
White	102	.62	83	.68
Black	220	.08	119	.12
Current Age		N.S.		N.S.
≤17	127	.27	54	.29
18	94	.21	63	.37
19	101	.27	85	.36
SES (years)		*		***
≤11	253	.23	139	.30
≥12	69	.32	63	.46
Family Stability		N.S.		N.S.
Ideal	141	.27	75	.39
Less ideal	83	.26	61	.28
Least ideal	98	.22	66	.35
Religiosity		N.S.		N.S.
Low	67	.18	56	.31
Medium	150	.26	94	.37
High	105	.29	52	.35
Age First Conception		*		N.S.
≤14	51	.28	34	.28
15	92	.25	54	.30
16	85	.18	53	.42
≥17	94	.30	61	.36
Pregnancy Intention		***		*
Wanted	98	.34	89	.40
Not wanted	224	.21	113	.30
Grand Mean	322	.25	202	.35
R^2		.40		.49
F-ratio		17.21***		15.37***

NOTE: Estimates are based on unweighted sample cases. N.S. = not significant; *p<.10; **p<.05; ***p<.01.

TABLE C.27 Adjusted Proportion of Premaritally Pregnant Women 15-19 Years of Age Whose First Pregnancy Ended in an Illegitimate Live Birth

Variable	1971 n	1971 Adjusted Proportion	1976 n	1976 Adjusted Proportion
Race		***		***
White	130	.29	135	.21
Black	248	.81	138	.72
Current Age		*		N.S.
15-16	70	.54	29	.36
17	82	.58	53	.49
18	107	.71	80	.48
19	119	.65	111	.49
SES (years)		N.S.		***
<9	129	.64	72	.62
9-11	165	.66	100	.50
12	63	.54	68	.37
≥13	21	.68	33	.27
Family Stability		N.S.		N.S.
Ideal	166	.62	108	.41
Less ideal	100	.63	85	.53
Least ideal	112	.65	80	.49
Religion		N.S.		N.S.
Fundamentalist Protestant	32	.57	24	.52
Other Protestant	270	.63	165	.44
Catholic	51	.68	46	.50
Other	25	.68	38	.52
Religiosity		N.S.		N.S.
Low	83	.67	93	.43
Medium	173	.63	118	.50
High	122	.62	62	.48
Age First Conception		***		**
≤14	59	.65	40	.59
15	106	.67	68	.54
16	95	.72	70	.40
≥17	118	.52	95	.42
Pregnancy Intention		N.S.		N.S.
Wanted	108	.58	95	.48
Not wanted	270	.65	178	.46
Grand Mean	378	.63	273	.47
R^2		.31		.45
F-ratio		9.10***		11.60***

NOTE: Estimates are based on unweighted sample cases. N.S. = not significant; *p<.10; **p<.05; ***p<.01.

TABLE C.28 Adjusted Proportion of Premaritally Pregnant White Women 15-19 Years of Age Whose First Pregnancy Ended in an Illegitimate Live Birth

Variable	1971 n	1971 Adjusted Proportion	1976 n	1976 Adjusted Proportion
Current Age		**		N.S.
≤17	40	.18	38	.14
18	42	.46	39	.15
19	48	.24	58	.20
SES (years)		N.S.		***
≤11	83	.33	77	.27
≥12	47	.23	58	.04
Family Stability		N.S.		N.S.
Ideal	77	.28	69	.15
Not ideal	53	.32	66	.19
Religion		N.S.		N.S.
Protestant	90	.28	77	.13
Catholic	29	.32	42	.23
Other	11	.29	16	.22
Religiosity		N.S.		N.S.
Low	48	.32	64	.19
Medium/high	82	.27	71	.15
Age First Conception		*		N.S.
≤16	81	.36	73	.18
≥17	49	.18	62	.16
Pregnancy Intention		**		N.S.
Wanted	46	.16	55	.19
Not wanted	84	.31	80	.16
Grand Mean	130	.29	135	.17
R^2		.13		.13
F-ratio		2.07**		2.14**

NOTE: Estimates are based on unweighted sample cases. N.S. = not significant; *p<.10; **p<.05; ***p<.01.

BIBLIOGRAPHY

Alan Guttmacher Institute (1976) *11 Million Teenagers*. New York: Planned Parenthood Federation of America.

Alan Guttmacher Institute (1978) *Contraceptive Services for Adolescents: United States, Each State and County, 1975*. New York: Author.

Alan Guttmacher Institute (1979) *Abortion 1976-1977: Need and Services in the United States, Each State and Metropolitan Area*. New York: Author.

Butz, W. P. and Ward, M. P. (1978) Countercyclical U.S. Fertility and the Implications. *Rand Paper,* P-6263. Santa Monica, CA: Rand Corporation.

Butz, W. P. and Ward, M. P. (1979) The Emergence of Countercyclical U.S. Fertility. *American Economic Review* 69: 318-328.

Cannon, K. and Richard, L. (1971) Premarital Sexual Behavior in the Sixties. *Journal of Marriage and the Family* 33: 37-49.

Card, J. J. (1977) *Long-Term Consequences for Children Born to Adolescent Parents*. Palo Alto, CA: American Institutes for Research.

Center for Disease Control (1977) *Abortion Surveillance: Annual Summary 1975*. Atlanta: Author.

Chilman, C. S. (1978) *Adolescent Sexuality in a Changing American Society: Social and Psychological Perspectives*. Washington, DC: Government Printing Office.

Chow, L. P., Gruhn, W., and Chang, W. P. (1979) Feasibility of the Randomized Response Technique. *American Journal of Public Health* 69: 273-276.

Clayton, R. (1972) Premarital Sexual Intercourse: A Substantive Test of the Contingent Consistency Model. *Journal of Marriage and the Family* 34: 273-281.

Coombs, L. C. (1977) Levels of Reliability in Fertility Survey Data. *Studies in Family Planning* 8: 218-232.

Cutright, P. (1971) Illegitimacy: Myths, Causes and Cures. *Family Planning Perspectives* 3(1): 26-48.

Cutright, P. (1972) The Teenage Sexual Revolution and the Myth of an Abstinent Past. *Family Planning Perspectives* 4(1): 24-31.

Davis, K. (1972) The American Family in Relation to Demographic Change. In C. F. Westoff and R. Parke (eds.) *Demographic and Social Aspects of Population Growth*. Washington, DC: Government Printing Office.

DeLamater, J. and MacCorquodale, P. (1975) The Effects of Interview Schedule Variations on Reported Sexual Behavior. *Sociological Methods and Research* 4: 215-236.

DeLamater, J. and MacCorquodale, P. (1979) *Premarital Sexuality*. Madison: University of Wisconsin Press.

Djerassi, C. (1970) Birth Control After 1984. *Science* 169: 941-951.

Easterlin, R. A. (1978) What Will 1984 Be Like? Socioeconomic Implications of Recent Twists in Age Structure. *Demography* 15: 397-432.

Easterlin, R. A., Wachter, M. L., and Wachter, S. M. (1978a) Demographic Influences on Economic Stability: The United States Experience. *Population and Development Review* 1: 1-22.

Easterlin, R. A., Wachter, M. L., and Wachter, S. M. (1978b) Changing Impact of Population Swings on American Economy. *Proceedings of the American Philosophical Society* 122: 119-130.

Evans, J., Selstad, G., and Welcher, W. (1976) Teenagers: Fertility Control Behavior and Attitudes Before and After Abortion, Childbearing or Negative Pregnancy Test. *Family Planning Perspectives* 8: 192-200.

Foreit, K. G. and Foreit, J. R. (1978) Correlates of Contraceptive Behavior Among Unmarried U.S. College Students. *Studies in Family Planning* 9: 169-174.

Freedman, D. S. and Thornton, A. (1979) The Long Term Impact of Pregnancy at Marriage on the Family's Economic Circumstances. *Family Planning Perspectives* 11: 6-20.

Furstenberg, F. F., Jr. (1976) *Unplanned Parenthood: The Social Consequences of Teenage Childbearing.* New York: Macmillan.

Gagnon, J. and Simon, W. (1973) *Sexual Conduct: The Social Sources of Human Sexuality.* Chicago: Aldine.

Goode, W. J. (1964) *The Family.* Englewood Cliffs, NJ: Prentice-Hall.

Hirsch, M., Seltzer, J., and Zelnik, M. (1981) Desired Family Size of American Teenagers. In G. E. Hendershot and P. J. Placek (eds.) *Predicting Fertility: Demographic Studies of Birth Expectations.* Lexington, MA: D. C. Heath.

Jessor, S. and Jessor, R. (1975) Transition from Virginity to Non-Virginity Among Youth: A Social-Psychological Study Over Time. *Development Psychology* 11: 473-484.

Kantner, J. F. and Zelnik, M. (1969) UNITED STATES: Exploratory Studies of Negro Family Formation—Common Conceptions About Birth Control. *Studies in Family Planning* 1(47): 10-13.

Kantner, J. F. and Zelnik, M. (1972) Sexual Experience of Young Unmarried Women in the United States. *Family Planning Perspectives* 4(4): 9-17.

Kantner, J. F. and Zelnik, M. (1973) Contraception and Pregnancy: Experience of Young Unmarried Women in the United States. *Family Planning Perspectives* 5: 21-35.

Knodel, J. and Piampiti, S. (1977) Response Reliability in a Longitudinal Survey in Thailand. *Studies in Family Planning* 8: 55-66.

Lindemann, C. (1974) *Birth Control and Unmarried Young Women.* New York: Springer.

Luker, K. (1975) *Taking Chances.* Berkeley: University of California Press.

McCarthy, J. and Menken, J. (1979) Marriage, Remarriage, Marital Disruption and Age at First Birth. *Family Planning Perspectives* 11: 21-29.

Moore, K. A. (1978) Teenage Childbirth and Welfare Dependency. *Family Planning Perspectives* 10: 233-235.

National Center for Health Statistics (1973) Natality, Vol. I. *Vital Statistics of the United States 1970.* Washington, DC: Government Printing Office.

National Center for Health Statistics (1975) Natality, Vol. I. *Vital Statistics of the United States 1971.* Washington, DC: Government Printing Office.

National Center for Health Statistics (1977) Teenage Childbearing: United States, 1966-75. *Monthly Vital Statistics Report* 26 (5, September supplement). Washington, DC: Government Printing Office.

National Center for Health Statistics (1978a) Advance Report Final Natality Statistics, 1976. *Monthly Vital Statistics Report* 26 (12, March supplement). Washington, DC: Government Printing Office.

National Center for Health Statistics (1978b) Natality, Vol. I. *Vital Statistics of the United States 1975.* Washington, DC: Government Printing Office.

National Center for Health Statistics (1980) Advance Report Final Natality Statistics, 1978. *Monthly Vital Statistics Report* 29 (1, April supplement). Washington, DC: Government Printing Office.

Presser, H. B. (1978a) Age at Menarche, Socio-sexual Behavior and Fertility. *Social Biology* 25: 94-101.

Presser, H. B. (1978b) Social Factors Affecting the Timing of the First Child. In W. B. Miller and L. F. Newman (eds.) *The First Child and Family Formation.* Chapel Hill: Carolina Population Center.

Reiss, I. (1967) *The Social Context of Sexual Permissiveness.* New York: Holt, Rinehart & Winston.

Reiss, I., Barnwart, A., and Foreman, H. (1975) Pre-Marital Contraceptive Usage: A Study and Some Theoretical Explanations. *Journal of Marriage and the Family* 37: 619-632.

Ryder, N. B. (1979) Consistency of Reporting Fertility Planning Status. *Studies in Family Planning* 10: 115-128.

Ryder, N. B. and Westoff, C. F. (1971) *Reproduction in the United States 1965.* Princeton: Princeton University Press.

Shah, F. and Zelnik, M. (1980) Sexuality in Adolescence. In B. B. Wolman and J. Money (eds.) *Handbook of Human Sexuality.* Englewood Cliffs, NJ: Prentice-Hall.

Shah, F., Zelnik, M., and Kantner, J. F. (1975) Unprotected Intercourse Among Unwed Teenagers. *Family Planning Perspectives* 7: 39-43.

Sklar, J. and Berkov, B. (1973) The Effect of Legal Abortion in Legitimate and Illegitimate Birth Rates: The California Experience. *Studies in Family Planning* 4: 281-292.

Sklar, J. and Berkov, B. (1974) Teenage Family Formation in Postwar America. *Family Planning Perspectives* 6: 80-90.

Sorensen, R. (1972) *Adolescent Sexuality in Contemporary America.* New York: World.

Udry, J. R. (1979) Age at Menarche, at First Intercourse, and at First Pregnancy. *Journal of Biosocial Science* 11: 433-441.

Udry, J. R., Bauman, K. E., and Morris, N. M. (1975) Changes in Premarital Experiences of Recent Decade-of-Birth Cohorts of Urban American Women. *Journal of Marriage and the Family* 37: 783-786.

United Nations (1978) *Demographic Yearbook 1977.* New York: United Nations Department of International Economic and Social Affairs.

U.S. Department of Commerce (1973a) Census of Population: 1970. Final Report PC(1)-D1. *U.S. Summary-Detailed Characteristics.* Washington, DC: Government Printing Office.

U.S. Department of Commerce (1973b) Census of Population: 1970. Final Report PC(2)-3A. *Women by Number of Children Ever Born.* Washington, DC: Government Printing Office.

U.S. Department of Commerce (1973c) Census of Population: 1970. Final Report PC(2)-4E. *Persons in Institutions and Other Group Quarters.* Washington, DC: Government Printing Office.

U.S. Department of Commerce (1973d) Census of Population and Housing: 1970 Evaluation and Research Program PHC(E)-2. *Test of Birth Registration Completeness 1964 to 1968.* Washington, DC: Government Printing Office.

U.S. Department of Commerce (1976) Premarital Fertility. *Current Population Reports,* Series P-23, No. 63. Washington, DC: Government Printing Office.

U.S. Department of Commerce (1977a) Marital Status and Living Arrangements: March 1976. *Current Population Reports,* Series P-20, No. 306. Washington, DC: Government Printing Office.

U.S. Department of Commerce (1977b) Estimates of the Population of the United States, by Age, Sex, and Race: July 1, 1974 to 1976. *Current Population Reports,* Series P-25, No. 643. Washington, DC: Government Printing Office.

U.S. Department of Commerce (1977c) Fertility of American Women: June 1976. *Current Population Reports,* Series P-20, No. 308. Washington, DC: Government Printing Office.

Vener, A. M. and Stewart, C. J. (1974) Adolescent Sexual Behavior in Middle America Revisited. *Journal of Marriage and the Family* 36: 728-735.

Westoff, C. F. (1977) Fertility Decline in the United States and Its Implications. In W. J. Cohen and C. F. Westoff, *Demographic Dynamics in America.* New York: Macmillan.

Yankelovich, D. (1974) *The New Morality: A Profile of American Youth in the 1970's.* New York: McGraw-Hill.

Zabin, L. S., Kantner, J. F., and Zelnik, M. (1979) The Risk of Adolescent Pregnancy in the First Months of Intercourse. *Family Planning Perspectives* 11: 215-226.

Zelnik, M. (1979) Sex Education and Knowledge of Pregnancy Risk Among U.S. Teenage Women. *Family Planning Perspectives* 11: 355-357.

Zelnik, M. (1980) Second Pregnancies to Premaritally Pregnant Teenagers, 1976 and 1971. *Family Planning Perspectives* 12: 69-75.

Zelnik, M. and Kantner, J. F. (1970) UNITED STATES: Exploratory Studies of Negro Family Formation—Factors Relating to Illegitimacy. *Studies in Family Planning* 1(60): 5-9.

Zelnik, M. and Kantner, J. F. (1972a) Some Preliminary Observations on Pre-Adult Fertility and Family Formation. *Studies in Family Planning* 3: 59-65.

Zelnik, M. and Kantner, J. F. (1972b) Sexuality, Contraception, and Pregnancy Among Young Unwed Females in the United States. In C. F. Westoff and R. Parke (eds.) *Demographic and Social Aspects of Population Growth.* Washington, DC: Government Printing Office.

Zelnik, M. and Kantner, J. F. (1972c) Probability of Premarital Intercourse. *Social Science Research* 1: 335-341.

Zelnik, M. and Kantner, J. F. (1973) Sex and Contraception Among Unmarried Teenagers. In C. F. Westoff (ed.) *Toward the End of Growth: Population in America.* Englewood Cliffs, NJ: Prentice-Hall.

Zelnik, M. and Kantner, J. F. (1974) The Resolution of Teenage First Pregnancies. *Family Planning Perspectives* 6: 74-79.

Zelnik, M. and Kantner, J. F. (1975) Attitudes of American Teenagers Toward Abortion. *Family Planning Perspectives* 7: 89-91.

Zelnik, M. and Kantner, J. F. (1977) Sexual and Contraceptive Experience of Young Unmarried Women in the United States, 1976 and 1971. *Family Planning Perspectives* 9: 55-73.

Zelnik, M. and Kantner, J. F. (1978a) First Pregnancies to Women Aged 15-19: 1976 and 1971. *Family Planning Perspectives* 10: 11-19.

Zelnik, M. and Kantner, J. F. (1978b) Contraceptive Patterns and Premarital Pregnancy Among Women Aged 15-19 in 1976. *Family Planning Perspectives* 10: 135-143.

Zelnik, M. and Kantner, J. F. (1979) Reasons for Nonuse of Contraception by Sexually Active Women Aged 15-19. *Family Planning Perspectives* 11: 289-296.

Zelnik, M. and Kantner, J. F. (1980) Sexual Activity, Contraceptive Use and Pregnancy Among Metropolitan-Area Teenagers: 1971-1979. *Family Planning Perspectives* 12: 230-237.

Zelnik, M., Kim, Y. J., and Kantner, J. F. (1979) Probabilities of Intercourse and Conception Among U.S. Teenage Women, 1971 and 1976. *Family Planning Perspectives* 11: 177-185.

ABOUT THE AUTHORS

MELVIN ZELNIK is Professor, Department of Population Dynamics, School of Hygiene and Public Health, Johns Hopkins University, with joint appointments in the Department of Behavioral Science, School of Hygiene, and the Department of Social Relations, Faculty of Arts and Sciences. He received his Ph.D. in sociology from Princeton University in 1959. Prior to joining the faculty of Johns Hopkins University, he taught at Pennsylvania State and Ohio State Universities, served as a research associate at the Office of Population Research, Princeton University, and worked, on two separate occasions, as a demographer at the Bureau of the Census. He also served one year in Surabaya, Indonesia, while on leave from Johns Hopkins University, as a Ford Foundation project specialist and has served as a consultant in Indonesia and the Philippines. In 1981 he was a recipient, with John F. Kantner, of the Carl S. Shultz Memorial Award for "sustained contributions to the field of population and family planning."

JOHN F. KANTNER is Professor and Chairman of the Department of Population Dynamics, School of Hygiene and Public Health, Johns Hopkins University, with appointments also in the Departments of Behavioral Science and Social Relations. He received his Ph.D. in sociology from the University of Michigan in 1953. Prior to joining the Johns Hopkins faculty in 1968, he taught at the College of William and Mary, the University of Indonesia, Punjab University, and the University of Western Ontario. He served at the U.S. Bureau of the Census for seven years as a specialist in the Soviet population and for five years he was a member of the staff of the Population Council. He is a corecipient, with Melvin Zelnik, of the Carl S. Shultz Memorial Award for their work on the fertility of the American teenager. He is President-Elect of the Population Association of America, the professional association for U.S. population scholars.

KATHLEEN FORD is an Assistant Professor in the Department of Population Dynamics, School of Hygiene and Public Health, Johns Hopkins University. She received a B.A. in mathematics from Boston College and M.A. and Ph.D. degrees in sociology from Brown University. Before joining the faculty of Johns Hopkins University, she was a demographic statistician at the National Center for Health Statistics. Besides this work on teenage fertility, she has also done research on contraceptive use in the United States, timing of births in the United States, the fertility of immigrants to the United States, abortion, and fertility models.

.Z44 c.2
Melvin.
pregnancy in
ence

Of Related Interest . . .

The Pregnant Adolescent
Problems of Premature Parenthood

by **FRANK G. BOLTON, Jr.**, *Arizona Department of Economic Security,*
with the research assistance of **S.P. KANE**

In a comprehensive and much-needed summary of current research findings and theories, Bolton offers fresh insights into the problems and prospects of the pregnant adolescent. He emphasizes the potential for child abuse and neglect, making an important—and relatively neglected—linkage. Throughout the book, he is concerned with the problems and policies needed to deal with this increasingly visible social problem: Of the 13 million sexually active female adolescents, 10% become pregnant each year. Over half bear their children. The price for related social services exceeds $8 billion . . . and is still rising.

"An exceptionally well-documented and clearly presented book on a newly recognized and important social problem."
—Richard Gelles, University of Rhode Island

*"**The Pregnant Adolescent** . . . provides an understandable, useful and up-to-date research prospective on one of America's most serious and perplexing social problems. . . . Packed with information on almost every aspect of adolescent pregnancy . . . [it] provide[s] a balanced view of this problem and its implications for women and infants . . . [and] identifies important stages where adolescent mothers can be helped to be better mothers. . . . Bolton has a firm grasp of the voluminous research on this subject, and he has carefully organized these data in a readable format. . . . **The Pregnant Adolescent** would be a welcome addition to any professional library."*
—The Annals of the American Academy of Political and Social Science

Sage Library of Social Research, Volume 100
ISBN 0-8039-1433-4 hardcover   ISBN 0-8039-1434-2 softcover

SAGE PUBLICATIONS   Beverly Hills   London